How to Open & Operate a Financially Successful
Independent Record Label

WITH COMPANION CD-ROM

Martha Maeda

HOW TO OPEN & OPERATE A FINANCIALLY SUCCESSFUL INDEPENDENT RECORD LABEL: WITH COMPANION CD-ROM

Copyright © 2012 Atlantic Publishing Group, Inc.
1405 SW 6th Avenue • Ocala, Florida 34471 • Phone: 800-814-1132 • Fax: 352-622-1875
Website: www.atlantic-pub.com • E-mail: sales@atlantic-pub.com
SAN Number: 268-1250

Library of Congress Cataloging-in-Publication Data

Maeda, Martha, 1953-
  How to open & operate a financially successful independent record label : with companion CD-ROM / by Martha Maeda.
     p. cm.
  Includes bibliographical references and index.
  ISBN-13: 978-1-60138-142-2 (alk. paper)
  ISBN-10: 1-60138-142-5 (alk. paper)
  1. New business enterprises. 2. Record labels. 3. Marketing. I. Title. II. Title: How to open and operate a financially successful independent record label.
  HD62.5.M324 2011
  384--dc23
                         2011026356

Printed in the United States

PROJECT MANAGER: Gretchen Pressley • gpressley@atlantic-pub.com
INTERIOR LAYOUT: Antoinette D'Amore • addesign@videotron.ca
PROOFREADER: C&P Marse • bluemoon6749@bellsouth.net
COVER DESIGN: Meg Buchner • meg@megbuchner.com
BACK COVER DESIGN: Jackie Miller • millerjackiej@gmail.com

Printed on Recycled Paper

A few years back we lost our beloved pet dog Bear, who was not only our best and dearest friend but also the "Vice President of Sunshine" here at Atlantic Publishing. He did not receive a salary but worked tirelessly 24 hours a day to please his parents.

Bear was a rescue dog who turned around and showered myself, my wife, Sherri, his grandparents Jean, Bob, and Nancy, and every person and animal he met (well, maybe not rabbits) with friendship and love. He made a lot of people smile every day.

We wanted you to know a portion of the profits of this book will be donated in Bear's memory to local animal shelters, parks, conservation organizations, and other individuals and nonprofit organizations in need of assistance.

– *Douglas & Sherri Brown*

PS: We have since adopted two more rescue dogs: first Scout, and the following year, Ginger. They were both mixed golden retrievers who needed a home.

Want to help animals and the world? Here are a dozen easy suggestions you and your family can implement today:

- *Adopt and rescue a pet from a local shelter.*
- *Support local and no-kill animal shelters.*
- *Plant a tree to honor someone you love.*
- *Be a developer — put up some birdhouses.*
- *Buy live, potted Christmas trees and replant them.*
- *Make sure you spend time with your animals each day.*
- *Save natural resources by recycling and buying recycled products.*
- *Drink tap water, or filter your own water at home.*
- *Whenever possible, limit your use of or do not use pesticides.*
- *If you eat seafood, make sustainable choices.*
- *Support your local farmers market.*
- *Get outside. Visit a park, volunteer, walk your dog, or ride your bike.*

Five years ago, Atlantic Publishing signed the Green Press Initiative. These guidelines promote environmentally friendly practices, such as using recycled stock and vegetable-based inks, avoiding waste, choosing energy-efficient resources, and promoting a no-pulping policy. We now use 100-percent recycled stock on all our books. The results: in one year, switching to post-consumer recycled stock saved 24 mature trees, 5,000 gallons of water, the equivalent of the total energy used for one home in a year, and the equivalent of the greenhouse gases from one car driven for a year.

DEDICATION

This book is dedicated to all the artists, producers, and technicians who enrich our lives with wonderful music, year after year.

TABLE OF CONTENTS

CHAPTER 3 : Writing a Winning Business Plan 89

CHAPTER 4: Financing Your Record Label..... 109

CHAPTER 5: Finding and Working with Artists 117

CHAPTER 6: Contracts and Agreements..... 139

CHAPTER 7: Music Publishing.......................181

CHAPTER 12: Promotion and Marketing 269

CONCLUSION: What Does the Future Hold? 301

APPENDIX A: Further Reading 305

INTRODUCTION

A record label is an entity that produces and markets music. A label can be a single person working from a home office with a laptop, or it can be a corporation with a large advertising budget and a full-time staff of producers, talent agents, sound engineers, graphic artists, marketing professionals, and distributors. You may want to start a record label to produce and sell your own music or because you feel that you have a talent for recognizing good musicians and helping them to develop their careers. Perhaps you have years of experience in the entertainment industry and are ready to strike out on your own. Managing your own label will give you artistic freedom and the power to make important decisions without having to answer to a committee of corporate executives. You may want to apply your knowledge of marketing and promotion to selling an exciting and rewarding product. Or you may simply have a passion for a particular genre of music and confidence that you can succeed.

Whatever your motivation, this book will help you with every aspect of setting up and running an independent record label. Learn how to set up your record label as a legal entity, how to prepare a business plan, how to keep accounts and prepare taxes, and how to protect your intellectual property. Read about the history of the music industry, current trends, and the anticipated directions the industry will take in the near future. Review helpful suggestions for discovering and working with talented musicians and artists, and producing and recording music. Craft legal contracts that protect the best interests of your label and your artists. Learn how to record and market music and the roles of producers, engineers, and artists. Explore multiple opportunities for publicizing and promoting your music, including social media and viral marketing. Learn how to work with distributors, music stores, and media outlets to make your products widely available. The more you know about the music business, the greater your chances of success.

The word "record" in this book refers to any form in which music is recorded and sold — a vinyl record, CD, DVD, tape cassette, MP3 file, audio download, and any new technology that has not yet appeared in the market. The world of music is evolving so rapidly that it is difficult to anticipate the next direction it will take. Trends in the music industry are

driven not only by new technologies, such as cell phones with universal wireless access, but also by new forms of social networking and sharing music, such as Facebook, YouTube, Pandora®, and Internet radio.

It takes years of dedication and effort to develop a successful record label. The entertainment industry is volatile; an artist or a genre that is extremely popular today may be almost forgotten next year. Be prepared for a roller coaster ride. You will learn to make the most of the peaks and to strategize your way through the valleys. Each independent record label is as unique as its founder(s) and the artists it promotes. Some thrive in a local scene; others sell to a global audience; still others have the support of a small but intensely loyal, genre market. For young people in particular, music is more than entertainment; it represents a brand and a lifestyle with which they thoroughly identify. Genres such as punk, indie, metal, and emo are associated with specific styles of clothing and fashion, behavior, attitude, and ideology. Music has become inextricably entwined with advertising and commercial entertainment products — some of today's successful artists first attracted attention when one of their songs was used in a popular TV show or commercial or when they participated in a televised talent quest. These trends present unique opportunities to break into mainstream music markets.

Since their inception, independent labels have been responsible for introducing some of the world's most beloved artists and genres to mainstream music audiences. However, the development of digital recording technology and the explosive growth of the Internet, digital downloads, and social networks has dramatically altered the arena in which independent labels operate. Today, a good recording can be made with a relatively small investment and marketed through the Internet. Hundreds of thousands of independent labels and artists compete for the attention of a global audience.

Independents use social networking and innovative marketing to engage their fans and develop a loyal following.

Recording a great album is only the first step. The real challenge is getting that album out into the marketplace, building an image and a following for your label, and making a living for yourself and your artists. You will need a wide range of skills to run a successful record label, including an intuition for good music, the ability to work effectively with artists and professionals, and an aptitude for marketing and distribution. Your label also needs a solid business foundation, or it will founder even in the face of runaway popularity. You will need money to invest in recording and advertising. If you are deficient in any of these areas, you must find partners or hire employees who have the skills and resources to complement your own.

Your record label is a reflection of who you are — your instincts, talent, musical tastes, creativity, business ability, and vision. Your personality will determine the character of your label, and your passion for music will be the driving force behind its development. The information in this book will help you to direct that passion into a lucrative and successful business. The music industry is vast; some topics can only be touched on briefly in this book. *Appendix A: Further Reading contains a list of suggested reading and resources where you can find more information on many of these subjects.*

CHAPTER 1

What is an Independent Record Label?

An independent record label, or "indie," is just that — it is funded and operated independently from the major record labels that dominate mainstream music markets. During the rise of punk music, which emphasized independence and a do-it-yourself ethic, a record label was defined as an indie only if it studiously avoided having anything to do with major record labels. Today, some independent labels collaborate with major record labels in distribution or production deals. Over the years, major record labels seeking to expand into new markets have purchased many independent labels. In some cases, these labels have retained artistic control and maintained their unique images while receiving support from the parent label.

Independent record labels are as old as the recording industry; the earliest were founded at the end of the 19th century and beginning of the 20th century by gramophone companies to manufacture the wax cylinders and discs played on their machines. Many independent labels were established to promote the music of a single band or artist or a particular genre or niche in the music market. Historically, independent record labels heralded the emergence of new styles of popular music, such as rhythm and blues (R&B), jazz, rock 'n' roll, punk, pop rock, heavy metal, and new age or world music.

As you can see from the stories of the Big Four record labels below, they all began with the merger of two or more smaller labels and grew by acquiring the brands and music catalogs of other labels until they became mega-corporations with the resources to catapult a new and relatively unknown artist to global stardom in a few short weeks.

The histories of the four major record labels are filled with successes and failures, colorful personalities, tales of beloved artists and musical groups, acquisitions and mergers, and ultimately, influxes of cash from international investment companies. Their executives had to be agile: jumping into new genres, finding ways to exploit overseas markets, keeping up with trends, quickly retiring outdated music, and always looking for "the next big thing." Their fortunes became entangled with the parent companies that funded them, fluctuations in the stock market, and dips in the economy. The biggest challenge of all has been the explosion of digital and file-sharing technologies over the last decade. No longer able to pull in huge profits from the sales of hard copies such as CDs and vinyl albums, record labels have had to find ways to make money from downloads and sales of single hit songs rather than compilations. They also had to deal with rampant piracy and illegal file sharing, which is almost impossible to control. Several companies experienced setbacks due to negative publicity when they sued their own customers for sharing files on their computers and others when the DRM (digital rights management) software they embedded in their music files to discourage illegal sharing inadvertently made computers vulnerable to viruses.

Independent record labels experience their own set of challenges, primarily the high cost of promoting artists and records. They must decide where to invest their limited resources to achieve the greatest results. Another challenge is finding production facilities and establishing distribution networks for their CDs and records. Even success can be a challenge: an independent label may not be prepared to supply its products in large quantities or deal with the sudden rise of one of its artists to international prominence. Successful independent labels usually operate within a specialized field or genre.

New technologies have made it much easier for you to start a record label of your own. Digital recording equipment and software make it possible to produce music with a relatively small financial outlay. On-demand printing and distribution companies allow you to order copies of CDs or DVDs as you need them instead of having to buy hundreds at a time. Digital music can be distributed through downloads without the need for hard copies. The Internet and social media such as Facebook, YouTube, and Twitter™ provide unprecedented avenues for promotion and publicity. Using the Internet, you can quickly do research, locate professional services, and compare prices without leaving your desk. Computers also enable you to do your bookkeeping, keep track of contracts, and produce your own high-quality photos, publicity materials, posters, and press releases. *Later chapters will cover these topics in detail.*

The Big Four

Four major record labels, known as the Big Four, represent as much as 75 percent of the annual music market. They are Sony Music Holdings, Universal Music Group, EMI Group, and Warner Music. Many familiar record labels, such as Columbia Records, which Sony Music Holdings owns, are subsidiaries of one of these major labels. An artist may be contracted directly to the major label or to one of its subsidiaries. Subsidiary labels may work somewhat independently, but the major label that owns them typically makes important financial decisions. In some cases, major labels offer distribution services to indie labels that coincide with their own markets.

Major labels pour massive resources into promoting and marketing their artists. The decision to sign a particular band or artist is made by a corporate hierarchy and is based on whether company executives believe the artist can achieve an acceptable level of sales. Once a contract is signed, hundreds of the label's employees work on producing, recording, releasing, and publicizing the artist's music. The label arranges radio play, publicity, concert tours, and distribution through its own well-established channels. In return, the artist must relinquish control over some aspects of his or her career and, in many cases, his or her artistic freedom.

Each of the major labels has a music publishing arm that manages the rights to its artists' music and lyrics. The music publishing branch is an important source of revenue because it earns money every time someone wants to copy, perform, or rerelease a song. Nightclub entertainers, high school glee clubs, orchestras, bands, and choirs must all pay to use the copyrighted music. Another important asset is the record label's catalog — its past hits and recordings that can be rereleased as compilations, box sets, and commemorative albums. Many catalogs are acquired when a label is purchased by another label. In 2010, Warner Music Group reported that its catalog had been responsible for 40 percent of its revenue and its publishing arm for 18 percent of its revenue for the previous year.

Activities of a Major Record Label

In its 2010 Form 10-K, the annual report every publicly traded company must file with the SEC, Warner Music Group describes its business activities:

"We play an integral role in virtually all aspects of the music value chain from discovering and developing talent to producing albums and promoting artists and their products. After an artist has entered into a contract with one of our record labels, a master recording of the artist's music is created. The recording is then replicated for sale to consumers primarily in the CD and digital formats. In the U.S., WEA Corp., ADA, and Word market sell and deliver product, either directly or through subdistributors and wholesalers, to record stores, mass merchants, and other retailers. Our recorded music products are also sold in physical form to online physical retailers, such as Amazon. com, barnesandnoble.com, and bestbuy.com, and in digital form to online digital retailers like Apple's iTunes® and mobile full-track download stores, such as those operated by Verizon or Sprint™. In the case of expanded-rights deals where we acquire broader rights in a recording artist's career, we may provide more comprehensive career support and actively develop new opportunities for an artist through touring, fan clubs, merchandising, and sponsorships, among other areas. We believe expanded-rights deals create a better partnership with our artists, which allows us to work together more closely with them to create and sustain artistic and commercial success.

"We have a decades-long history of identifying and contracting with recording artists who become commercially successful. Our ability to select artists who are likely to be successful is a key element of our Recorded Music business strategy and spans all music genres, all major geographies, and includes artists who achieve national, regional, and international success. We believe that this success is directly attributable to our experienced global team of A&R (artists and repertoire) executives, to the longstanding reputation and relationships that we have developed in the artistic community, and to our effective management of this vital business function.

"In the U.S., our major record labels identify potentially successful recording artists, sign them to recording agreements, collaborate with them to develop recordings of their work, and market and sell these finished recordings to retail stores and legitimate digital channels. Increasingly, we are also expanding our participation in image and brand rights associated with artists, including merchandising, sponsorships, touring, and artist management. Our labels scout and sign talent across all major music genres, including pop, rock, jazz, country, R&B, hip-hop, rap, reggae, Latin, alternative, folk, blues, gospel, and other Christian music. WMI markets and sells U.S. and local repertoire from its own network of affiliates and numerous licensees in more than 50 countries. With a roster of local artists performing in various local languages throughout the world, WMI has an ongoing commitment to developing local talent aimed at achieving national, regional, or international success."

Warner Music Group

Warner Bros. movie studio started Warner Bros. Records in 1958 to release its movie soundtracks after one of its actors, Tab Hunter, scored a hit with "Young Love" for Dot Records, a subsidiary of rival Paramount Pictures. At that time, the popularity of rock 'n' roll and pop music was just taking off, and the label was soon a major entity in its own right. In 1963, Warner Bros. Records purchased Frank Sinatra's label, Reprise Records. In 1968, Seven Arts Productions bought Warner Bros. and acquired Atlantic Records, a dominant jazz and R&B label. In 1969, Kinney National Services purchased Warner-Seven Arts for $400 million. In 1970, Kinney paid $10 million for Elektra and its sister company, Nonesuch Records.

In 1971, the company changed its name to Warner Communications, but became known in the music industry as WEA (Warner Elektra Atlantic). Through its purchases, the company acquired rights to many of Atlantic's rock artists, including Led Zeppelin, Cream, Crosby Stills & Nash, Yes, Average White Band, Dr. John, King Crimson, Bette Midler, and Foreigner, as well as to its earlier catalog of soul and blues recordings. Elektra brought in The Doors, Judy Collins, The Stooges, and a rich variety of folk, classical, and world music. When its distributor was unable to keep up with the demand for newly emerging Grateful Dead albums, the company established an in-house distribution arm. The acquisition of Asylum Records in 1972 brought in Linda Ronstadt, The Eagles, Jackson Browne, and Joni Mitchell. WEA was instrumental in the U.S. success of Fleetwood Mac and the pioneer heavy metal bands Led Zeppelin, Black Sabbath, and Deep Purple. Alice Cooper, Montrose, and Van Halen were among the first U.S. metal bands to sign with the label.

In 1977, WEA became the distributor for several punk rock and new wave bands including the Ramones, the Dead Boys, and Talking Heads for Sire Records, which it acquired in 1978. WEA jump-started the U.S. careers of Madonna, Ice-T, Depeche Mode, Echo & the Bunnymen, The Pretenders, and The Cure, and later successfully promoted Seal, k.d. lang, Tommy Page, and Ministry. WEA labels also signed contracts with The Cars and Prince. During the 1980s, WEA also distributed a number of successful independent labels.

In 1988, WEA acquired the German classical label Teldec and the UK Magnet Records. In 1989, it bought Italian CGD Records and Japanese MMG Records. From 1981 to 1984, Warner Communications was a partner in the launch of MTV. In 1990, Warner Communications merged with Time Life® to create Time Warner Cable, the largest media company in the world at that time. The same year, WEA purchased French label Carrere Disques. In 1991, WEA was renamed Warner Music. In 1992, it acquired the French classical label Erato and in 1993 the Spanish DRO Group, Hungarian Magneoton, Swedish Telegram Records, Brazilian Continental Records, and Finnish Fazer Musiiki. In 1992, Time Warner acquired a 50 percent stake in the Rhino Records label. Rhino signed an agreement that allowed it to begin reissuing recordings from Atlantic's back catalog. By 1998, Time Warner completely owned Rhino Records.

In 1994, the Warner publishing division, now Warner/Chappell Music, became the world's largest owner of song copyrights and the world's largest publisher of printed music when it purchased CPP/Belwin. In 1996, Time Warner took over the Turner Broadcasting System. In 2000, Time Warner consolidated with AOL but suffered reverses when the dot-com bubble burst. In 2004, Time Warner sold Warner Music Group (WMG) to a group of investors led by Edgar Bronfman Jr. for $2.6 billion. In 2009, WMG acquired Rykodisc and Roadrunner Records.

During the first decade of the 21st century, like all major record labels, WMG evolved to adapt to rapid changes in the way music is distributed through digital media. It moved out of record production and sold off its manufacturing operations in 2003. At the end of 2007, Warner became the third major label to sell digital music without Digital Rights Management (DRM), the technology that inhibits the use of digital media, through Amazon MP3 (Amazon.com's digital music store). In November 2008, WMG's Atlantic Records reported that 51 percent of its revenue from music sales in the U.S. had come from digital products. WMG as a whole reported that digital sales had made up 27 percent of its total revenue. By mid-2010, digital music made up 30 percent of WMG's revenues worldwide and 47 percent of its U.S. revenues.

Universal

Universal Music is not the biggest record label, but according to the IFPI (International Federation of the Phonographic Industry), it is the top-selling label, thanks to its more than 100 subsidiaries. Universal Music originated as MCA, Inc. (Music Corporation of America), a U.S. talent agency founded in 1924 that pioneered the practice of booking tours for musicians and entertainers. In 1962, MCA merged with Decca Records, acquiring Universal Pictures in the process. At that time, Decca Re-

Elton John performs at Minsk Arena in Minsk Belarus.

cords owned Coral Records and Brunswick Records. MCA formed Uni Records in 1966 and bought Kapp Records in 1967. In 1967, it began releasing its labels' records outside the U.S. as MCA Records. In 1971, it merged Decca, Kapp, and Uni into MCA Records in California; the first U.S. release from MCA Records was Elton John's *Crocodile Rock* in 1972.

Elton John's *Goodbye Yellow Brick Road* album and The Who's double album *Quadrophenia* were both released in the U.S. by MCA in October 1973 and vied for the top two positions on the U.S. Billboard 200 albums chart for weeks. In 1977, MCA set up its Infinity Records division in New York City to strengthen MCA's presence on the East Coast; it was fully absorbed into the parent company in 1980. In 1979, MCA acquired ABC Records along with its subsidiaries Paramount Records, Dunhill Records, Impulse! Records, Westminster Records, and Dot Records. The expense of this acquisition combined with rising costs for the production of vinyl caused financial losses from 1979 until 1982, and the company did not begin to gain ground until the mid-1980s.

In the late 1980s, MCA launched Mechanic Records to release heavy metal music and signed bands such as Voivod, Dream Theater, Bang Tango, and Trixter. It acquired Motown Records in 1988 and sold Motown to PolyGram in 1993. In 1989, MCA created a new holding company called MCA Music Entertainment Group, which acquired GRP Records and Geffen Records. The Matsushita group bought the MCA parent company in 1990. In 1995, Seagram Company Ltd. acquired 80 percent of MCA and renamed its music division Universal Music Group (UMG).

MCA Records adopted a new logo in 1997, which highlighted the parent company's former full name. In 1998, Seagram merged PolyGram (owner of British Decca) with its music holdings. In 2001, the French company Pernod Ricard bought Seagram's drinks business and sold its media holdings (including Universal) to Vivendi (now Vivendi SA). In spring 2003, the UMG label Geffen Records absorbed MCA Records. Today, Universal Music Enterprises and Geffen manage MCA's rock, pop, and urban back catalogs (including those from ABC Records and Famous Music Group). MCA's jazz, classical music, and musical theater are managed by other UMG subsidiaries.

In May 2007, Vivendi purchased BMG Music Publishing for $2.4 billion and became the world's largest music publisher.

Sony Music Holdings

Sony Music Holdings is the second largest of the four major record labels and controls 25 percent of the music market. Sony originated from the American Record Company (ARC), formed in July 1929 by a merger of four smaller record companies. In October of the same year, ARC was taken over by Consolidated Film Industries. During the Great Depression, the company bought up many record labels at bargain prices, including American Columbia Phonograph Company and its subsidiary Okeh Records, and gained control of their music catalogues. At the end of 1938, Columbia Broadcasting System (CBS) purchased ARC for $700,000. CBS made the American Columbia label its flagship (the UK Columbia label became successful under EMI Records). In 1951, CBS arranged to distribute its music internationally through Philips Records.

Carlos Santana performing at the George Amphitheater

In 1953, CBS founded Epic Records, and in 1958, it founded Date Records to market rockabilly music (later, in 1966, the label changed to soul music). During the 1960s, CBS launched and developed is international arm, CBS Records. In 1967, CBS Records, plunged into rock music, signing Janis Joplin with Big Brother & the Holding Company, then Laura Nyro, Jimmie Spheeris, Electric Flag, Santana, The Chambers Brothers, Bruce Springsteen, Andy Pratt, Chicago, Billy Joel, Blood, Sweat & Tears, and Pink Floyd. By 1970, the company had doubled its market share.

In March 1968, CBS entered a joint venture in Japan with Sony, CBS/Sony Records. In 1970, CBS Records revived Embassy Records in the United Kingdom and Europe to release budget reissues of albums that had originally been released in the U.S. under Columbia Records. In 1983, thanks to its joint venture with Sony, CBS began releasing some of the first compact discs in the U.S. market. During the 1980s and early 1990s, a CBS subsidiary, CBS Associated Records, signed artists such as Ozzy Osbourne, The Fabulous Thunderbirds, Electric Light Orchestra, Joan Jett, and Henry Lee Summer.

In November 1987, the Sony Corporation of America purchased CBS Records for $2 billion. CBS Corporation granted Sony a temporary license to use the CBS name until 1991 when Sony renamed the company Sony Music Entertainment (SME). CBS Associated was renamed Epic Associated, and Sony reintroduced the Columbia label after acquiring the international rights to the trademark from EMI. (In Japan, rights to the Columbia name belong to an unrelated company, Nippon Columbia.)

In 2004, Sony Music and Bertelsmann Music Group (BMG) merged to form Sony BMG Music Entertainment. In 2005, Sony BMG was fined $10 million after the New York attorney general's office determined that it had been paying radio stations and disc jockeys to play the songs of various artists, an illegal practice known as **payola**. In 2008, Sony acquired Bertelsmann's 50 percent stake in Sony BMG and renamed the company Sony Music Entertainment Inc. (SME), now Sony Music Holdings.

EMI Group (Electric & Musical Industries Ltd.)

EMI Group (Electric & Musical Industries Ltd.) is the fourth largest of the four major record labels. It was formed in March 1931 by a merger between the U.K. Columbia Graphophone Company and the Gramophone Company. Electric & Musical Industries Ltd. produced both recordings and sound and playback equipment. The Gramophone Company's subsidiaries throughout the British Commonwealth continued to dominate the popular music industries in India, Australia, and New Zealand until the 1960s. The year it was founded, the company opened a recording studio at Abbey Road, London.

During the 1930s, antitrust action taken by its U.S. competitors forced EMI to sell Columbia USA; it retained the rights to the Columbia name elsewhere in the world until the Columbia name was retired in 1972. Among its artists during the 1930s and 1940s were Arturo Toscanini, Sir Edward Elgar, and Otto Klemperer. EMI released its first long-playing records (LPs) in 1952 and its first stereophonic recordings in 1955.

In 1951, Columbia America cut its ties with EMI. EMI re-entered the U.S. market when it bought 96 percent of the stock of Capitol Records in 1957. The company was very successful from the late 1950s to the early 1970s, with pop and rock artists including Frank Sinatra, Cliff Richard, The Shadows, The Beach Boys, The Hollies, Cilla Black, and Pink Floyd. The Beatles, now estimated to have sold more than 1 billion records, were signed by EMI in 1962.

In 1979, EMI Ltd. merged with THORN Electrical Industries to form Thorn EMI. Thorn EMI acquired Chrysalis Records in 1991. One of its most expensive acquisitions was Virgin Records in 1992. In 1996, shareholders voted to separate Thorn Electrical Industries from EMI. The new media company was named EMI Group PLC.

In 2000, EMI licensed its catalogue in a digital format to Streamwaves, the first company to launch an Internet subscription service with major label content. EMI's album sales declined with the rapid increase of digital downloads. In 2007, EMI announced a loss of almost $420 million for the previous fiscal year. After rejecting a takeover bid from Warner Bros., EMI was bought by Terra Firma, a private equity group. Some of its artists left the company because they doubted a private equity firm could adequately handle their affairs. In February 2010, EMI announced pretax losses of $2.82 billion due to debt, in spite of making a profit of $481 million during the previous fiscal year. In February 2011, Citigroup took ownership of EMI Group from Terra Firma and wrote off $3.5 billion of debt.

The Big Four

	UNIVERSAL MUSIC GROUP	WARNER MUSIC GROUP CORPORATION (WMG)	SONY ENTERTAINMENT	EMI
Annual Revenue from Recorded Music (Sept. 30, 2010)	$5.87 billion for the 12-month period ending September 30, 2010	$2.455 billion for the 12-month period ending September 30, 2010	$1.728 billion for the 6-month period ending March 2009	$1.65 billion in 2009
Net Income for fiscal year ending in 2010	$756 million	$143 Million		$481 million for the 12-month period ending February 2010
Share of recorded music market in 2009	28%	15%	23%	10%
Subsidiary Labels	Decca Classics, Deutsche Grammophon, ECM, EmArcy Records, Fonovisa Records, Disa Records, Hip-O Records, Interscope-Geffen-A&M, Island Def Jam Music Group, Island Records Group, Lost Highway Records, MCA Nashville Records, Mercury Music Group, Mercury Nashville Records, Polydor Records,	Asylum, Atlantic, Cordless, East West, Elektra, Nonesuch, Reprise, Rhino, Roadrunner, Rykodisc, Sire, Warner Bros. and Word	Arista, Columbia, Epic, J Records, Jive, LaFace, Legacy, RCA, Red Music, Distribution, SoSo, Def, Zomba Music Group (including Rough Trade and Pinnacle)	Angel Records, Back Porch Records, Blue Note Records, Astralwerks Records, Capitol Records, Caroline Records, Charisma Records, Definitive Jux Records, Delabel (France), EMI Gospel, EMI Records, Forefront Records, Gyroscope Records, Imperial Records, Liberty Records, Manhattan Records, Mute

	UNIVERSAL MUSIC GROUP	WARNER MUSIC GROUP CORPORATION (WMG)	SONY ENTERTAINMENT	EMI
Subsidiary Labels (cont'd)	Show Dog-Universal Music, Universal Chronicles, UM3, Universal Classics and Jazz, Universal Music Latin Entertainment, Universal Motown Republic Group, V2 Records, Verve Music Group			Records, Nature Sounds, Parlophone, Priority Records, Sparrow Records, Stones Throw Records, The Front Line, Venture Records, Virgin Records

The Independents

Historically, independent record labels have played an important role in introducing new forms of popular music to the world. After World War II, independent labels specializing in jazz, country, folk, blues, and rock 'n' roll and catering to small, but devoted audiences, gave artists the creative freedom to develop unique styles. Individual artists who wanted

more control over their careers established independent labels such as the Beatles' Apple Records, Rolling Stone Records, and Elton John's Rocket. Many of these labels later became defunct or were absorbed by the major record labels, but some of them remain in business today.

One of the most notable indie labels was Sun Records, founded in 1952, which gave Elvis Presley, Carl Perkins, Roy Orbison, Jerry Lee Lewis, and Johnny Cash their first recording contracts. The label remains in business as Sun Entertainment Corporation, which currently licenses its brand and classic hit recordings to independent reissue labels. Its subsidiaries include SSS International Records, Plantation Records, Amazon Records, Red Bird Records, and Blue Cat Records.

During the 1970s, when punk rock emerged as a reaction to the excesses of mainstream rock, independent labels proliferated. An essential characteristic of punk rock and its offshoots was a do-it-yourself ethic and the determination to avoid any kind of involvement with major record labels and their distribution channels. Punk labels developed their markets by having their bands tour aggressively to support new releases, playing wherever they could, and creating an entire culture around them. During the early 1990s, numerous artists started their own labels when they failed to attract the interest of major record labels.

Each successful independent record label has a unique story, but all of them share some things in common.

- Their founders were passionate about music and were often musicians themselves.

- The founders were able to sign at least two or three artists who produced hit records.

- The founders learned by trial and error; they responded to each new challenge in creative ways that allowed them to keep growing.

- Many of the founders were young and knew little about business when they started, but they had a vision for their labels. Their flexibility and creativity allowed them to change with the times, quickly moving into digital music, streaming, Internet downloads, and social media.

Here, in brief, are the stories of a few independent labels:

Dischord Records

Ian MacKaye and Jeff Nelson founded Dischord Records in 1980 to release *Minor Disturbance* by their band, The Teen Idles. Dischord is a local label that supports punk rock music in the Washington, D.C., area. In addition to being a musician, MacKaye is a sound engineer and producer, and he is responsible for the exceptional quality of the label's early releases. The label is known for its strict do-it-yourself ethic; it produces all of its albums by itself and sells them at discount prices without the help of major distributors.

Epitaph Records

Epitaph Records was founded in 1981 by Bad Religion guitarist Brett Gurewitz to promote his band's albums. The label began as nothing more than "a logo and a P.O. box"; it started without any equipment or a physical location. It released a debut album in 1987 for the grunge band L7 and soon signed several punk bands including NOFX, Pennywise, Down by Law, Coffin Break, The Offspring, Rancid, RKL, SNFU, Total Chaos, and Claw Hammer. Epitaph became widely known in 1994 when four of its bands (Bad Religion, which had left Epitaph by this time; NOFX; Rancid; and The Offspring) released hit records. From 1994 to 2001, Gurewitz left Bad Religion in order to devote himself full time to running Epitaph. Epitaph continued to grow, and today it is one of the largest independent labels. Its sister labels include Hellcat records, which handles a roster of mainly psychobilly and ska bands, ANTI- and Epitaph Europe. Epitaph actively solicits submissions of demos from new artists.

Merge Records

Laura Ballance and Mac McCaughan founded Merge Records in 1989 to release music from their band Superchunk. The first releases were cassette tapes by WWAX and Bricks, followed by the first Superchunk (then known only as "Chunk") vinyl 7-inch single. The founders borrowed cash from their friends to finance projects. The label launched its first full-length CD in 1992. From 2000 to 2010, Merge releases by Arcade Fire, Spoon, and She & Him reached the top of the charts in the U.S. and the U.K. In 2010, when Touch and Go Records, the company that had handled Merge's releases since its beginning, announced that it would no longer manufacture and distribute records for independent labels, the company had to quickly find another distributor.

CASE STUDY:
ARCADE FIRE –
AN INDEPENDENT
SUCCESS STORY

Canadian-American indie-rock band Arcade Fire, which has released three top-selling albums, has remained with Merge for its entire career. Arcade Fire was established in 2001 and was signed the same year by Merge Records, who recognized the promise in their early live performances. In 2004, Arcade Fire released its debut album *Funeral*, which appeared on many top ten album lists in 2004 and 2005 and was named album of the year by *Pitchfork, Filter, No Ripcord*, and the MTV2 2005 Review. By November 2005, more than half a million copies had sold worldwide. *Funeral* was the first Merge Records album to make the *Billboard* 200 chart and its biggest selling album to date. Their second album, *Neon Bible*, premiered at No. 1 on the Canadian Albums Chart and the Irish Album Charts and No. 2 on the U.S. *Billboard* Top 200 charts and the U.K. Top 40 Album Chart for the week of March 12, 2007, as well as being No. 1 on the Rock and Indie album charts. The band's third album, *The Suburbs*, won the 2011 Grammy® Award for Album of the Year and Best International Album at the 2011 BRIT Awards. It also received nominations for the Best Alternative Music Album Grammy for all three of its studio albums.

The band records its albums in its own studios, located in a renovated church, and retains ownership of the music, which it licenses to Merge. Merge helps to finance production and takes care of distribution and promotion. In an August 2010 interview with Sasha Frere-Jones for the *New York Times*, Scott Rodger, Arcade Fire's manager, described the role of Merge Records as "manufacturing and distribution — floating the expense, executing the marketing and retail plans we have approved, and insuring the music is available on all credible D.S.P.s. (digital service platforms)."

Naxos

Klaus Heymann, a German-born resident of Hong Kong, founded Naxos (Naxos Records) in 1987 by. Naxos is now the largest independent classical label in the world and one of the two top-selling classical music labels. In 2009, it began distributing streaming Web radio and podcasts. It is known for its budget-priced CDs with simplified covers and artwork. During the 1980s, Naxos minimized recording costs by recording central and eastern European symphony orchestras, often with lesser-known conductors. In the 1990s, it began recording with British and American orchestras. Naxos avoids duplicating the repertoire of other labels and has made extensive recordings of modern composers and little-known works of Japanese classical music, Jewish-American music, wind band music, film music, and early music. Naxos launched the online Naxos Music Library (**www.naxosmusiclibrary.com**), a paid service that allows subscribers to listen to more than 50,850 CD-length recordings from the catalogs of 320 independent labels. It offers access to librettos, musical scores, and artist biographies.

Orange Mountain

In 2001, Kurt Munkacsi, producer of most of Phillip Glass' recordings and head of Euphorbia productions, set out to archive all the master recordings made by Philip Glass. The result was Orange Mountain Music. This label's mission is to release some of the hundreds of hours of recordings made by Phillip Glass in the process of creating operas, film scores, musical theatre pieces and records; performances of his solo, operatic, orchestral and small ensemble work; and recordings by other artists and organizations that have collaborated with Philip Glass. Orange Mountain quickly established itself as a serious producer of quality music and soon began producing releases of new music as well as archival releases. By 2011, the label had produced 68 high-quality releases and continues to receive regular reviews in *The New York Times*, in *The Gramophone*, and in international music publications.

Rounder Records

University students Ken Irwin, Bill Nowlin, and Marian Leighton-Levy established Rounder Records in 1970 as a mail-order business to release recordings of blues, blues-rock, string band, and bluegrass music. Its catalog expanded to include folk, soul, soca (a modern form of calypso), Cajun, and Celtic music, and at one point, it handled sales and distribution for as many as 450 other labels and had 100 employees. Its founders have an intellectual and emotional commitment to recording and preserving cultural musical traditions. In a 2010 interview for the *The Boston Globe*, Leighton-Levy noted that Rounder's customers continue to purchase large numbers of CDs rather than digital downloads.

In 1985, Rounder was one of the first labels to produce compact discs. Bluegrass artist Alison Krauss has chosen to remain with the label for the duration of her career, rejecting numerous offers from major labels. In 2004, the company launched Rounder Books. In 2010, the label was acquired by the Concord Music Group, which does all of its distribution through Universal Media Group.

SST Records

SST Records was formed in 1978 in Long Beach, CA, when Greg Ginn repurposed his mail-order electronics company, Solid State Transmitters, to release the music of his band, Black Flag (Panic). Ginn was frustrated because a label called Bomp! Records seemed to be dragging its feet about releasing a recording of his music. During the 1980s, SST released recordings by the Minutemen, Saccharine Trust, the Meat Puppets, Minneapolis hardcore group Hüsker Dü, as well as numerous other punk artists. In the early 1980s, there was a strong public reaction against punk music, and the movement was mostly underground, with punk bands playing in small venues such as parties and clubs.

When SST released Hüsker Dü's double album *Zen Arcade* in 1984, it knew the record would be a hit, but money was tight. The label decided to press only 5,000 copies because it had never made more than 5,000 copies of any of its releases. The album received critical acclaim from several mainstream reviewers and sold out quickly; it remained out of print for months before the label could resupply its retail outlets.

In 1987, the label decided to economize on promoting Black Flag albums by releasing them quickly, one after another, and supporting these releases with a heavy touring schedule. SST released 80 titles in 1987 and apparently overextended itself because several of its artists became dissatisfied with its services and signed with other record labels. In 1986, SST bought New Alliance, and it later created two sublabels — Cruz Records and a short-lived label, Issues Records, for spoken-word recordings. After being one of the dominant indies of the 1980s, the label lost prominence as Ginn gravitated toward jazz and many punk artists left the label.

Sub Pop Records

Sub Pop Records began as fanzine, *Subterranean Pop* or "Sub Pop," started by Bruce Pavitt and dedicated to underground bands in the northwestern U.S. Pavitt sometimes printed the magazine and sometimes released compilations of his favorite bands on tape cassettes. In 1986, Pavitt and Jonathan Poneman created the Sub Pop label to release the **EP (extended play** — a recording that includes more than a single song but is not long enough to be an album and is often used to promote upcoming releases) of a friend's band, Soundgarden. At that time, punk music was often released as limited runs of 7-inch vinyl singles that soon sold out in record shops, which was frustrating for fans that could not get copies. In 1988, Sub Pop initiated a Singles Club, charging an annual $35 subscription fee and guaranteeing that members would receive a new single every month. The first single sent out was a single by Nirvana. As Nirvana's popularity skyrocketed, Sub Pop became synonymous with the Seattle grunge music scene.

According to Sub Pop, its success was due to carefully orchestrated branding and unorthodox marketing. In addition to the Singles Club, Sub Pop created a uniform look and feel for its early releases. Its logo appeared everywhere — in its early days, Sub Pop sold more T-shirts bearing the Sub Pop logo than records. Sub Pop courted the attention of the British music press and made sure its logo appeared in interview photos of its artists. Sub Pop signed and promoted bands such as Tad, Dwarves, Mudhoney, Sleater-Kinney, The Postal Service, and Iron and Wine. As punk moved into the mainstream music market, Sun Pop found itself competing with the major labels for artists. The cost of its aggressive promotions became prohibitive, and by 1991, the company was in financial difficulties. The staff was downsized from 25 to five. The company was saved by its share of the royalties on Nirvana's album *Nevermind,* though Nirvana had already moved to a major label. In 1995, Sub Pop signed a deal giving Warner Bros. 49 percent ownership, which has existed until the present. According to Poneman, the label made several mistakes after joining with Warner Bros. It opened satellite offices in Toronto and Boston, spent too much on band advances, restricted its policy for new artists, and established contracts with all its employees. Pavitt left the label in 1996.

The company, however, was well poised to take advantage of the shift to digital distribution and lower profit margins. Between 2001 and 2006, it released five of its six best-selling CDs. The company stopped paying oversized advances for bands and videos. Its bands are made as self-sufficient as possible, with tours intended to make money rather than be subsidized by the label. Realistic recording budgets give bands an opportunity to earn royalties even on modest sales. Sub Pop takes advantage of the opportunity for cheap promotion of new music through online channels. In 2007, Sub Pop launched the imprint Hardly Art under a new business model, in which bands own their master recordings and split profits with the label rather than receiving royalties. Contracts are made for one release at a time.

Functions of a Record Label

A major record label or a large independent label has a staff of employees organized into departments that handle each aspect of the business. The departments of a typical record label include:

- **A&R (Artists and Repertoire)** — The A&R department scouts and signs new artists, then works with them to produce recordings. A&R participates in song selection and choosing a producer and recording studio, and it makes all the practical arrangements for recording. A&R also communicates with other departments and makes sure the terms of the contract with the artist are met.

- **Business Affairs** — This department manages finances, oversees the budget, and takes care of bookkeeping, payroll, and taxes.

- **Legal Department** — The Legal Department prepares contracts, resolves legal issues between the artists and the label, and protects the label's and artists' copyrights.

- **Art Department** — The Art Department supervises all design jobs, including CDs and cover art, logos, letterheads, business cards, ads for trade and consumer press, posters, and promotional materials. The art department is responsible for maintaining a consistent brand and image for the label.

- **Marketing** — The marketing department creates and carries out a marketing plan for each new release and coordinates the label's participation in promotions, sales, and publicity campaigns.

- **Public Relations (PR)** — The PR department arranges interviews and radio and television appearances; prepares and sends out press releases; solicits feature stories and record reviews in local and national newspapers, magazines, and Web-based zines; and coordinates with the artists' publicists.

- **New Media Department** — The new media department produces and promotes music videos for the label's artists, as well as maintains a visual presence on Internet sites. The media department may be responsible for the label's website and other online content, as well as marketing through social media, and works closely with the Art and PR departments.

- **Artist Development** — This department works to develop the public image of the label's artists through consistent marketing and promotions. Many labels no longer devote resources to developing their artists' careers, preferring instead to focus on promoting individual releases and signing artists who already have established fan bases.

- **Sales and Distribution** — This department handles all aspects of the label's retail sales and develops working relationships with distributors and key retail outlets. Sales works closely with the Marketing and Promotion departments.

- **Promotion Department** — The Promotion Department devotes itself to securing airplay for the label's new releases on traditional, satellite and Internet radio, and it works closely with the New Media, Marketing, Sales, and PR departments to ensure marketing strategies are well coordinated and fully implemented. The Promotion Department may be responsible for arranging concert tours and public appearances.

- **Label Liaison** — At a large record label, the Label Liaison coordinates the activities of the label's distributors with the needs of the record label, ensuring that product is available in stores when a new release is announced or when an artist goes on tour.

If you will be running your record label by yourself or with one or two partners, you will be busy carrying out many different tasks. Some responsibilities may take up too much time and interfere with your ability to focus on selling music, but they cannot be neglected. Instead of maintaining a full-time staff, many smaller labels outsource various responsibilities to third-party services, such as production studios and distribution companies, and contract with lawyers and accountants to provide services as needed.

How is a Major Record Label Different from an Independent?

The basic difference between a major record label and an independent label is a difference of scale. A major record label has the financial backing, staff, and distribution network to mass-market a newly released CD, placing it simultaneously in retail outlets all over the country, getting extensive airplay on commercial radio stations, and booking international tours. Major labels add to their profits by mass-producing their CDs, DVDs, or vinyl records. They print their labels and posters for pennies each in overseas facilities and sell them with big markups. Shipping and distribution cost much less on a large scale. Independent labels typically focus their marketing efforts on a particular geographical region or **niche market** (a specialized group of loyal fans) and rely on direct contact with fans and alternative marketing techniques to sell their records.

A major label signs an artist for either a **developmental deal** or a recording contract. In a developmental deal, the label pays the artist to make one or more recordings, sometimes covering additional costs such as purchasing musical instruments or equipment, and decides later whether to do a full-scale release of the recording(s). With a **recording contract**, the label pays the artist an advance and then records and promotes his or her music. The advance is typically recoupable, which means it is paid back to the record label out of the profits from sales of the recording(s). An independent label looks for artists who are ready to sign recording contracts and already have a fan base. Major record labels often sign artists for multiple albums, while independent labels typically contract one recording at a time.

Under a contract with a major label, the artist typically must accept the label's choice of recording studio, producer, and recording engineers. The label often retains the right to make final edits and changes to the recording and may exercise control over artwork and publicity photos. The artist may be required to commit to a touring schedule the record label establishes. An independent label may not pay the artist as much up front, but it allows the artist more freedom and control over the finished product and more input in planning promotions and tours.

Independent labels operate more like a service, working side-by-side with a band or an artist to build a grassroots fan base, arranging appearances at local venues and festivals, and organizing distribution of the artists' CDs. The label produces recordings and implements a marketing and retail plan appropriate to the artist's genre, including making the music available on DSPs (digital service platforms, such as MP3 files and streaming down-loads). The staff members of an independent label often develop personal relationships with promoters and other influential people in a particular genre, making it easier to arrange concerts and public appearances. Many independent labels have unique cultural images of their own that help to brand the artists who associate with them.

Major record labels have large publicity budgets and many employees. In order to make a profit, they must sell hundreds of thousands of recordings. The decline in the sales of CDs in favor of digital downloads has cut into the profits of major labels. A major label might have to sell 500,000 CDs to make an acceptable profit from a release, while an independent label can pay its bills and make a profit if it sells just a few thousand. On the other hand, an independent label may lack the financial resources for large-scale promotion.

Why start an independent record label?

A better question might be, "Why not?" The initial steps of registering a business name and getting an occupational license or permit are relatively simple. If you are about to launch a recording of your own music, or

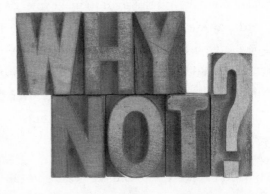

you are helping an artist with a first release, why not establish a brand right away? There will probably be a second and a third recording after that. You will be able to build your image around your label, and in the future, to extend that brand to include other artists.

If you are involved in some aspect of the music business and have a passion for a particular type of music, your record label might become the catalyst that gives new artists exposure to audiences who can appreciate them or revives old favorites so younger generations can enjoy them. The independent labels mentioned earlier in this chapter all played vital roles in launching the careers of many artists and in preserving musical traditions.

A record label is a legal entity that can own and manage copyrights, royalties, and publishing rights. If something happens to you in the future, your label can continue to operate as a business and protect the interests of its artists. Buying and selling music catalogs and publishing rights is one way a label can make money.

There has never been a better time to start your own label. Computers give you the tools to do many things yourself that you would have had to pay someone else to do in the past, such as bookkeeping and printing press releases, posters, and promotional materials. Using today's software and equipment, a recording engineer with sound equipment can single-handedly create sophisticated digital recordings. CDs are relatively inexpensive to replicate and ship, and it costs very little to provide audio downloads. Many companies offer **turnkey solutions** — complete services that manufacture, package, and ship CDs and make audio downloads available for sale, all for a set price. Three websites — iTunes, Amazon, and Rhapsody — are responsible for 95 percent of all digital download sales. Companies such as Tunecore® (**www.tunecore.com**), InGrooves (**www.ingrooves. com**), and The Orchard® (**www.theorchard.com**) allow you to sell your digital music on multiple sites. Distribution companies like CDBaby® (**www.cdbaby.com**) and Amazon's CreateSpace® (**www.createspace.com**) make it possible for you to sell hard copies of your CDs online.

Today's social media and the Internet provide multiple channels for publicizing new releases and building a fan base with a tiny budget. Platforms such as MySpace and YouTube provide a marketplace and exposure for new music. Some industry commentators believe independent labels are the future of recorded music and that major record labels are in decline because they have not been able to adapt to the rapid changes in the way people discover and listen to music.

Once you have built a reputation and a repertoire for your record label, you can sell the business to someone else. If your business becomes too much for you to handle, you can sign a distribution deal with a major label or another independent label. A major label bought many well-known independent labels after one or two decades.

CASE STUDY: L-MA KING

Kingdome Records

L-Ma King is a singer and songwriter of gospel and holy music based in Kissimmee, Florida. She is preparing to launch her second CD, Now Is the Time, *in July 2011.*

I wrote my first song in January 2004 and started singing in 2005. I did not have any formal voice training and did not grow up singing in a church choir, but song has always been a part of my life, and I began to feel tremendously inspired. When I began working on my first CD, I found my way through prayer and word-of-mouth. One person led to another. When I needed a keyboardist, I looked through the yellow pages and found someone named Sugarcane. I thought, 'With a name like that, he has to understand my type of music!' I called Sugarcane, and he introduced me to a wonderful musician who is a band and recording engineer all in one. We set up a recording studio in a room at our church. He brings in his equipment and does all the tracks himself — keyboard, bass, and percussion. We send our recording to a company that does the final mixing and creates the master.

In 2009, I released my first CD, *God's Blessings — Songs for the Now*, and began handing out copies to pastors, family, and church members — everyone I knew. Bishop B. G. Shearrill of Montgomery, Alabama, was the first person to receive my CD and play it on his Internet radio station, WMGY 800/AM (**http://wmgyradio.com**). He became my mentor, helping to take my music to new heights. Bishop Jesse Harris, owner of *The Gospel News magazine* in Tuskegee Institute, Alabama, urged me to start my own record label. He assured me it would be simple, but in fact, it has been quite an investment of time and money, filling out all the paperwork and paying the various registration fees. It cost $300 to register a fictitious name here in Florida. I had to get an occupational license and register with the state of Florida to pay sales tax. If I fail to submit the sales tax return on time each month, there is a $50 penalty. It cost another several hundred dollars to have a logo designed and copyrighted.

I will have to sell quite a few CDs to pay for setting up the record label. Right now, all of my financial resources are invested in producing and promoting my CDs. Maybe there will be something leftover for me later!

I got the name for my label when I was trying to register a domain name for a website. The name "Kingdom" was already taken, of course, and one of the alternative suggestions was "Kingdome" with an "e."

Bishop Shearrill took my CD around to dozens of other Internet gospel stations, but for the moment, I am only working with WMGY 800/AM and Rev. Ray Manning of Ray Manning Singers (**http://Raymanningsingers. com**). I also got ads in gospel magazines, such as *The Gospel News*, *Gospel USA*, and *Gospel Now*. *The Gospel News* magazine eventually featured me on the cover and in an interview. My song, "The Holy Wine Blessing," made it to No. 1 on the Ray Manning's radio station playlist in the June/July 2010 issue of *Gospel USA*.

Each of my CDs has a companion book explaining the inspirations for all of the songs, a sort of journal about how they were written and recorded. I perform live wherever I can and tell everybody I meet about my music and my mission — pastors, church members, even people standing in line next to me at a cash register. My main purpose is to spread the good news and to bring hope and inspiration to as many people as I can reach. But I will be thrilled if I reach the top of the charts.

Why You Might Not Want to Start an Independent Record Label

Like any other business, running a record label is hard work. If you are working alone or with a small staff, you will be the one responsible for fulfilling all the label's commitments. You may be overseeing production of recordings, booking tours and performances, writing press releases, and staying up late at night packaging CDs to ship to retailers. You may find yourself taking care of an artist who is going through a personal crisis or resolving a dispute between band members. If you are a musician yourself, all of this work is in addition to writing songs, practicing, and performing. If you neglect or overlook some aspect of your business, your sales might decline or you might miss out on a valuable opportunity to expand your success.

Producing and promoting a new release takes money and is always a gamble. You may find your finances stretched thin until you begin making a profit. If your record takes off suddenly, you may need to come up with money to manufacture large quantities of CDs or vinyl albums to supply your retailers. Every new artist you sign represents new financial burdens along with the possibility of making money.

The owner of a successful independent label possesses passion, good intuition, and a mind for business. If you know you are lacking in one of these areas, it is better to seek a partnership with someone who complements your weaknesses or to work as an employee in a music business until you know what you are doing.

How Record Labels Make Money

A record label makes money by selling new releases of its artists, as well as past releases from its catalog, compilations, box sets, and memorial albums. Although sales of digital formats are rapidly expanding, CDs are still the main form in which recordings are sold. Music is still sold as tape cassettes, and as you will read in *Chapter 10*, vinyl records are making a comeback. CDs, tapes, and vinyl records are sold online and through specialty stores, entertainment retailers, discounters, and mass-marketers such as big box chain stores. Online sales of CDs are made through online retailers such as Amazon.com; the websites of traditional retailers such as Barnes and Noble®, Best Buy®, and Walmart®; and websites of record labels, affiliates, and individual artists.

Digital music is sold as individual tracks or whole albums, subscriptions, and streaming services. Music is increasingly sold as downloads on mobile devices through companies such as iTunes, Napster®, MOG, Rdio™, Rhapsody®, MTV, Nokia, Spotify, Sprint, T-Mobile®, Verizon Wireless, Orange™, Vodafone, eMusic, Virgin Mobile®, China Mobile, YouTube, and MySpace Music and as ringtones for cell phones.

Depending on its contracts, a record label can earn a percentage of the royalties whenever its artist's music is broadcast on television, radio, cable, and satellite; performed live at a concert, arena, nightclub, or other venue; played at sporting events, in restaurants, or bars; performed as part of a staged theatrical production; used in films, TV programs, or TV commercials; or used as background for a music video or a video game. It can earn money by licensing copyrighted music and lyrics for use in printed sheet music.

Memorabilia for sale outside a concert

Finally, a record label can earn money when its name and logo are used on merchandise such as posters, T-shirts, musical instruments, pennants, and dolls. The label can also produce and sell merchandise associated with its music, such as books, clothing, and commemorative booklets, or it can sell memorabilia associated with its artists.

The ease with which digital music can be downloaded and shared has presented a challenge for the music industry. It is impossible to collect royalties when someone copies a song on a CD or flash drive and gives it to a friend. Record labels have been trying many strategies to deal with this threat to their bottom line, including educating the public, developing subscription-based audio and visual streaming, adding value to paid downloads, embedding software that blocks file copying, and even taking their customers to court. The issue of protecting the value of intellectual property is under continual study. Record labels and artists are now embracing the fact that controlling illegal downloading and file sharing is difficult and seek to profit from the popularity of their artists in other ways, such as sales of merchandise, concert tickets, and high-quality gift sets. Some websites offer free downloads to their visitors and pay for these downloads by selling advertising space. Many songs now appear in TV shows or commercials within weeks of their first release.

Standard distribution deal

The most common arrangement between an artist and a record label is a distribution deal in which the record company advances the money for the cost of recording an album and handles the manufacturing, distribution, press, and promotion. The artist gets a percentage of the sales as royalties after all those costs are repaid. The record label owns the copyright to the recording indefinitely.

The "360" deal

In the past, major record labels made a profit of $2.50 to $4 on the sale of each CD. With the advent of digital music sales, the business model has changed. Customers prefer to buy individual songs rather than whole albums, and the profit on the sale of a digital file is measured in pennies, not dollars. To compensate for the decline in revenue from record sales, major record labels are increasingly signing **360 (or multiple rights) deals** — contracts that allow them to receive a percentage of the earnings from all of a band's activities. In addition to revenue from record sales, the label claims a percentage of the profit from concert ticket sales, merchandise sales, music publishing, endorsement deals, and any other use of the artist's brand or music. In return, the label commits itself to developing the band's career over the long term, finding new promotional opportunities, and devoting more of its resources to marketing the band's image.

Major labels acknowledge that, in the near future, most music downloads probably will be free and will serve mainly to increase the sales of event tickets and merchandise. They claim they cannot afford to promote artists based on sales of recordings alone, and that 360 deals allow them to focus on developing artists instead of concentrating on the promotion of individual chart-topping hits or albums. In a speech to a Web 2.0 Summit audience in 2008, Warner Music Group CEO Edgar Bronfman caused a stir when he announced his label now required all new artists to sign 360 deals and that a third of its signed artists were under those contracts.

Artists, on the other hand, are reluctant to give up income from concert tickets, publishing rights, merchandise, and endorsements that have traditionally been their domain. Conflicts of interest can arise when a company associated with one of the major label's competitors offers an endorsement deal or an opportunity to appear on television or at a live event. The major label's efforts to create a brand for a band sometimes end up stifling the band's image instead of strengthening it. Many 360 deals cover the release of multiple albums by the artist, an obligation that can take years to fulfill. Although record companies claim they need an extended time to recover their financial investment in an artist, ten years can be a long time from the developing artist's point of view. Most artists would prefer to retain some control over their careers. Some record labels continue to claim a percentage of the revenue from touring, merchandise, and publishing even after the contracted albums have been completed. These deals often have terms that are unfair to artists, such as claiming a percentage of gross (total) revenue from concert ticket sales without allowing the artist to deduct his or her travel expenses.

A 360 deal can be mutually beneficial if the financial obligations of each party are spelled out clearly and in cases where a relatively unknown artist will benefit from a major record label's highly orchestrated promotion in ways the artist could not achieve otherwise — for example, when a band's music is particularly suited to commercial pop radio.

License deal

In a license deal, the artist retains the copyrights and ownership of the master, and the record label licenses the right to exploit him or her exclusively for a specific number of years (typically seven). After that, the artist regains the right to license the use of his or her music for TV commercials, movies, and rereleases. This type of deal is appropriate for artists who have already produced their own recordings and do not need much creative guidance. The record label might not be as motivated to invest in the promotion of a new release because it will only benefit from it for a short period.

Net profit deal

Many independent record companies now follow a "net profits" business model. The contract gives the record label the right to recoup all the costs of producing and promoting a record, including costs that are normally borne by the label under a traditional contract, such as manufacturing, distribution, and marketing. The artist and record company then share the remaining net profits on a 50/50 (or other percentage) basis. The formula is structured so the record company gets a favorable return on its investment in the record and does not need to seek additional revenue from the band's other activities.

Manufacturing and distribution deal

In a manufacturing and distribution deal, the record label handles only the manufacturing and distribution. The artist does everything else. This kind of deal works well for a record label that already has an extensive distribution and marketing network for a particular genre of music. The label does not stand to make as much money because the artist retains ownership and licensing rights to the album.

Self-release

Innovative recording equipment and software such as Pro Tools has made it possible to record album masters on a low budget. A band may be able to finance its own recordings and retain ownership of the copyrights, licensing only the distribution and promotion to a record label.

Tales from the Industry

M.C. Hammer:
Thinking and Spending Big

M.C. Hammer, the first hip-hop artist to obtain diamond status for an album and a known innovator of pop rap, has always managed his own recording business. He brainstormed and produced acts such as Oaktown's 3.5.7, Common Unity, Special Generation, Analise, One Cause One Effect, Teabag, Geeman, Pleasure Ellis, B Angie B, Stooge Playaz, Ho Frat Ho, and Wee Wee.

In the mid 1980s after a record deal fell through, Hammer decided he, too, would start a record label business. He borrowed a cool $20,000 each from former Oakland A's players Mike Davis and Dwayne Murphy to start Bust It Productions. He sold records from his car and basement and eventually founded the independent label Bustin' Records (later Oaktown Records). Throughout his career, he moved Oaktown from one label and distributor to another while collaborating with and mentoring other artists.

In 1987, the label released his debut album, *Feel My Power*, which sold more than 60,000 copies. Hammer also released the single "Ring 'Em," which, through relentless street marketing by Hammer and his wife, became popular at San Francisco Bay Area dance clubs. Hammer developed a dynamic stage show with a troupe of dancers, musicians, and backup vocalists that caught the attention of a Capitol Records executive. Hammer signed a multi-album record deal with Capitol and received a $750,000 advance. A revised version of *Feel My Po*wer was re-issued as *Let's Get It Started* and sold two million copies. His next album, *Please Hammer, Don't Hurt 'Em* ranked number one for 21 weeks and has sold about 18 million records to date. Although criticized by rap fans for his sometimes-repetitive lyrics, his clean-cut, good boy image, and his perceived dependence on sampling, M.C. Hammer navigated a successful career that included extensive touring in Europe and Asia. In 1991, PepsiCo sponsored him, and PepsiCo International CEO Christopher A. Sinclair went on tour with him.

Unfortunately for Hammer, his success was matched by a lavish lifestyle that included a $12 million mansion in California and a payroll of 200 employees. The concert tour for his fourth album, *Too Legit to Quit*, had to be canceled midway because, though the album reached #5 on the charts, album sales could not support the expense of the elaborate stage show. The music video for the album included a number of celebrities and was one of the most expensive music videos ever produced. As his style of pop rap became less popular with fans, sales of later releases did not match the income from his earlier albums. In 1996, when Hammer declared bankruptcy, he had gone through $33 million in royalties and was $13 million in debt. His mansion sold for a tiny portion of its original price.

Hammer's financial difficulties did not stop him from continuing to release successful albums and singles, making a foray into gospel music, and appearing in films and on television. Today he lives much more modestly and applies his know-how and drive to developing a series of new business ventures including clothing lines (J Slick and Alchemist Clothing), and most recently, Alchemist Management, a company that manages and markets ten martial arts fighters.

CHAPTER 2

Setting Up
Your Record Label

N othing can stop you from declaring yourself a record label, creating a logo and a website, and selling your own CDs. If you achieve any measure of success, however, you will soon find yourself in trouble of one kind or another. When you sell anything retail or through commercial channels, you may have to pay state sales tax and report your profits as personal income on your tax return. If you do this incorrectly, you will be in violation of the law and may be subject to IRS audit. If you do not register copyrights for your music and lyrics, they can be stolen and performed by anyone who happens to like them. When someone else turns that song into a hit, you will have to engage in a complicated legal battle to claim any rights to your own composition. Your band's name and your cool logo can be copied and used by somebody else to promote his or her product if you do not register them as a trademark. Just when you are reaching the heights of success, your brand could be stolen from under you.

Other types of problems arise when you start promoting someone else's music. Unless you register your label as a separate business entity, you could become personally liable to fulfill the financial obligations of a contract and lose everything you have, including your house and your car. A casual partnership between friends can quickly turn sour when someone has to take the blame for a mistake. You can avoid many pitfalls by setting up your record label correctly as a business entity from the beginning and by being aware of the situations that could arise as your business grows.

Many companies offer to help you set up your business — for a substantial commission. You can save money by doing most things yourself. Often, all you have to do is fill out some online forms, pay a fee, and in some cases, provide documentation such as a driver's license or proof of a business license. Federal, state, and local government websites walk you step-by-step through the registration process and provide telephone contacts or live chats to answer your questions. If you encounter difficulties you cannot resolve by yourself, you often can get assistance from your local U.S. Small Business Administration (SBA) office. The SBA website (**www.sba.gov**) offers valuable guidance. Standard templates are available for articles of incorporation and other registration documents (see companion CD). You can also purchase business software packages that include templates for legal documents, such as the one sold by RecordLabelResouce.com (**www. recordlabelresource.com**).

Filling out your own registration forms helps you understand the legal obligations of a business and may force you to think through aspects you might not have considered, such as how decisions will be made and the responsibilities of each person involved in your company. You also will know how to alter your business organization in the future and know when reports and annual fees are due without depending on a third party who will charge you additional sums to do this work.

If you need to customize legal documents, you can pay a business or an entertainment lawyer by the hour to advise you. Do as much of the work as you can yourself and prepare your questions in advance so you will be able to explain your needs clearly to the lawyer and quickly determine what needs to be done.

Determine the Legal Structure of Your Business

The legal structure of your business will set the stage for your everyday operations and influence how you proceed with financial, tax, and legal issues. It will even play a part in how you name your company, as you will be adding Inc., Co., or LLC at the end of your name to specify what type of company you are. Your business structure will dictate what type of documents you will need to file with various government agencies and how much and what type of documentation you must make accessible for public scrutiny. In addition, it will define how you will actually operate your business.

Most independent labels begin as sole proprietorships, partnerships, or LLCs. If you are promoting your own music, you do not need to be too concerned about legal and financial liability. When you begin signing other artists to your label, an LLC protects you from being personally liable if an artist takes you to court for breach of contract or holds you responsible for theft or damage to expensive equipment. A corporation is usually not formed unless the label seeks financing from outside investors or becomes an employee-owned business.

The chart below compares different legal structures and lists the documents you may need to file with state and federal agencies, depending on where you live.

Business Entity Chart

LEGAL ENTITY	COSTS INVOLVED	NUMBER OF OWNERS	PAPERWORK	TAX IMPLICATIONS	LIABILITY ISSUES
Sole proprietorship	Local fees assessed for registering business; generally between $25 and $100	One	Local licenses and registrations; fictitious name registration	Owner is responsible for all personal and business taxes.	Owner is personally liable for all financial and legal transactions.
Partnership	Local fees assessed for registering business; generally between $25 and $100	Two or more	Partnership agreement	Business income passes through to partners and is taxed at the individual level only.	Partners are personally liable for all financial and legal transactions, including those of the other partners.
LLC	Filing fees for articles of incorporation generally between $100 and $800, depending on the state	One or more	Articles of organization; operating agreement	Business income passes through to owners and is taxed at the individual level only.	Owners are protected from liability; company carries all liability regarding financial and legal transactions.
Corporation	Varies with each state; can range from $100 to $500	One or more; must designate directors and officers	Articles of incorporation to be filed with state; quarterly and annual report requirements; annual meeting reports	Corporation is taxed as a legal entity; income earned from business is taxed at individual level.	Owners are protected from liability; company carries all liability regarding financial and legal transactions.

Sole Proprietorship

A sole proprietorship is the easiest and least costly way of starting a business such as a record label. It is the most prevalent type of legal structure that startup or small businesses use. There are likely to be fees for business name registration, a fictitious name certificate, and necessary licenses. Attorney fees for starting the business will be less than those for the other forms of business because fewer documents are required, and the owner has absolute authority over all business decisions.

A sole proprietorship is owned and operated by one owner. You will have absolute control of all operations. Under a sole proprietorship, you own 100 percent of the business, its assets, and its liabilities. Some of the disadvantages are that you are wholly responsible for securing all monetary backing, and you are ultimately responsible for any legal actions against your record label. The advantages are that it is relatively inexpensive to set up, and with the exception of a couple of extra tax forms, there is no requirement to file complicated tax returns in addition to your own. Your business expenses can be deducted from your income for tax purposes. Until your business is bringing in a profit, a sole proprietorship is the easiest structure to maintain. Most business owners who start small begin their operations as sole proprietors.

As a sole proprietor, you can operate under your own name or you can choose to conduct business under a fictitious name. *See the section on Protecting Your Name below.*

General Partnership

A partnership is almost as easy to establish as a sole proprietorship, with a few exceptions. In a partnership, all profits and losses are shared among the partners. A profit is the positive gain after expenses are subtracted from a company's revenue, while a loss occurs when a company's expenses exceed its revenues. The two most common types of partnerships are general and limited partnerships. A general partnership can be formed by an oral agreement between two or more persons, but a legal partnership agreement drawn up by an attorney is advisable. Legal fees for drawing up a partnership agreement are higher than those for a sole proprietorship, but they are usually lower than fees for incorporation. A formal partnership agreement helps to solve disputes that might arise later on. Each partner is responsible for the other partners' business actions, as well as his or her own.

Not all partners in a partnership necessarily have equal ownership of the business. Normally, the extent of each partner's financial contribution to the business determines the percentage of the business that partner owns. This percentage is applied to sharing the organization's revenues, as well as its financial and legal liabilities.

One key difference between a partnership and a sole proprietorship is that the business does not cease to exist with the death of a partner. If a partner dies, the deceased partner's share can either be taken over by a new partner or the partnership can be reorganized to accommodate the change. In either case, the business is able to continue without much disruption. Many partnerships have a life insurance policy for each partner that will allow the partnership to buy his or her share from the deceased partner's heirs in case of death.

Sometimes as a sole proprietorship grows, the needs of the company outgrow the knowledge and capabilities of the single owner, requiring the input of someone who has the expertise and experience necessary to take the company to its next level. Not all entrepreneurs benefit from turning their sole proprietorships to partnerships, but many businesses benefit significantly from the knowledge and expertise each partner contributes.

When establishing a partnership, it is in the best interest of all partners involved to have an attorney develop a partnership agreement. Partnership agreements are simple legal documents that normally include information such as the name and purpose of the partnership, its legal address, how long the partnership is intended to last, and the names of the partners. It also addresses each partner's contribution, professionally and financially, and how profits and losses will be distributed. A partnership agreement also needs to outline how changes in the organization will be addressed, such as death of a partner, the addition of a new partner, or the selling of one partner's interest to another individual. The agreement ultimately must address how the assets and liabilities will be distributed should the partnership dissolve.

A Partnership Agreement should include the following:

- Type of business

- Amount of money or property invested by each partner

- Responsibilities or duties of each partner

- How profit or loss will be divided among partners

- How each partner will receive compensation (salaries or a percentage of profits)

- How assets will be distributed when partnership is dissolved

- How long the partnership will continue

- Procedures for changing or dissolving the partnership

- How disputes will be settled

- What restrictions will be placed on each partner's authority to make decisions and to spend money

- How the partnership will be reorganized if one of the partners dies or becomes incapacitated

Worksheet for a Successful Partnership

Before entering into a partnership, it is important that all partners agree on important matters such as compensation, decision-making, and reinvestment in the business. The following exercise will help you and your future partner(s) to understand each other's expectations:

Write down your responses to these questions and have your partner do the same. Then trade worksheets and discuss your opinions and answers to the following topics:

1. My philosophical vision for the company

2. My business strategy

3. I came to this strategy through the following education, practice, and life lessons.

4. My work ethic

5. What "commitment to the business" means to me

6. My talents

7. My partner's talents

8. My skills

9. My partner's skills

10. My role as I see it in the company

11. My partner's role in the company

12. Our method of compensation for partners

13. Our compensation plan for key employees and other employees

14. Our record keeping will be done through _____ (method) or by _____ (person)

15. We plan to create capital by…

16. We will finance debt through these methods…

17. We will deal with OSHA regulations and safety by…

18. When big decisions need to be made, we will…

19. If we disagree on a decision that has a major impact on the company, we will…

20. Things we enjoy outside of working hours include…

Limited Liability Company

A limited liability company (LLC), often wrongly referred to as limited liability corporation, is not a corporation, but it offers many of the same advantages. Many small business owners and entrepreneurs prefer LLCs because they combine the limited liability protection of a corporation with the "pass through" taxation of a sole proprietorship or partnership, which means each owner pays personal income tax on his or her share of the profits instead of the company as a whole paying tax. The owners of an LLC, referred to as members, enjoy the same protection from liability as a corporation and the flexible recordkeeping of a partnership, which is not required to keep meeting minutes or records. In an LLC, the members are not personally liable for the debts incurred for and by the company, and profits can be distributed as the members deem appropriate. All expenses, losses, and profits are passed through the business to the individual members who ultimately pay either business taxes or personal taxes, but not both on the same income.

LLCs are a comparatively modern type of legal structure; the first one was established in Wyoming in 1977. It was not until 1988, when the Internal Revenue Service ruled the LLC business structure would be treated as a partnership for tax purposes, that other states followed suit by enacting their own statutes establishing the LLC form of business. LLCs are now allowed in all 50 states and Washington, D.C. An LLC is easier to establish than a corporation but requires more legal paperwork than a sole proprietorship. It is appropriate for a business whose operations require adequate protection from legal and financial liabilities for its members, but it is not large enough to warrant the expenses incurred in becoming a corporation or the recordkeeping involved in operating as a corporation.

Regulations and procedures affecting forming LLCs differ from state to state, and they can be found in the "corporations" section of your state's secretary of state website. *A list of the Secretary of State department that handles LLCs and corporations in each state can be found later in this chapter.*

Two main documents normally are filed when establishing an LLC. One is an operating agreement, which addresses the management and structure of the business, the distribution of profit and loss, the method of voting, and how changes in the organizational structure will be handled. The operating agreement is not required by every state.

Articles of Organization, however, are required by every state, and the required form generally is available for download from your state's website. The purpose of the Articles of Organization is to establish your business legally by registering with your state. It must contain, at a minimum, the following information:

- The limited liability company's name and the address of the principal place of business

- The purpose of the LLC

- The name and address of the LLC's registered agent (the person who is authorized to physically accept delivery of legal documents for the company)

- The name of the manager or managing members of the company

- An effective date for the company and signature

For instance, Articles of Organization for an LLC filed in the state of Florida will look something like this:

ARTICLE I — Name

The name and purpose of the Limited Liability Company is:

Fictitious Name International Trading Company, LLC
Purpose: To conduct...

ARTICLE II — Address

The mailing and street address of the main office of the Limited Liability Company is:

Street Address: 1234 International Trade Drive
　　　　　　　　 Beautiful City, FL 33003

Mailing Address: P.O. Box 1235
　　　　　　　　　 Beautiful City, FL 33003

ARTICLE III — Registered Agent, Registered Office, and Registered Agent's Signature

The name and the Florida street address of the registered agent are:

　　　　　　　　 John Doe
　　　　　　　　 5678 New Company Lane
　　　　　　　　 Beautiful City, FL 33003

After being appointed the duty of registered agent and agreeing to carry out this service for the above mentioned Limited Liability Company at the location specified in this certificate, I hereby agree to take on the assignment of registered agent and will perform in this capacity. I further agree to adhere to all statutes and provisions associated with the proper and complete performance of my tasks, and I am knowledgeable with and agree to the conditions of my position as a registered agent as outlined in Chapter 608, Florida Statutes.

_____

Registered Agent's Signature

ARTICLE IV — Manager(s) or Managing Member(s)

Title	Name & Address
"MGR" = Manager	
"MGRM" = Managing Member	

MGR

Jane Doe
234 Manager Street
Beautiful City, FL 33003

MGRM

Jim Unknown
789 Managing Member Drive
Beautiful City, FL 33003

ARTICLE V — Effective Date

The effective date of this Florida Limited Liability Company shall be January 1, 2009.

REQUIRED SIGNATURE:

_____

Signature of a member or an authorized representative of a member

---

Corporation

Corporations are the most formal type of legal business structure, as well as the most common form of business organization. A corporation can be established as public or private and is chartered under the laws of the state where it is headquartered. A public corporation is owned by its shareholders (also known as stockholders) and is public because anyone can buy stocks in the company through public stock exchanges. Shareholders own shares or stocks, which represent a financial interest in the company. Many corporations start out as individually owned businesses and grow to the point where they seek additional financing by offering shares for sale in the open market. The first offer of shares to the public is called an **initial public offering** (IPO). Selling shares of your company diminishes your control over it by giving decision-making power to stockholders and a board of directors. Control is exercised through regular board of director meetings and annual stockholders' meetings. Records must be kept to document decisions made by the board of directors. Small, closely held corporations can operate more informally, but recordkeeping cannot be eliminated. Officers of a corporation can be liable to stockholders for improper actions.

A private corporation is owned and managed by a few individuals who are normally involved in the day-to-day decision-making and operations of the company. If you own a relatively small business but still wish to run it as a corporation, a private corporation is the optimal legal structure because it allows you to stay closely involved in the operation and management. Even as your business grows, you can continue to operate as a private corporation. There is no rule that says a private corporation must change to a public corporation when it reaches a certain size.

Whether private or public, a corporation is a separate legal entity capable of entering into binding contracts and being held directly liable in any legal issues. Its finances are not directly tied to anyone's personal finances, and it is taxed separately from its owners. These are only some of the many advantages to operating your business in the form of a corporation.

A business may incorporate without an attorney, but legal advice is highly recommended. The corporate structure is usually the most complex and is more costly to organize than the other two business forms. Forming a corporation can be a lengthy process, and the legal paperwork can put a strain on your budget. In addition to the startup costs, there are ongoing maintenance costs, as well as legal and financial reporting not required of partnerships or sole proprietorships.

To legally establish your corporation, it must be registered with the state in which the business is created by filing Articles of Incorporation. Filing fees, information to be included, and its actual format vary from state to state. However, some of the information most commonly required by states is listed as follows:

- Name of the corporation

- Address of the registered office

- Purpose of the corporation

- Duration of the corporation (how long it will remain in operation)

- Number of shares the corporation will issue

- Responsibilities of the board of directors

- Status of the shareholders, such as quantity of shares and responsibilities

- Stipulation for the dissolution of the corporation

- Names of the incorporator(s) of the organization

- Statement attesting to the accuracy of the information contained therein

- Signature line and date

Most states provide instructions for filing the Articles of Incorporation on their secretary of state corporate division website, along with a schedule of fees.

State Offices Responsible for Filing Articles of Incorporation

The name of the government office that provides services to businesses and corporations is different in every state. Here is a list by state of the appropriate office for filing Articles of Incorporation:

STATE	NAME OF DIVISION RESPONSIBLE FOR FILING ARTICLES OF INCORPORATION
Alabama	Corporations Division
Alaska	Corporations, Businesses, and Professional Licensing
Arizona	Corporation Commission
Arkansas	Business / Commercial Services
California	Business Portal
Colorado	Business Center
Connecticut	Commercial Recording Division
Delaware	Division of Corporations
Florida	Division of Corporations
Georgia	Corporations Division
Hawaii	Business Registration Division
Idaho	Business Entities Division
Illinois	Business Services Department
Indiana	Corporations Division
Iowa	Business Services Division
Kansas	Business Entities
Kentucky	Corporations
Louisiana	Corporations Section
Maine	Division of Corporations
Maryland	Secretary of State
Massachusetts	Corporations Division
Michigan	Business Portal
Minnesota	Business Services
Mississippi	Business Services

STATE	NAME OF DIVISION RESPONSIBLE FOR FILING ARTICLES OF INCORPORATION
Missouri	Business Portal
Montana	Business Services
Nebraska	Business Services
Nevada	Commercial Recordings Division
New Hampshire	Corporation Division
New Jersey	Business Formation and Registration
New Mexico	Corporations Bureau
North Carolina	Corporate Filings
North Dakota	Business Registrations
Ohio	Business Services
Oklahoma	Business Filing Department
Oregon	Corporation Division
Pennsylvania	Corporation Bureau
Rhode Island	Corporations Division
South Carolina	Business Filings
South Dakota	Corporations
Tennessee	Division of Business Services
Texas	Corporations Section
Utah	Division of Corporations and Commercial Code
Vermont	Corporations
Virginia	Business Information Center
West Virginia	Business Organizations
Washington	Corporations
Washington, D.C.	Corporations Division
Wisconsin	Corporations
Wyoming	Corporations Division

S Corporation

An S corporation is a legal structure designed for small businesses. Until the inception of the LLC, the S corporation was the only legal structure that afforded small business owners some form of limited liability protection from creditors, yet provided the benefits of a partnership. An S corporation is taxed in much the same way as a partnership or sole proprietorship. Each year's profits and losses are passed through to the shareholders, who must report them on their personal income tax returns. According to the IRS, shareholders must pay taxes on the profits the business realized for that year in proportion to the percentage they own of the company's stock.

In order to qualify as an S corporation under IRS regulations, the following requirements must be met:

- It cannot have more than 100 shareholders.

- Shareholders are required to be U.S. citizens or residents.

- All shareholders must approve operating under the S corporation legal structure.

- It must be able to meet the requirements for an S corporation for the entire year.

Form 253, "Election of Small Business Corporation," must be filed with the IRS within the first 75 days of the corporation's fiscal year.

Electing to operate under S corporation status is not effective for every record label business. However, many employee-owned and family-owned companies over the years have benefited from it. In 1966, the S Corporation Association of America (**www.s-corp.org**) was established to lobby in Washington, D.C., on behalf of small- and family-owned businesses against too much taxation and government regulation. The association represents the 4.5 million owners of S corporations in the U.S.

FINANCIAL STATEMENT REQUIREMENTS AND DISCLOSURE AT A GLANCE BY BUSINESS STRUCTURE			
Business Type	**Regulatory Requirement**	**Management Requirement**	**Investor and Lender Requirement**
Sole Proprietors	None	Generally, rely on common accounting software and reports. Financial statements are not relied on and audited statements are rare.	Lenders normally limit loan sizes and rely on owner's income tax returns and other personal information when making loan decisions. Loans are backed by the sole proprietor's personal property, in addition to business assets.
Partnerships	None	May rely on common accounting software. May have an accounting firm compile financial statements if a particular need arises.	Similar to the sole proprietor, except two or more partners provide personal resources to guarantee loans.
Private C-Corp	Generally none. Some states require annual disclosure of total assets and liabilities but not a full set of financial statements.	Typically the largest of the private business structures. Senior management uses financial statements to manage daily operations, to provide the board of directors with ability to oversee the entire company, to keep investors informed, as a requirement of bylaws, and to obtain loans. Stock option programs may make audited statements a requirement in the process of valuing the company and establishing a stock price.	Lenders frequently require GAAP conforming audited financial statements and include covenants about the total amount a company can borrow from all sources against assets. Investors normally require unaudited quarterly statements and audited annual statements to track financial performance.
Private S-Corp	Generally none. Some states require annual disclosure of total assets and liabilities but not a full set of financial statements.	The need for financial statements is made at management discretion. Accounting software may not give adequate oversight of the business, and with up to 100 investors, the corporate bylaws may mandate annually audited statements.	Similar to Private C-Corps. Lenders frequently require annual audited statements depending on loan sizes and associated risk. Investors that do not actively manage the business may require statements to verify management is competent.

FINANCIAL STATEMENT REQUIREMENTS AND DISCLOSURE AT A GLANCE BY BUSINESS STRUCTURE			
Business Type	**Regulatory Requirement**	**Management Requirement**	**Investor and Lender Requirement**
Private LLC	Generally, none. Some states require annual disclosure of total assets and liabilities but not a full set of financial statements.	Generally, the same as Private S-Corps, but there can be more investors influencing the need.	Generally, the same as Private S-Corps, but there can be more investors influencing the need.
Public C-Corp	All financial statements publicly disclosed as defined by the SEC. Includes annual audited and quarterly unaudited reports along with other requirements.	Management regularly relies on financial statements to guide decision-making. Extensive public analysis requires management thoroughly understand information behind the numbers and be able to explain significant changes. Board of directors determines the outside firm to conduct the annual audit.	Lender requirements are similar as those for Private C-Corps. Investors can obtain copies from the SEC EDGAR database and have an opportunity to ask questions of management at the annual shareholders meeting.

Selecting a Name for Your Record Label

The name you select for your record label will become your brand and the central element of all your marketing efforts. If you are successful, your name will become synonymous with a certain type of musical experience and even with a culture, as Sub Pop did in the 1980s. Loyal customers will want to buy and listen to new releases just because your name is on them. It is important to choose a name that evokes the right images and emotions in your target audience and a name that has significance for you. Large corporations spend millions of dollars creating and testing potential product names with surveys, focus groups, and psychological evaluations because they know the "feel" and emotional connotations of a name are crucial to successful marketing.

As an independent label, put careful thought into the name you select. It should be a name that everyone in your company likes and agrees on. It also should be short, unique enough to stand out from the crowd, and easy to remember. A name containing more than two or three words will cause all sorts of problems when you are designing logos, letterheads, and posters, and people will misspell it more often in Internet search engines.

You can set up a sole proprietorship, obtain licenses, and operate a business using just your first and last name. If you use your own name, you can avoid the expense of registering a fictitious name with your state government. Most personal names, however, do not have the right look and feel for a record label. In choosing a name, you must consider your future plans for your label. What will happen if you sell your label to another company, expand your business to include other types of music, or become a corporation controlled by shareholders? If you are creating a label to market your own music, do not use the name of your band unless you have no intention of adding any other bands to your catalog. Your name and your band's name are valuable trademarks and marketing tools in themselves. It is better to preserve them for independent use. In the future, if you want to branch out into a new genre or a new project, you can always create a sublabel with a unique name, such as Epitaph's Hellcats or SST's Cruz Records. Each label name, however, means additional expense to advertise and promote it.

You may already have decided on a name for your record label. If not, brainstorm with your partners, friends, and family members. Write down all the suggestions and discuss how each name makes you feel and the visual images it evokes. Think of words that inspire the images you want, and look up words with similar meanings in a thesaurus. Experiment with adding numbers or the names of colors, plants, and gemstones, or combining syllables. Try different spellings. Translate words into other languages. Test other peoples' reactions to your list of names. Narrow down your list to a handful of possible names, and repeat the process until you feel satisfied you have found suitable names.

Even when you have found the perfect name for your record label, there is a possibility someone else is already using it. Make a list of four or five alternatives in case your first choice is not available. You do not want to use a name to which you do not have all legal rights. Imagine the nightmare that could arise if you are forced to change your record label's name after you are already well established. You would have to alter your name on every one of your contracts and legal documents; destroy all your business stationery, posters, and promotional materials; and launch a massive advertising campaign to reclaim your loyal followers.

Conduct a thorough search to confirm no one else is using the name. Start with the Internet. Search the database of the U.S. Patent and Trademark Office (**www.uspto.gov/trademarks/index.jsp**) to see if the name is already registered. Type the name into several Internet search engines and even Wikipedia (**www.wikipedia.org**). See how other companies are using the words in your name. Play around with the search engine results. Remember to test misspellings and words that have different spellings but sound the same as your name. Add the names of countries where you might want to market your music to your name in the search box to see if your name is used in another part of the world. Next, check some online business directories such as The Yellow Pages (**www.theyellowpages. com**™), WhoWhere.com (**www.whowhere.com**), and Business.com (**www.business.com**). Some libraries will do a name search for you for a small fee. You can find lists of record labels on numerous websites, including A2G Music (**http://a2gmusic.com/content/record_label**), All Record Labels.com (**http://allrecordlabels.com**) and Wikipedia (**http:// en.wikipedia.org/wiki/List_of_record_labels**).

Before you can register your company name with the secretary of state's office in your state, you must prove no other business in that state is using the same name. Most of the state websites where you can submit a business name registration begin with a name search of all businesses registered in that state. Your local county clerk has a record of all the fictitious names (or assumed names) registered in your county.

Finally, check to see if your name is available as an Internet domain name. Your label's Internet presence will be crucial for promotions and sales of digital downloads and successful marketing through social media. You do not want your fans to encounter any obstacles when they look for your label online. If "yourcompanyname.com" is not available, consider using a different name. You can search for domain names on the InterNIC website (**http://internic.net/whois.html**) or on any website that sells them, such as GoDaddy.com® (**www.godaddy.com**) or Network Solutions® (**www. networksolutions.com**).

Protecting your name

As soon as you have decided on a name, claim it. If you are using it as the name of your corporation, file your incorporation documents as soon as possible. If you are a sole proprietorship or partnership, register it as an assumed name with the office of the secretary of state in your state and locally with your county clerk. From now on, all your contracts and legal documents will read "Your personal name or partnership name, DBA (doing business as) your record label name."

Begin putting the symbol TM (trademark, used to distinguish a product) or SM (service mark, used to distinguish a service) after your name wherever you use it. (You do not have to register a trademark or service mark to use these symbols.) You can officially register a service mark or trademark with the U.S. government for $325 — a small amount to pay for the assurance that no one else can legally use your name.

Register your domain name immediately with an inexpensive registrar (such as GoDaddy.com or Network Solutions), along with possible misspellings and obvious variations. Each domain name costs only $7 to $10 per year (some of the new suffixes cost more). Again, this is a small amount to pay to prevent some opportunist from siphoning off your Web traffic. When you set up your website, you can arrange for all of these domain names to redirect to your site. Registering your domain name in other countries is more complicated because some countries require your business to have a physical presence registered in the country first. You may have to employ the services of an agent in that country.

Tip: Keep your domain names up to date.

Be sure to renew your domain names on time or set up automatic renewals; someone could be waiting to grab your domain name the moment your registration expires.

Designing a Logo for Your Label

Your company logo, like your name, is an important element of your branding and your marketing strategies. Your logo is a visual symbol that instantly identifies your products. Just like the words in a name, the colors and forms of a logo convey specific feelings and messages. A logo can be your company name or initials, a simple shape, or an elaborately designed symbol. Even if you have already designed your logo, it is a good idea to get a graphic designer to create it for you using illustration software so that you will have high-quality images to use in print and on websites. A professional artist will make sure that your logo design is balanced and aesthetically pleasing. If you cannot afford to hire a professional, look for a student or a friend who has experience with graphic design software. Or do it yourself using the logo design tools on Guru Corporation's Logosnap.com (**www.logosnap.com**) or

HP®'s Logomaker (**www.logomaker.com**). Your logo will appear on business cards and stationery, on your website, and on all of your products.

Registering Your Business

You will have to register your business locally with the city or county that has jurisdiction over the area where it is physically located, and you may be required to get certain licenses or permits. Failure to register your business correctly could result in fines or penalties. Every county and has its own rules for business registration. Contact the office of your local county clerk, or look up the regulations on its website. If you are running your business out of your home, you may be required to purchase an occupational license that must be renewed every year. If you are using an assumed name for your record label, make sure the correct name is listed on the registration.

You can use the Business Licenses and Permits Search Tool (**www.sba.gov/content/search-business-licenses-and-permits**) at the SBA.gov website, the official business link to the U.S. government, to get a listing of the federal, state, and local permits, licenses, and registrations you will need to operate your business.

Most states do not require a sole proprietorship to register if it is operating under the owner's personal name. Businesses with assumed, or fictitious, names must be registered with the state.

As discussed earlier in this chapter, a corporation must register by filing its Articles of Incorporation with the state. A public corporation is required to file an annual audited financial report and quarterly unaudited reports along with other documents such as notices of changes to the corporate structure. All of this information is made available to the public on the SEC EDGAR database (**http://www.sec.gov/edgar.shtml**). Detailed information about corporations whose shares are trading on a stock exchange is available on the stock exchange's website and investment websites.

Keep copies of all your licensing applications, registration documents, and official forms. You may be required to display your business licenses in a prominent place. Maintain a list of all your licenses and registrations, along with their renewal dates. Mark renewal dates on a calendar. Remember that you may need additional business licenses if you expand your business to include new activities or services, such as warehousing, retail sales of merchandise, or event organizing.

How to Obtain an Employer Identification Number (EIN)

All employers, partnerships, and corporations must have an employer identification number (EIN), also known as a federal tax identification number. You must obtain your EIN from the IRS before you conduct any business transactions or hire any employees. The IRS uses the EIN to identify the tax accounts of employers, certain sole proprietorships, corporations, and partnerships. The EIN is used on all tax forms and other licenses. To obtain an EIN, fill out Form 55-4, which you can obtain from the IRS at **www. irs.gov/businesses/small**. Click "Small Business Forms and Publications." *A copy of this form is included on the companion CD.* There is no charge. If you are in a hurry to get your number, you can get an EIN assigned to you by telephone at 800-829-4933.

A sole proprietor who does not have employees can use his or her Social Security number on tax forms instead of an EIN.

State Sales Tax Permit

Anything you sell retail, such as CDs or digital music downloads on your website or T-shirts and posters at events, will be subject to state sales tax, and you could end up with a hefty fine by not reporting and paying sales tax as required by your state.

You can apply for a sales tax permit on the website of your state's Department of Revenue. Before you can apply, you will need to have your local business license, EIN, registered business name and address, and other information about your company. Find out how and when the sales tax permit has to be renewed and how and where to file and pay sales tax. Some states require you to pay monthly; others allow you to pay quarterly (every three months) if the sales tax you owe does not exceed a certain amount. In addition to paying sales tax, you must file regular sales tax reports. Most states allow you to file and pay online; sign up for this feature if you can. Otherwise, you will probably be given a coupon book with a detachable form for each month and mailing envelopes to send in each month's sales tax report and payment. Be careful to pay on time and not miss filing deadlines, or you will have to pay fines and penalties.

You must collect sales tax for each retail sale. The sales tax should be calculated and listed separately from the item prices on the sales receipt. Cities and counties within the same state may charge different percentages of sales tax. The amount of sales tax is determined by the physical location of the buyer. You will need to program your cash registers to calculate the correct sales tax for the area where the sales are made. You must record the sales tax you collect in your accounting system, usually in a liability account called "Sales Tax Payable." *See the following section on Bookkeeping.*

You do not have to charge sales tax when you are selling goods wholesale to a reseller (a merchant who sells your product to retail customers). Anyone who is buying wholesale and not paying sales tax should have a resellers permit. Keep a copy of the resellers permit on file in case of a tax audit.

Sales tax on Internet sales

Sales tax on merchandise sold on the Internet has been extended to digital downloads of music, video, e-books, ringtones, and other digital products by many states, beginning with New Jersey in 2007. In July 2010, Wyoming became the most recent state to charge sales tax on downloads kept for permanent use by the buyer. Below is a list of all the states that charge sales tax on digital downloads. Each state defines digital products differently, and some products are exempt in some states.

STATES THAT CHARGE SALES TAX ON DIGITAL DOWNLOADS	
Alabama	New Jersey
Arizona	New Mexico
Colorado	North Carolina
District of Columbia	South Dakota
Connecticut	Rhode Island
Hawaii	Tennessee
Indiana	Texas
Kentucky	Utah
Louisiana	Washington
Maine	Wisconsin
Mississippi	Wyoming
Nebraska	

Even when a state requires its residents to pay sales tax on digital downloads or merchandise sold online, online retailers are required to collect the sales tax only when they have **nexus**, a legal term referring to a physical presence, in that state. The criteria for determining whether a business has nexus are different from one state to another. (Refer to your state sales tax office for more information.) A business might be considered to have nexus if it has a physical location in the state; it has resident employees working in the state; it has employees, such as sales reps, who regularly solicit business in that state; or it owns property (including intangible property) in that state. In the past, to have nexus for sales tax purposes, a business had to have a physical location in the state, but more recently, this requirement has been expanded to include affiliates who sell a company's products. The billing address for the credit card used to make the purchase determines the state in which the sale was made and the amount of sales tax to be charged. In sales of merchandise, such as a CD or T-shirt, physically shipped to a buyer, the shipping address determines the state in which the sale was made and the amount to be charged. Sales tax is calculated as a percentage of the final price including shipping. You only have to collect and pay sales tax for sales made to customers living in states where your company has nexus. Customers living in the other states where online sales are taxable are expected to report and pay sales tax on their state income tax returns for items they bought online. Whether they will comply remains to be seen.

Sales tax rates and regulations are continually changing. Online shopping cart software programs automatically calculate and add sales tax when it is appropriate and use the services of a tax rate provider, a company that constantly updates tax information to comply with the latest regulations. Accounting software programs such as QuickBooks™ include sales tax modules that calculate how much sales tax should be charged for each sale based on your physical location and the shipping or billing address of your customer and keep track of the amount you owe each month.

Open a Bank Account

If you are a sole proprietorship promoting your own music and your record label is still a business in name only, you do not need a separate business bank account. You might not want to pay the fees to maintain a separate business account until you have regular business income. As soon as your label grows and you reach the point where your personal finances must be kept separate from your business finances, a business bank account is essential. A partnership, LLC, or corporation should have a bank account in its name.

To establish a business checking account, most financial institutions will require a copy of the state's certificate of fictitious name filing from a partnership or sole proprietor or an affidavit to that effect. An **affidavit** is a written declaration sworn to be true and made under oath before someone legally authorized to administer an oath. To open a business checking account for a corporation, most banks will require a copy of the Articles of

Incorporation, an affidavit attesting to the actual existence of the company, and the EIN acquired from the IRS.

Meet with a bank representative when you go to open a business checking account and inquire about the services available for businesses, such as online banking, business credit cards, and business lines of credit. A **line of credit** account is an arrangement whereby the bank extends a specified amount of unsecured credit to the borrower.

If you expect to enter the international market, look for a banking institution with an international department, such as Bank of America, Wachovia, Global Connect, or Regions Bank, that will be able to handle and process specialized transactions, such as foreign exchange payments. Look for speed in handling transactions, electronic banking, a strong but flexible credit policy, and a solid relationship with other financial institutions overseas.

Finding a Location for Your Record Label

The physical location of your record label is not important because you will not be relying on walk-in traffic. Much of your work will be done over the phone and outside the office at production facilities, rented studios, and performance venues. All you need is enough space to organize your files, store paperwork and CDs, accommodate your staff, and house recording equipment if you have it. Many independent labels begin by operating out of a home office. Later, as your business expands and you add full-time employees, you can look for a suitable office to rent or buy.

It is natural for an independent label to set up shop in a geographical region where its particular genre is popular — for example, country western in Nashville, indie in Austin, grunge in Seattle, or jazz in New York. It is much easier to network and find new artists when you are part of a local music scene and to establish personal relationships with local musicians and local performance venues. The less distance you have to travel to connect with artists and business associates, the better. Geographical location is not as important for a label that is only promoting one band or is focused on rereleases. If you are doing a lot of recording with different bands, urban areas where there is an active music culture have a greater selection of studio and production facilities.

Though you may often be on the move, you will need to communicate constantly with your artists, staff, and business associates. A good laptop computer and cell phone are essential. Learn to organize your "mobile office" so that you can access files, documents, websites, e-mails, and financial records with the touch of a button, no matter where you are.

Get a Post Office Box

Whether you are working from a temporary office at home or have a separate physical address for your business, it is a good idea to secure a post office box (P.O. box) at your nearest post office. You can rent a P.O. box online at the U.S. Postal Service website (**www.USPS.com**). Look under "Products and Services" for "P.O. Boxes Online."

Having a post office box for your company helps keep your business correspondence separate from your personal correspondence. Most important, it will prevent you from having to reprint any business stationery should you ever relocate your office. Continuity in any business means stability.

Accounting and Bookkeeping

Disciplined and accurate bookkeeping is essential to the success of a record label. In addition to the usual business expenses, such as office supplies, rent, payroll, and the cost of wholesale product, you will find yourself making substantial financial outlays to publish and produce recordings, hire studio facilities, rent venues for performances, pay travel expenses for tours, and buy advertising in local newspapers. You may be advancing money to artists when they sign a record contract. When money does start coming in, it will come from multiple income streams including online sales of digital downloads and ringtones, sales of CDs and merchandise, profits from event ticket sales, and royalties from the use of your music and recordings. A percentage of that income will belong to your artists, according to the terms of their contracts. Without an accurate bookkeeping system, you will never know where you stand financially or whether your business is making or losing money. You could also end up in legal trouble if you fail to pay your artists what they are due. You need up-to-date information about your finances to make important decisions, such as how much to spend on advertising for a tour or how much merchandise to order. A mistake could quickly land you in a financial bind.

If you or one of your partners understands bookkeeping and basic accounting principles, you can set up and maintain your own accounting system until your record label grows large enough to require the services of a full-time accountant. Many of the third-party online sales channels (such as iTunes and Amazon.com) keep track of sales tax and automatically subtract their costs and fees from each sale and provide you with reports. Shopping cart software programs often include accounting components and customized reporting. *These will be discussed in more detail in Chapter 9.* If you use checks, debit cards, or credit cards to pay for expenses, most banks now offer online reports that show how your money is being spent. You can import your bank statements directly into Microsoft® Excel® or another spreadsheet program or into your accounting software and sort and categorize your expenses. If you are not comfortable using computerized spreadsheets, purchase accounting ledgers at an office supply store and keep manual ledgers.

Accounting Software Programs

Accounting software packages offer complete accounting systems that do just about everything: keep track of income, expenses, and sales tax; create invoices; do your payroll; process credit card transactions; import data from your bank statements and online shopping carts; print checks; produce instant customized reports; and create budgets, forecasts, and business plans.

One of the most widely used packages, known for its versatility and ease of use, is QuickBooks financial software. The basic version of this program, QuickBooks Pro, sells for less than $230 at office supply retailers. An online version is available starting at $13 per month. QuickBooks' Premier Edition is a complete accounting system sells for approximately $400. QuickBooks can also be purchased online directly from the QuickBooks website at **www.quickbooks.intuit.com**, or other sites such as Amazon.com (**www.amazon.com**).

Another popular accounting package is Sage Peachtree Complete Accounting 2011 (**www.peachtree.com**), which sells for about $300 and offers more inventory options than QuickBooks. Although the setup is a little complicated, it is easy to use once you have it up and running.

You can find in-depth reviews of the top ten small business accounting software packages at Top Ten Reviews™ (**http://accounting-software-review.toptenreviews.com**).

All of these software packages have live support options and add-ons, such as credit card processing services, for an additional cost. They can be customized to fit your business needs. Have an accountant or someone who knows the program well help you set it up so that it does exactly what you need it to do. Once the program is set up, all you have to do is enter your records on a regular basis.

The person who is taking care of your bookkeeping should be responsible for paying sales tax each month and renewing licenses, permits, memberships, and domain names regularly and on time.

If accounting and recordkeeping are not your strengths, hire a part-time bookkeeper to update your records on a regular basis. Many experienced bookkeepers work from home, and you can find their services advertised on Craigslist (**www.craigslist.org**) and in local classified ad services. Ask friends, family, and other business owners to recommend someone. An accounting student would be happy to work on your books for a few hours every week or month. Be sure to check references and hire someone reliable and knowledgeable. Depending on the extent of your activities, it might be wise to have an accountant set up your bookkeeping system initially, review your accounts and business records at the end of the year, and help you with tax preparation.

Tip: Do not become a victim of fraud.

It is happening every day, in companies of all sizes: a trusted employee is discovered to have diverted tens or hundreds of thousands of dollars of the company's money to his or her own pocket. More than 96 percent of these employees have no criminal background; they just find themselves in a situation where it is easy to steal and cannot resist the temptation. Every year U.S. businesses lose an estimated 7 percent of their annual revenues to fraud. Do not let someone steal your hard-earned money. Fraud occurs when the accounting system is poorly organized and when one individual is given control of multiple accounting functions, such as approving invoices and writing checks. The best way to prevent and detect fraud is to regularly review your accounts for irregularities and to require more than one person to approve expenditures. All expenses should be documented with sales receipts and/or invoices. Have an outside accountant review your account records from time to time, especially if one individual is doing all the bookkeeping. Follow your intuition; if you sense that something is wrong, investigate. An honest mistake can quickly be discovered and the person's name cleared. A dishonest employee could continue to undermine your business for years and deprive hard-working employees and artists of their rightful earnings.

Taxes

A corporation reports income and pays taxes as a separate legal entity. In all the other types of business organizations — S corporations, LLCs, partnerships, and sole proprietorships — each year's business income and expenses are "passed though" to the individual owners and reported on their personal income tax returns. All legitimate business expenses are deducted from business revenues, and the balance is reported as income on the owners' tax returns. If expenses exceed revenue, that amount is reported as a loss on tax returns. For that reason, you do not want to overlook any expense that could legitimately be deducted.

According to IRS Publication 535 (**www.irs.gov/publications/p535**), a business expense must be "ordinary and necessary" to be deductible. An ordinary expense is one that is common and accepted in your industry, for example, the cost of manufacturing CDs. A necessary expense is one that is helpful and appropriate for your trade or business, such as printing posters to put in music stores. An expense does not have to be indispensable to be considered necessary. You may need the help of a tax accountant to determine which of your expenses qualify as "ordinary and necessary."

Certain expenses, such as the cost of goods sold, expenses associated with starting up your business, and the purchase of land, vehicles, and equipment, are not deductible and must be **capitalized** (classified as long-term investments rather than current business expenses) instead. The cost of these items can be recovered by deducting a specified percentage each year as depreciation, amortization, or depletion.

You can deduct expenses such as mileage when you use your personal vehicle for business, travel, interest on money borrowed for your business, office supplies, and entertaining clients. It is important to keep receipts and statements that document these expenses. Make a habit of keeping all your receipts for business-related purchases and filing them away for future reference.

When you run your business out of your home, you can also deduct a portion of your utility bills, mortgage interest, and home maintenance costs as business expenses. The amount you can deduct is determined by the percentage of your home that is completely dedicated to your business — the number of square feet you use for your office, studio, or storage space.

It is important to be aware of tax rules so you can comply with them from the beginning and get the maximum tax deduction. Learn from other business owners, and consult a tax accountant or lawyer.

Expenses that can be deducted from your income on your tax return:

DEDUCTIBLE BUSINESS EXPENSES:
Supplies
Studio rental fees
CD production costs
Travel expenses
Vehicle-related expenses
Hotel rooms during business travel or touring
Half of your meal expenses while traveling or on tour
Fees paid to publicist, booking agent, accountant, lawyer, etc.
Promotional expenses (fliers, business cards, merchandise to give away, etc.)
Equipment rental fees
Parking and tolls
Gifts to industry professionals (up to $25 is deductible)
Music business books, directories, or software for your business
Copyright and trademark fees
Office supplies
Home office or studio

CAPITAL EXPENSES, DEDUCTIBLE AS AMORTIZATION, DEPRECIATION, OR DEPLETION:

Computers

Instruments, mics, amps

Recording equipment

Vans, buses, vehicles

Real estate

Business expenses must be itemized on IRS Schedule C and filed with your Federal Form 1040. If you are self-employed, you will probably have to also file a Schedule SE. According to IRS Publication 533, you must pay self-employment taxes (SE taxes) if your net earnings from self-employment activities were more than $400. SE tax is a Social Security and Medicare tax for individuals who work for themselves, similar to the Social Security and Medicare taxes withheld from the pay of most wage earners. A self-employed individual is required to file an annual return and pay estimated tax quarterly. Use the worksheet in IRS *Form 1040-ES, Estimated Tax for Individuals* (**www.irs.gov/pub/irs-pdf/f1040es.pdf**) to find out if you are required to file quarterly estimated tax. You may have to pay a penalty to the IRS if you fail to make quarterly estimated income tax payments.

The amount of SE tax you must pay each quarter is calculated based on the income reported in your income tax *Form 1040* from the previous year. If this is your first year being self-employed as a record label business owner, you will need to estimate the amount of income you expect to earn for the year. Form 1040-ES contains blank vouchers you can use to mail in your estimated tax payments, or you can make your payments online using the Electronic Federal Tax Payment System (EFTPS). If you overestimated your earnings for one quarter and paid too much tax, complete another Form 1040-ES worksheet to refigure your estimated tax for the next quarter. If you estimated your earnings too low, complete another Form 1040-ES worksheet to recalculate your estimated taxes for the next quarter. You can find more information on SE tax online at the Self-Employed Individuals Tax Center (**www.irs.gov/businesses/small/article/0,,id=115045,00. html#obligations**).

Each time you hire a new employee, he or she must fill out an IRS *Form W-4, "Employer Withholding Allowance Certificate."* The Form W-4 determines how much income tax, Social Security, and Medicare tax is withheld from each paycheck. The frequency with which you have to deposit these withheld taxes with the IRS is determined by the amount of taxes you reported for your company two years previously (the look-back period). Payroll software automatically calculates withheld taxes when it prints paychecks. You can find more information in *IRS Publication (Circular E), Employer's Tax Guide* (**www.irs.gov/pub/irs-pdf/p15.pdf**).

When you hire someone, such as a cameraman, to do occasional work for you, or to do **work for hire** (work on a one-time project), that person is treated as an independent contractor, and you do not have to withhold taxes on his or her behalf. Payments to an independent contractor that total $600 or more for the tax year must be reported to the IRS on Form 1099-MISC, "Miscellaneous Income," and a copy must be given to the independent contractor. The independent contractor is responsible for paying his or her own income and SE taxes to the IRS. Your record label will probably be using the services of many individuals on a part-time or one-time basis. If you are uncertain about how to treat these workers for tax purposes, read "Independent Contractor (Self-Employed) or Employee?" on the IRS website (**www.irs.gov/businesses/small/article/0,,id=99921,00.html**), or consult a tax accountant or lawyer.

CHAPTER 3

Writing a Winning Business Plan

A successful record label needs a good business plan. A business plan transforms your hopes and ideas into substantial reality. It lays out, on paper, why you are forming a record label, who your customers and competitors are, your strengths and weaknesses, how you plan to finance and run your business, and what you have to do to get started. In the beginning, you may not know enough about the music industry or about what you can achieve to craft a detailed business plan. Start by writing down what you do know — your reason for founding a record label, your goals, the type of music you intend to promote, the qualities that will make your label unique, and the first steps you will take to start operating your business. As you gain experience, you can develop a professional business plan you can show to lenders, investors, and artists to convince them you are a solid and viable operation.

A business plan is a thorough assessment of what you want to accomplish, how you plan to go about it, and what your financial resources are. Creating a written business plan helps you to develop and think through your ideas and foresee all eventualities. You are forced to consider every aspect of your new business, including how much you will spend to establish and operate it, assets and skills you can contribute to the business, sales and profit expectations, strategies for expanding the business, and how you will exit the business. Will you be producing recordings in a studio, or promoting music that an artist has already recorded? What will be your main sources of income?

Your business plan is also your sales pitch to prospective investors and business partners, lenders from whom you wish to borrow money for the business, suppliers from whom you want to buy on credit, and artists whom you hope to promote. A well-constructed business plan shows you understand your business thoroughly and are planning for the future. Finally, a business plan serves as a yardstick to measure your progress and help you adjust your goals and expectations as the business grows.

Evaluate your situation today and visualize where you want your record label business to be in three to five years. Set yourself goals to reach along the way; these will serve as benchmarks on your road to success. Your first goal might be to register your business name and logo and set up your company. Your next goal might be to record and produce a CD. After that, you will aim to sell a certain number of CDs, and so on. Each record label is unique, and there are many ways to market and sell music. You might not foresee exactly how you will accomplish each of your goals or even what direction your label eventually will take. As your business grows, you will learn from your experiences and probably come up with many creative ideas that would never have occurred to you in the beginning. Digital technology and entertainment media are evolving so rapidly that it is difficult to predict how music will be promoted and sold even three years from now. Your business plan will also evolve as you adapt to new opportunities.

Writing a complete business plan takes a lot of thought, research, and preparation. There are numerous books on the subject, software programs, and even professional business plan writers, but because you are starting a small business with few physical assets, you should be able to write your own plan. An independent record label typically starts small and builds gradually on its successes. It may never have more than a handful of employees. Use the *Business Plan for a Record Label* template on the companion CD as a guide. A typical business plan is between ten and 30 pages long, but yours may be shorter in the beginning.

Save your business plan on your computer, and keep a paper copy in a file or binder. As your business grows, add copies of important documents such as partnership agreements, contracts, budgets, lists of prospective artists, marketing strategies, and contact information for companies and individuals who provide services. From time to time, review and update your business plan to reflect your current circumstances. Your business plan can help you to make important decisions based on whether they fit in with your original business ideas and to get back on track when your business starts to deviate from its original purpose. Either you will refocus your business activities or alter your business plan to incorporate the new direction you are taking. When you seek additional financing or take on a new partner, your business plan can be rewritten in a more professional manner with the help of business plan software or books to present a clear picture of your business to your prospective partners. An accountant or entertainment lawyer can also help you create a professional business plan. Remember, the business plan is the résumé of your record label. Make sure it is a true reflection of the best of your business.

Structure of a Business Plan

A business plan for any type of business typically contains the following elements:

I.   Cover sheet
II.   Statement of purpose
III. Table of contents
IV.   Mission Statement
V.   Executive Summary
VI.   The business
    1. Description of business
       a) Industry background
       b) Product description
    2. Marketing analysis
       a) Target market
       b) Product description
       c) Market approach strategy
       d) Competition
       e) Strengths and Weaknesses
    3. Personnel — Management and Staffing
       a) Résumés, strengths
       b) Roles and responsibilities
       c) Operating procedures
    4. Financial Management
       a) Capital, assets
       b) Accounting system
       c) Financing

      d) Payment of principals and employees

      e) Business Insurance

VII. Financial data (you will add to this section as your business progresses)

VIII. Supporting documents

Your initial business plan may not contain all these elements if you are starting out as a sole proprietor and selling your own CDs. As your business acquires more stakeholders (people who have a substantial interest in your business, such as investors, partners, and artists who sign with you), you will be adding legal documents and financial statements. Your business description will change as you learn from experience and discover new ways to market your music. You will add more sections when you apply for a loan, add a new business partner, or sign a contract with a distributor.

Cover Sheet

The cover page should be evenly laid out with all the information centered on the page. Always write the name of your company in all capital letters in the upper half of the page. Several line spaces down, write the title "Business Plan." Last, write your company's address, the contact person's name (your name), and the current date.

NAME OF COMPANY

Business Plan

Address
Contact Name
Date

Statement of Purpose

This section should contain one to three paragraphs explaining the purpose of your business plan and may be altered to suit different purposes. A statement of purpose for an initial business plan explains why you are starting the business and what you hope to accomplish, while a business plan submitted with a loan application would explain (briefly) why you are applying for the loan and how the money will be used. For example, the statement of purpose for an initial business plan might read something like this:

> *"XXX RECORDS was formed in July 2010 to produce and promote the music of YOUR NAME, a well-known New Orleans jazz vocalist and trumpet player. After graduating in 2001 from the New Orleans Institute of Jazz, YOUR NAME began performing in local clubs. YOUR NAME was soon invited to appear at jazz festivals all over the southeastern U.S. and was recognized with the MUSICIAN OF THE YEAR AWARD at the 2005 JAZZ FESTIVAL.*

> *"XXX RECORDS produces and sells albums and individual songs recorded by YOUR NAME and is now expanding its marketing and promotional activities to the national and European markets."*

A Statement of Purpose accompanying a business plan submitted with a loan application might read:

> *"XXX RECORDS was formed in July 2010 to produce and promote the music of YOUR NAME, a well-known New Orleans jazz vocalist and*

trumpet player. After graduating in 2001 from the New Orleans Institute of Jazz, YOUR NAME began performing in local clubs. YOUR NAME was soon invited to appear at jazz festivals all over the southeastern U.S. and was recognized with the MUSICIAN OF THE YEAR AWARD at the 2005 JAZZ FESTIVAL. YOUR NAME is recognized for her unique vocal style and mastery of the trumpet. Her renderings of New Orleans jazz standards, as well as her original jazz compositions, have attracted a loyal following throughout the U.S. and Canada.

"XXX RECORDS produces and sells albums and individual songs recorded by YOUR NAME and is now expanding its marketing and promotional activities to European markets.

"In January 2011, XXX RECORDS applied for a loan from the MUSICIANS BANK in the amount of $25,000.00. The loan will be used to record a new album by YOUR NAME, purchase the recording rights for two copyrighted songs, and market the CD through XXX RECORDS' established distribution channels. Loan repayments are made from the sales of CDs and digital music downloads, as well as any use of the music for other purpose such as in commercials, films, or TV shows. The loan is secured by the copyrights to YOUR NAME's recordings and song lyrics until such time as the loan is paid off in full."

Your Mission Statement

A mission statement is a well-written paragraph (sometimes two paragraphs) stating the purpose of your business, the products and services you provide, and something about your company's attitude toward its employees and customers. If written and advertised correctly, your mission statement can become a valuable marketing tool by helping to shape your label's public image. It will also set the tone for your company's internal policies, help you affirm your purpose, and guide your business in the direction you want it to go.

To create a mission statement, list your top priorities and discuss them with your business associates, friends, and family to see how they react. Try to explain why these priorities are important to you. Think about what you are trying to bring to the music industry, such as helping solo jazz artists find an outlet to publish and distribute their music. Experiment with words and phrases until you have created a statement that is clear and understandable. Try to keep it simple and avoid clichés or vague language. A good mission statement will serve as a reminder of your original intentions for your business.

Many companies put all or part of their mission statements on the "About Us" sections of their websites. Reading the mission statements of companies similar to yours will give you an idea of what you might or might not want to include in your own statement. Some sample mission statements:

From TAXI® (**http://www.taxi.com/about.html**), an independent agency that acts as a liaison between artists and music companies:

"We're the world's leading Independent Artist & Repertoire Company. As a matter of fact, we invented independent A&R more than a decade ago. Since 1992, TAXI has specialized in giving artists, bands, and songwriters real access to the people in the music business who have the power to sign deals."

From Wounded Bird Records:

"Wounded Bird Records (**www.woundedbird.com**) was formed in 1998 as a label that specializes in the reissue of albums from the 60s, 70s and early 80s on compact disc. All of our releases are properly licensed from the owner of the original masters, in most cases the original record label and sometimes the artists themselves. We strive to reproduce the original album cover artwork, converted to accommodate the CD size format."

What is your BHAG (big, hairy, audacious goal)?

James Collins and Jerry Porras first introduced the concept of a "big, hairy, audacious goal" (BHAG) in their 1994 book, *Built to Last: Successful Habits of Visionary Companies*. They described a BHAG as a clear and compelling long-term goal that has the power to change your life, as well as the way you do business. Think of it as the ultimate dream for your business. A BHAG should be ambitious and almost unattainable, take at least ten years to achieve, and require you to extend yourself beyond your comfort zone. It should be action-oriented and exciting, something others can easily understand and relate to when you share it with them. Finally, it should be something you can measure and quantify. It may take you some time to come up with a goal to which you can make a ten-year commitment. Once you have identified your BHAG, break it down into smaller milestones and revisit it regularly to remain focused. Examples of famous BHAGs:

Google: "Organize the world's information and make it universally accessible and useful."

Amazon: "Every book, ever printed, in any language, all available in less than 60 seconds."

Microsoft: "A computer on every desk and in every home."

Executive Summary

The executive summary is a summary of the information in your business plan and should be about one to two pages in length. It should be written after you have completed the rest of your business plan. The executive summary contains essential information about your business, such as your target market, how the business will be managed, the expertise of your staff, the types of contracts signed with your artists, and how your music will be marketed and distributed. Write the executive summary to prompt the reader to look deeper into the business plan. It is a good idea to discuss the various elements of your business plan in the order you address them in the rest of the document.

Body of the Business Plan

The body of the business plan describes in detail how your record label will operate and make money and how it will achieve the goals set forth in your mission statement. It can be divided into four distinct sections:

1. A description of the business

The essential business of a record label is making money by owning and exploiting copyrights to music. Your business plan should explain how you will obtain rights to music and how you will promote and sell that music. Especially when asking for loans, it should say how your business would make money. Describe how your record label will operate: selling and promoting music you create yourself, recording and selling the music of other artists and sharing the profits, or purchasing rights to existing recordings and published music.

Your business description should include a brief overview of the music industry in which you will be participating. Include a thorough analysis of your market, including facts and figures such as the volume of digital music sales in the U.S. for the past year and examples of similar businesses that have recently experienced success. Identify your competition and explain what sets your company apart from others in the same field. The information in this section should inspire you (and your future clients, investors, partners, and lenders) to believe your company will be taking advantage of an excellent business opportunity. It should also prepare you to answer any questions you may be asked during a presentation or sales pitch with confidence and self-assurance.

Describe your product — the genre of music, the artist(s), the degree to which you will be involved in the creative process (composing, performing, and recording music), and the form your product will take (digital downloads, CDs, vinyl records, music videos, ringtones, etc).

2. The marketing plan

The marketing plan should be one of the most comprehensive sections of your business plan and can be several pages long, depending on the number of products involved and the market you intend to cover. Identify your target market (teens, college students, country music fans, baby boomers, lovers of folk music, opera buffs). In the jazz music example above, your target market would include jazz music enthusiasts in the U.S. and Europe, high school students in jazz bands, and companies that produce TV commercials. Include additional information about the music industry for that particular market and cite the sources where you found this information, such as *Billboard* magazine or Nielsen SoundScan. Elaborate on the characteristics of the principal market you intend to target, such as demographics, market trends, and geographic location of the market.

Describe, in detail, the strategies you intend to employ to reach this target market. For example, you might distribute your CD to record stores specializing in jazz; plan a tour of jazz clubs, college campuses, and jazz festivals; and approach college radio stations to play your record on their jazz shows. Discuss major changes that have taken place in the industry in the recent past, which will affect how you will conduct business. Estimate the cost of implementing various marketing strategies. This should include the cost of setting up and maintaining a website, purchasing advertising on the Internet and radio, touring and promotional events, and producing one-sheets and sample CDs to give out to anyone who might publicize your music.

Based on demographics and industry statistics, estimate how much **revenue** (the total amount of money received by a company for its goods or services) you can expect to receive from sales of your products.

Analyze your competition, including large record labels and other independent labels in the same genre. Include the threats posed by illegal downloads, piracy, and copyright infringement, and describe any steps you will take to counter these threats.

Finally, evaluate the strengths and weaknesses of your business. Your strengths are anything that gives your company a market advantage. Strengths might include your knowledge and experience in the music industry, an existing fan base for your music or your band, relationships or partnerships with businesses or individuals who can help you break into the market, and your intuitive grasp of the local music scene. Your skills and those of your partners or employees are also strengths — you might have the ability to produce CDs or do all your graphic design in-house, which would save money and allow you to respond quickly to new opportunities. Weaknesses could include inexperience or lack of knowledge about important aspects of your business, such as accounting, financing, distribution, or sound engineering. Limited financial resources are also a weakness because they restrict your ability to market on a large scale if one of your artists suddenly becomes a runaway success. Another weakness might be legal clauses in contracts that allow artists to retain certain rights to their recordings or to back out of commitments too easily. Explain how you will employ each strength to the maximum advantage of your business. Describe what you are doing to correct or compensate for each weakness.

3. Personnel — management and staffing

In this section, give a brief résumé for each of the principals in your business (a principal is an owner, partner, or executive who makes business and policy decisions for a company). Emphasize the qualities and experiences each person contributes to your business. Outline the role and responsibility of each principal. If you will be operating your business single-handedly, explain which aspects of the business you will handle yourself and which you will outsource to other individuals or companies. Include a brief description of other staff members and their responsibilities. Describe how decisions are made in your company, who makes them, and how they are put into practice. If your business is already operating, outline how each person carries out his or her responsibilities — for example, the procedure followed when a new artist is signed or the procedure for arranging promotional tours.

Discuss how orders are filled, turnaround time (the time it takes to fill an order after it is received), and company policies regarding returns and damaged items.

This is also where you should mention any labor policies, such as a drug-free workplace, whether consumption of alcohol is allowed during recording sessions, and penalties for employees or artists who are late or do not show up for scheduled events.

4. Financial management

This section should begin with a list of your capital and assets (contracts, copyrights, recordings, equipment, vehicles) as well as major financial liabilities (debts, commitments to artists, necessary expenses). Many independent labels start out with little capital — the owners' wallets — and expand their operations as they realize income from sales. Include income projections for the next year and the next three years.

Describe your accounting system, who will do your bookkeeping, and how income and expenses will be documented. Explain how principals and employees will be paid: hourly wages, fixed salaries, or a percentage of profits. Explain how artists will be paid. Outline policies for expense accounts or spending limits for business expenses. The more detail you can give in this section, the more clearly you will be able to understand the financial situation of your business later on.

Identify possible sources of financing and how this financing might be secured if the need arises. It is also a good idea to establish an exit plan, a strategy to close your business and cut your losses if you fail to make a profit for an extended period. This can be as simple as saying, "If I am not making a profit in two years, I will close the business." When partners or investors are involved, they should agree on specific indicators that will trigger a financial review of the business, such as repeated failures to sell as many records as expected.

Describe the insurance policies held by your business, the coverage they offer, and the cost of insurance premiums. *See the reference to life insurance in the section on Partnerships in Chapter 2.*

Business Insurance

Business insurance protects businesses from financial losses due to events that may occur during the normal course of business. Theft or damage to instruments, computers and electronic equipment; liability for injury to an employee or an artist during recording or performance; or penalties assessed in a legal judgment over copyright infringement could send you into bankruptcy. Insurance is a necessary expense; it protects you from risk and guarantees you will not have to close your business because of misfortune.

A small home office or home recording studio may be covered under a homeowner's insurance policy. Take pictures, create an itemized list of your equipment, and keep an updated record of models, serial numbers, and receipts. A copy of this record should be on file with your insurance agent. Your insurance company may suggest purchasing additional insurance if the value of your equipment exceeds that of normal home electronics systems.

A record label actively involved in recording and promoting contracted artists is vulnerable to many types of financial loss, and if you are the sole owner or a partner, you may be personally responsible. For example, you could be liable if a band's amplifiers are stolen while its members are on a tour you organized; expensive instruments are damaged by rain during an outdoor concert; equipment is broken in a rented recording studio; a dishonest employee steals company money; or an event is canceled. Many insurance companies now offer specialized insurance policies for recording studios and record labels, including:

- Allen Financial Insurance Group
  (**www.eqgroup.com/afrecpgm.htm**)

- CSI Insurance Group
  (**www.csicoverage.com/Other/RecordingStudio.aspx**)

- Heath Lambert (**www.heathlambert.com**)

- Robertson Taylor (**www.robertson-taylor.us.com**)

If the price of entertainment business insurance is beyond your budget or you need a specific type of coverage, look for a local insurance agent who can customize a policy for you. You can obtain a list of licensed agents in your state through your state's department of insurance or the National Association of Insurance Commissioners.

When talking to an insurance agent, find out exactly what is covered and whether the policy covers replacement costs or only the market value of damaged or stolen equipment. Does the insurance cover damage from fire, storms, flooding, or earthquakes? What about lost income or legal liability due to computer viruses? What are the deductibles (the amount you must pay out of pocket before the insurance takes over)?

5. Financial data (you will add to this section as your business progresses)

This section of your business plan should contain all information and documents pertaining to your financial status, including:

a. Startup costs

Startup costs are one-time expenses that are necessary to get your business up and running. The startup costs for an independent record label are relatively small compared to other types of businesses because you do not need to have a physical location, furnishings, or manufacturing equipment. Your main expenses will be fees for licenses, registrations, legal assistance, and the cost of producing and marketing your first recording or CD. Your startup costs will be higher if you are establishing a corporation or are taking over an existing business that already owns contracts or music catalogs.

b. Loan applications

Attach copies of any loan applications you have submitted to banks or lenders.

c. Available capital and avenues of funding

Attach a list of all your sources of capital.

d. Capital equipment and supply list

e. Balance sheet

A **balance sheet** is like a snapshot of a business's financial condition at a given point in time, such as the last day of its financial year. It usually has three sections: a list of assets and their values, a list of liabilities, and ownership equity. **Assets** are everything the company owns including cash, physical property, inventory such as unsold CDs and merchandise, and intangible assets such as copyrights and contracts. **Liabilities** are the business's financial obligations, including unpaid bills, taxes, and loans. Ownership equity is the difference between total assets and total liabilities. Good-quality accounting software, if it is set up correctly, can provide you with an up-to-date balance sheet anytime you need it.

f.   Break-even analysis

A break-even analysis is a calculation of the amount of sales volume needed to pay for production costs. When sales volume exceeds that amount, your business will make a profit. If sales volume is lower than that amount, you will lose money. A break-even analysis helps you set realistic goals for your record label and decide how much you can afford to spend on promotion and marketing. For example, sales of music, event tickets, and merchandise must bring in enough cash to justify the expense of taking an artist on tour.

g.   Pro-forma income projections (profit and loss statements)

A pro-forma income projection is an estimate of the company's expected revenues for a future period, based on market prices, the cost of goods and services, and allowances for loss.

a.   Three-year summary
b.   Detail by month, first year
c.   Detail by quarters, second and third years
d.   Assumptions upon which projections were based

h.   Pro-forma cash flow (Include same points as for number 7)

A pro-forma cash flow is a picture of what your company's cash flow should look like over a certain period. It shows all the cash coming into your business, including your contributions and money from loans or investors as well as revenue from sales, and all the money that will be paid out over the period, including payments to artists and loan repayments.

6. Supporting documents

Supporting documents are legal documents providing concrete evidence that the other sections of your business plan are accurate. This includes rental property leases, agreements with distributors and manufacturers, contracts with artists, insurance policies, and any other document that contains important information pertaining to your company. By looking at these documents, a prospective lender or investor can see what you are saying about your record label is true. Personal information about you and your partners, such as copies of previous tax returns, résumés and personal financial statements, shows you are qualified to run a successful business and that your financial liabilities will not cripple the company. By looking at your tax returns, a loan officer can see how much you have been earning from the business in recent years. Supporting documents include:

1. Tax returns of principal officers for the last three years

2. Personal financial statement(s) (all banks have these forms)

3. Copy of proposed lease or purchase agreement for office or studio

4. Copy of licenses and other legal documents.

5. Copy of résumés of all principal officers

6. Copies of letters of intent from suppliers, contracts with artists, agreements with distributors and manufacturers, etc.

7. Copyright registrations

Putting Your Business Plan to Work

You may have put a lot of thought and effort into writing your business plan, but it is only the first step. Your business plan gives your business form and structure; now it is time to add the details that will make it successful. Go over your entire business plan, starting with the Statement of Purpose, and break each section down into smaller, more concrete goals and milestones. What actions will you take to accomplish each of those goals? How many of those actions can you complete yourself, and which ones will require another person's expertise or another company's services? Exactly what will each member of your team do? When will you start? When do you expect to complete each activity?

Create a schedule for yourself with specific dates for achieving milestones and a checklist of the actions that must be taken to accomplish each one. Having specific goals and deadlines will push you to set priorities, get things done, and prevent you from getting bogged down in details. Measure yourself against your schedule at regular intervals to see how well you are keeping up with your goals. Your business timeline will gradually alter as you discover new avenues of opportunity, encounter unexpected obstacles, and find ways to streamline some of your work. Eventually your timeline will become a template for future projects. You will learn from experience how to set realistic goals and how much time to schedule for each step of a new record release.

CHAPTER 4

Financing Your Record Label

Your business plan estimates how much it will cost to start your record label and to complete and market at least your first record. If you do not have this much cash available, you must seriously consider how you are going to fund your first project. Without the money to promote your record, you will not be able to sell it. You will not start receiving revenue from selling your record until several weeks after it enters the market. *See Chapter 11 for more information on how record labels are paid by distributors.* In the meantime, you will have additional expenses and, if you have signed other artists, you might have to begin paying them. Independent record labels rely on a variety of funding sources.

Bank Loans

A bank is unlikely to give a small business loan to a record label startup because the risk is too high. There is no guarantee that you will succeed in

selling your record, and once the money is spent, the company will own no physical assets, such as machinery or real estate, that can be sold to recoup losses. After your record label has established itself and released several successful records, you might be able to approach a bank with a well-documented business plan and convince it to lend you money.

You are more likely to succeed in getting a personal loan from a bank, such as a home equity loan. To do this you will have to put up your

home or another piece of personal property as collateral. If you are unable to repay the loan, you will lose it. Unless you can afford to lose your home, it is not advisable to take out a personal loan to finance your record label.

Raise the Money Yourself

One way to get the money you need is to raise it yourself. Define a financial goal and look for every possible opportunity to perform. Set aside as much of the earnings as you can. Performing will give you valuable experience as a musician and help you build a loyal following of fans that will purchase your CD when it comes out. When you are ready to sell your CD, you will already have a reputation and a relationship with many venues where you can promote it. As you become more popular, you will be able to get better bookings and earn more.

While you are working to raise the money, you can look for private investors and start to build an online sales network. Record live performances or demo singles, and sell them as inexpensive downloads on your website or through online distribution services. *See Chapter 11 for more information.*

Private Investors

Private investors are individuals or companies who lend money directly to a business in exchange for a share of the revenue or a high interest rate. Venture capitalists typically have a good working knowledge of the industry they are investing in and look for business opportunities they believe have a good chance of succeeding. They usually insist on having a certain amount of control and sometimes want to be actively involved in the business or to mentor you. Negotiating a deal with a venture capitalist may mean giving up some of your artistic freedom and having to defer to your investor when making business decisions. You can look for investors through websites such as Fundingpost.com (**www.fundingpost.com**) and 3iC LLC (**www.help-finance.com/who1.htm**), at music conferences, and at venture capital expos.

Angel investors are wealthy individuals who are willing to invest money in a project with the expectation of sharing in the record label's future success. Angel investors often enjoy the excitement and prestige of being associated with a rising star and involved in the music business. They are less likely than venture capitalists to interfere directly in the day-to-day affairs of record labels and are willing to wait longer to see a return on their investments. Nevertheless, they can place demands and restrictions on labels. Angel investors are often found by networking and word-of-mouth. Tell everyone, everywhere you go, that you are looking for funding for a new recording. An angel investor might be a friend or family member who wants to support your project, or someone who admires the artist and appreciates the genre.

Whether you are borrowing money from a friend or a business consortium, get everything in writing, and have your lawyer look over the contract before you sign. Have a clear understanding of what is expected from each party, when the loan is to be repaid, and the amount of control the lender will have over the label's business affairs.

Tales from the Industry

SPV Experiences Insolvency After Overextending Itself

SPV (Schallplatten Produktion und Vertrieb), founded in Hanover, Germany, by Manfred Schütz in 1984, is considered one of the leading international heavy metal labels. SPV has worldwide distribution and an incomparable reputation for audio quality, archive research, and visual presentation. Its subsidiaries Steamhammer, Synthetic Symphony, Oblivion and Red hold a substantial back catalog from artists including Motörhead, Saxon, Kreator, Kamelot, Iced Earth, Helloween, Gamma Ray, Type O Negative, Dio, The Mission, Fields Of The Nephilim, Bad English, Suicidal Tendencies, Sepultura, Prong, and non-metal acts such as John Lee Hooker.

On May 25, 2009, SPV became insolvent and filed for bankruptcy after its revenue proved insufficient to sustain the costs of maintaining its extensive operations, which included two U.S. offices, several subsidiaries, and numerous artists. The company experienced problems supplying large retailers such as Amazon.com and Musicmarkt. Schütz conceded that the company had made "homemade mistakes" including unrealistic advances for big-name artists. SPV's insolvency created difficulties for its artists because the company was unable to provide the services it promised and to distribute new releases efficiently.

The label went into receivership and began casting around for investors. At the end of 2009, SPV Gmhb went back into production after resizing its business and entering into a partnership with Sony Music Entertainment, which purchased the rights for some of the German label's main artists and for a part of the catalog. To solve its distribution problems, it allied with a new inventory management and logistics partner, Bremer Versandwer, which had the expertise to handle CD, DVD, digital distribution, software, and console game products as well as accessories, hardware, and merchandise. The company closed its U.S. offices and reduced its staff. The label is now prospering by concentrating on selling and exporting its back catalog and promoting small and mid-size front-line acts that are financially safe.

Grants

A number of government and private entities give grants to support artists and music projects. Most grants are for specific types of projects, and the application process can be grueling. Competition is stiff, but if you can get a grant, you will not have to pay it back. Below is a list of some organizations that offer grants for recording music. State and local arts organizations also offer grants and subsidies for musicians in their regions. Look on their websites, and check with music schools and universities for information on available grants.

ORGANIZATIONS AND AGENCIES OFFERING GRANTS IN THE U.S. AND CANADA	
U.S.	
The National Academy of *Recording* Arts and Sciences, Inc. American Composers Forum	**www.composersforum.org**
American Music Center	**http://amc.net/grants/default.aspx**

ORGANIZATIONS AND AGENCIES OFFERING GRANTS IN THE U.S. AND CANADA	
American Musicological Society Awards and Travel Grants	**www.ams-net.org**
American Society for Composers, Authors, and Publishers Foundation Grant and Award Programs	**www.ascap.com/concert/programs.html**
Association for Recorded Sound Collections Research and Travel Grants	**www.arsc-audio.org/grants-committee.html**
BMI Awards, Scholarships, Internships, and Funds	**www.bmi.com/index.php**
Creative Capital Foundation	**www.creative-capital.org**
Electronic Music Foundation Studios	**www.emfstudios.org**
Electronic Music Foundation	**www.emf.org/about.html**
Foundation Center — Reference Guide for Musicians	**www.grantspace.org/Tools/Knowledge-Base/ Individual-Grantseekers/Artists/Funding-for- musicians**
Musical Online	**www.musicalonline.com/foundation_grants.htm**
National Association for Music Education	**www.menc.org/resources/view/grants-information**
National Endowment for the Arts	**www.arts.endow.gov/grants/apply/Music.html**
New York Foundation for the Arts NYFA Source	**www.nyfa.org/source**
Society for American Music	**http://american-music.org/awards/ AwardInformation.php**
The Aaron Copland Fund for Music	**http://grants.coplandfund.org/recording-program**
Western Arts Alliance	**www.westarts.org/links.html**
List of State Arts Agencies	**http://wdcrobcolp01.ed.gov/Programs/EROD/ org_list.cfm?category_ID=SAA**
Canada	
Canada Council for the Arts	**www.canadacouncil.ca**
Foundation to Assist Canadian Talent on Recordings (F.A.C.T.O.R.)	**www.factor.ca**
Canada Music Fund	

Cooperatives

Cooperatives are membership organizations through which artists and independent labels pool resources and support each other. Most are based in a geographical region, such as the Washington, D.C., Azalea City Recordings (**www.azaleacityrecordings.com**) and Sun Machine Cooperative (Minnesota, Iowa, Indiana and Illinois) (**www.sunmachine.coop**). Cooperatives usually offer services on favorable terms and expect the artist or label to do most of the promotion and sales. They are appropriate for independent artists and small labels, but may not be a good fit for a label with multiple artists that is trying to establish a strong identity for itself.

Joint Ventures

Once you have established yourself with solid CD sales and an artist who is attracting attention, a major label or a larger independent label may offer you a deal. The larger label pays the cost of production and promotion and then deducts this from the sales revenue along with a small percentage for administrative overhead. The larger label's distributor gets a percentage, and whatever is left is divided between the larger label and your label. A large label will not propose a joint venture unless it believes your artist has potential for success. You benefit because you do not have to advance the money for making and promoting the record, and you have access to the larger label's distribution network, but if the record does not sell well, you will only receive a portion of the income you would have received if you had financed it yourself.

Raising Funds Online

Some independent labels and artists pay for a record by selling CDs in advance. You can sell preorders online with the promise to ship the CD on the release date.

Websites such as Kickstarter (**www.kickstarter.com**), PledgeMusic (**www.pledgemusic.com**) and Sellaband (**www.sellaband.com**) provide online platforms where fans can invest in an artist's recording project by pledging money that the artist or label gets only when the target amount is reached. Artists offer various rewards to their investors, including free CDs, personalized copies of special limited editions, merchandise and tour tickets, concerts at a venue of the fan's choice, and sometimes a share of revenues.

CHAPTER 5

Finding and Working with Artists

A record label is an agency that helps artists promote and sell their music. It is a partnership between the artists, who contribute their music and talent, and the record label, which contributes everything else: financing, production and recording expertise, manufacturing and shipping, distribution, and publicity. Both partners must work hard to make sure the music receives all the attention it deserves. When music stops receiving attention, it stops selling. It is important that the artists and the staff of the record label are deeply committed to the success of their partnership.

Many independent record labels are founded by individuals or bands that want to market their own music, either because they are tired of waiting for recognition from a major record label or because they want to retain artistic control and independence. If you are one of those individuals, you are already thoroughly familiar with your genre, and you have music to sell. If you are starting an independent record label because you want to get into the business, or if you have experienced some success with your own music and are ready to add new artists to your label, you will need to scout for unsigned musicians and groups with the potential to grab public attention by producing a hit record.

Major record labels have A&R (Artists and Repertoire) agents who travel all over the country (and world) looking for new artists and new material. Many of them are musicians of a similar age and genre to the artists they

are trying to recruit. These agents spend all their time networking with musicians and other industry professionals. They attend live performances, listen to demos, talk to artists, and cultivate musicians who may not be ready to release a record. When an agent negotiates a contract with an artist, he or she is supported by a whole department of entertainment lawyers and has all the resources of the label at his or her command. A&R staff participate in selecting songs for an album and finding back-up musicians to accompany the artist. You, as an independent label, are probably working alone or with a handful of assistants. You might pay a lawyer by the hour to review your contracts, outsource much of your production and distribution, handle the promotion yourself, and make all the important decisions single-handedly. Because your resources are stretched thin, it is important to streamline your operation and try to make the most of your time and money by selecting your artists carefully.

Selecting the right artist is essential to the success of your record label. You will be investing your money, time, and energy in this person or band. All of your efforts to make a great CD, distribute it, and promote it could be sabotaged if the artist fails to deliver. Your artists become part of your label's identity and image. When you are ready to sign your next new artist, he or she will look at your label's "track record" of past successes. A trail of mediocre CDs and a history of failure will not inspire other artists to sign with you in the future. Inexperience and lack of professionalism can add thousands of dollars to your production costs. A band that is unavailable for tours and public appearances makes promotion difficult. Your artist may lack that special something that captures the heart and imagination of your audience.

Major record labels sign many artists who never make it to the big time. They record demos, work with the artists, and observe them carefully before deciding to throw millions of dollars into launching their careers on a national level. It is purely a business decision. An independent label operating on a shoestring budget does not have the resources to experiment. You will have to make business decisions, too, such as selecting an artist you know you can sell over one who is interesting and has promise, but is not a sure bet.

Where to Find Artists

Thousands of artists are out there, waiting to be discovered and signed by a record label. They are performing at clubs, raves, festivals, basement parties, talent quests, open mic nights (events where amateurs are allowed to perform on stage for a few minutes each), and even on street corners. They are posting their videos on YouTube and Facebook and submitting their **demos** (sample recordings) to every label that will accept them. Your job is to search through the crowd of musicians trying to get your attention and find an artist who has real talent, is a skilled musician, has great songs, is not signed by another record label, and wants to work with you.

Identify with your genre

Your passion for music will be the driving force behind the success of your record label. By identifying your label with a particular genre or style of music, you automatically will attract the attention of the people who love that music. In time, your name and logo will become synonymous with that type of music. Your target audience will be willing to buy a CD or download by an unknown artist because it has your logo on it; it will know it can look forward to an enjoyable listening experience, especially if they are already interested in the genre your promote.

Some genres, such as gospel, R&B, soul, country, jazz, heavy metal, and hip-hop, are easily identifiable. Other genres are gradually emerging and may not be as clearly defined. New genres are typically part of a recognizable scene — a particular age group, attitude, activity, and style of dress. Traditional genres are constantly evolving, borrowing from other styles, or branching off into sub-genres. The music played on country radio stations today barely resembles the music of country music stars from three decades ago, while the music played on pop radio stations now incorporates many conventions of country music, such as the use of simple chord progressions, plaintive vocals, and the sounds of banjos and harmonicas. Genres such as modern zydeco (evolved from Louisiana Creole dance music) and reggaeton (Latin urban music) are quickly evolving mixtures of older genres. Identify yourself with one genre or sub-genre and focus on it until you have two or three successes under your belt. After you have established a solid reputation for your label, you can consider experimenting with a new direction.

Immerse yourself in your chosen genre. Listen to the newest artists as well as the old favorites. Read reviews, blogs, zines, and magazines. Listen to Internet radio, college radio stations, and commercial radio stations to see what songs are being played. Attend music festivals and go to clubs. Study the audiences; observe how they are dressed, how they behave, and how they react to the performers. Take note of what other record labels of the same genre are doing to promote their artists. Talk to fans. Develop an understanding of your market. The more you become involved in your particular scene, the sharper your intuition will become and the better you will be able to recognize potential in a new artist.

Tales from the Industry

Marvin Gaye: "Here, My Dear," an Album Ahead of Its Time

When Marvin Gaye's first wife, Anna Gordy, filed for divorce in 1975, he was in financial difficulties because of extravagant spending on numerous expensive cars and several vacation homes in the U.S. and abroad. Marvin's attorney came up with a unique way for him to pay Gordy the $600,000 he owed her in alimony and child support: a contract giving her half the royalties from his next project. In the spring of 1976, Gaye set out to give Motown a "lazy, bad" album, but as he worked on the music, his feelings about his troubled marriage and divorce were expressed in songs such as "I Met a Little Girl," "Anna's Song," "You Can Leave, But It's Going To Cost You," "Anger," and "Falling In Love." Initially, Gaye was reluctant to release the album because it was so personal, but under pressure from Motown, it was released with the title *Here, My Dear*, in December of 1978.

Consumers hated the album, and critics called it "bizarre" and "un-commercial." An angry Gaye refused to promote it any further and went into self-imposed exile until 1982. In early 1979, only months after it came out, Motown also stopped promoting *Here, My Dear*. The album was Gaye's lowest-charting studio album of the 1970s, peaking at number four R&B and number 26 pop and falling off the charts after only two months. Its only single, "A Funky Space Reincarnation," peaked at number 23 on the R&B charts.

In 1994, the album was rereleased in remembrance of the tenth anniversary of Gaye's untimely death. It reached number one on *Billboard*'s R&B catalog chart. Audiences in the 1990s identified with the raw emotions and intensely personal messages in the songs, and appreciated the Latin beats and Jazz fusion that had repelled listeners in the 1970s. Today *Here, My Dear* is considered a landmark in Gaye's career. *Mojo Magazine* (1995) named it as one of the greatest albums in music history. In 2003, it was ranked #462 in *Rolling Stone Magazine*'s critics' poll, "500 Greatest Albums of All Time."

Start locally

You will probably not find your next artist all by yourself — someone will recommend the artist to you, or you will notice that a particular artist is attracting crowds at local venues. Begin to build a network of eyes and ears — contacts that will remember you and let you know when they spot real talent. Start by becoming a regular at local clubs and music venues. Talk to sound engineers, DJs, and bartenders about popular local musicians, and ask them to let you know when and where these artists are performing. Before approaching an artist, you will want to see several performances. You have to pay for cover charges and drinks when you spend your evenings hanging out at local clubs, but it is less expensive than traveling around the country looking for talent.

It also pays to become friendly with local bar owners. When they know why you are there, club owners may give you free admission to live performances. Ask to be put on the guest list for CD launch parties and other promotional events put on by clubs and radio stations. These same people will help you when you are ready to schedule promotional opportunities for your own artists.

Read the music reviews in local newspapers and news magazines. Attend performances in music stores and open mic nights on college campuses and in coffee shops. Go to outdoor events where local bands are entertaining. When a tour or group visits your area, go talk to their entourage. See who is opening for a well-known act. Tell everyone you are looking for unsigned artists for your label and that you welcome submissions of demos. Solicit demos on your website. If you eventually become overwhelmed, hire someone with a taste for good music to listen to demos and pick out the best ones for your review.

Attend music conferences, network with music professionals, and listen to the live performances. Two of the largest conferences are the Annual Conference of the Society for American Music (**www.american-music. org**) and the annual Music and Media Conference & Festival by South by Southwest (SXSW, Inc.) (**http://sxsw.com**), but there are many regional and local conferences. Unsigned artists perform at these conferences in hopes of landing a deal with a record label.

What to Look for in an Artist

Musical talent alone does not guarantee the success of a record. A record launch is a business project; if it does not bring in a positive return on your investment, the artist(s) will not be able to continue making music, and you will not be able to continue making records — or money. To succeed, an artist not only has to sound good, but he or she also has to appeal to your audience, be able to stick to a recording budget, and actively participate in the promotion of the record when it is released. Once you have located a prospective artist, evaluate him or her carefully before you commit to a contract. To produce a successful record, your company will have to compensate in some way for the artist's inexperience, shortcomings, and weaknesses. In the beginning, it is better to select artists who have already achieved some success and who are easy to work with. You must decide how large a project you can afford to take on.

When you have discovered that great vocalist or the unsigned band attracting crowds everywhere it plays, here are some questions to help you decide whether this is the right artist for your label:

Does this artist have unique and original qualities?

Dozens of performers are excellent musicians and can put on a great show, but they sound just like another well-known band or popular artist. Copycat artists are good entertainers, but they are not a good choice for a young independent label. You need an artist who adds a new twist to the genre with unique vocal qualities, creative musical styling, and/or original lyrics. Music fans are always looking for something new. If your artist can give them something they have never heard before, he or she will capture their attention, become a rising star, and your record label will rise as well. You will gain a reputation for introducing exciting new talent. After the first album becomes a hit, you want an artist who will be able to follow up with fresh material for the next album and who will grow musically and personally with experience.

Does this artist have charisma?

A good artist combines musical ability with a captivating voice and personality. Audiences unconsciously identify with the person singing the words and playing the music. Physical attractiveness helps, but even more important is the artist's persona — the "self" that the audience sees and hears. The artist's persona is expressed by his or her music, lyrics, behavior on stage, style of dress, and the images portrayed in music videos and publicity photos. Janis Joplin, one of the greatest female rock vocalists, was not considered a physical beauty, but her unique vocal quality, emotional intensity, and look captivated audiences across the world.

Is this artist a good fit for my label?

Does this artist fit your label's image and genre? Will he or she appeal to your audience and target market? A brilliant artist who does not match the genre and style of the other recordings on your label may confuse your market. Loyal followers who have come to expect a certain type of experience may be disappointed and drift away. To accommodate this artist, you will have to change the way you have done things in the past. You might have to find a different producer and sound engineer who are familiar with this new type of music and a different recording studio. You will not be able to market this music to the same audience and will need to develop new ways to promote it. Your distribution channels may have to be changed. All of this will require extra work and effort, and you may not be able to use the streamlined processes your company has developed to speed production.

Perhaps you are confident this artist will produce a hit, or you are ready to take your label in a new direction. Some independent labels establish sublabels to develop new genres. Before signing a contract, develop a marketing plan, refer to your business plan, and work out all the production details. Is the extra work and expense worth the gamble?

Is there a market for this artist's music?

Consider who will buy this artist's songs. An artist may be talented and a good performer, but if his or her genre is not popular right now or is appreciated by only a tiny segment of the population, you cannot expect the CD to become a runaway bestseller. That does not mean you cannot make a profit. If you have a way to promote the music directly to your target audience, you can create a marketing campaign to sell a limited release. An example is Rounder Records, which has specialized in recording and selling Roots music — traditional and folk music played by indigenous musicians — for 40 years. Their market is not the general public but the people who enjoy and understand each musical tradition. Your production and marketing plan for a particular album should be tailored to the target market for that artist.

Country music singer

Does this artist have the right image?

Every genre of music is associated with a lifestyle, a certain type of dress and behavior. The artist's appearance on stage and visual image will help to market his or her music. Does this artist dress and act in a way that will appeal to your audience? You can create an image by grooming an artist to look and behave in a certain way, but an artist who already cultivates the right image will make your work much easier. Some genres, such as heavy metal and punk rock, are associated with extreme styles of dress that require considerable personal investment and possibly modified behavior. An artist who does not delight in dressing to fit his or her genre will need extra attention from your staff.

Does this artist have an established fan base?

A new CD by an unknown artist attracts little attention among the thousands of other CDs in a music store. Independent labels do not typically have the resources to launch a nationwide media blitz or get extensive airplay on commercial radio for a new artist. They rely on the artist's fans to spread the news of a new release and sell CDs directly to the crowds at live performances. Thus, your new artist's fans will be a vital part of your marketing strategy. A pre-existing fan base gives your sales a jump-start. News of a release spreads like wildfire through social media — every fan wants to be the first to tell others about the new album and register an opinion.

Crowds of loyal fans at a club or festival are also proof an artist has audience appeal and knows something about the music business. Fans do not appear magically from nowhere. The artist, or the artist's manager or publicist, has been working hard to network, book live performances, and spread the news. The artist has been performing regularly and knows how to work a crowd. This hard-working and knowledgeable band or musician will be a good partner for your label.

Is this artist able to give consistent live performances?

Some artists make beautiful recordings in the studio but are unable to hold their own on the stage in front of a live audience. Live performances are central to a successful marketing strategy. A great artist should be able to create an intensively moving experience for live audiences, night after night and sometimes several times in one day. Not everyone has the ability to generate a commanding stage presence whenever and wherever it is required.

Once you have identified an interesting artist, find out where he or she is performing live and go to see the performance. Observe the audience, and watch the artist closely to see how he or she handles awkward moments and interacts with listeners. If possible, talk to stagehands or the club manager about the artist. Try to discover whether the artist is punctual and cooperative and interacts well with other musicians and staff. If there have been incidents of bad behavior, substance abuse, or complaints, you will probably hear about them in casual conversation. Try to find out what bands the artist has performed with, and how long he or she has been performing in public.

Attend several live performances before you make up your mind. A fantastic performance in one venue might be followed by a flop in front of another audience. Do not let the artist know you are in the audience or that you are interested in signing him or her until you have seen several performances.

Is the artist willing to travel and make public appearances?

Some artists may not be available for live performances because they are tied to a job or other responsibilities. Sometimes an artist will not want to make public appearances at certain venues, such as parties, music stores, or festivals. Find out about the artist's availability before you create a marketing plan. Determine to what extent the artist will be able and willing to participate actively in the promotion of a record. If the artist's availability is limited, be aware that you will have to plan your promotion schedule around that.

Does this artist have experience recording in the studio?

Many bands that can put on a heart-stopping performance on stage have difficulty generating the same energy when they are in a studio without a live audience. Listen to the artist's demos. How do they compare to the live performances? Experienced artists already know how to recreate their sound in a studio environment and how to work with producers and sound engineers. They also know you are paying for every hour in the studio. A band or artist who understands the recording process will save you time and money by preparing in advance, cooperating with the sound engineer, and making the most of the time in the studio. Ask your candidate if he or she has ever made a recording in a studio or released a full-length recording.

Is this artist an accomplished musician?

An artist with a trained voice and virtuosity on musical instruments has a wide range of artistic possibilities you can use and build upon. An amateur may be lucky enough to produce one or two good songs but may not have the talent or musical repertoire to expand this success to a whole album, let alone two or three. You want to stay with your new artist and invest in his or her career for some time, not have the fame fizzle after one hit. An accomplished musician can work easily with other musicians, pick up quickly on new ideas, and provide an enriched musical backdrop for recordings. If you are looking at a raw beginner, consider whether your company has the resources to invest in educating and training him or her to a professional level. Do you have other musicians who can make up for the artist's vocal shortcomings, for example, with instrumental backup? Will the artist have enough varied material for an extended live performance?

An artist who may be a beginner but who continues to improve his or her performance by taking lessons and pursuing musical training is a good find. Such an artist will produce even better work in the future and keep fans coming back for more.

Does this artist have a professional demeanor?

Observe the artist's behavior carefully. Does he or she show up on time for appointments and respond to telephone calls and e-mails? Does the artist treat others with respect and cooperate well with other musicians, sound staff, and stagehands? Has he or she ever canceled a live performance? Creative people sometimes have difficult personalities. If temperamental or unstable behavior is likely to interfere with production or jeopardize live performances, think twice about signing. A "bad boy" or "bad girl" image is a plus in some genres, but the bad behavior should not extend to professional relationships. You need an artist who will make a good impression on club managers and media representatives, be gracious to fans, and willingly participate in promotional events.

You can learn a lot about an artist's personality by observing and by talking to the people who work with him or her. Perform a background check on the Internet. Search the artist's name and look for news articles and blogs that might reveal something of importance. This artist is a business investment for your record label. Will the artist's success be enough to overcome the possible negative consequences of irresponsible behavior?

Does the artist write his or her own material?

In some genres, it is common practice for a musician to perform songs written by independent songwriters. However, musicians of modern genres such as rap, reggae, punk, and emo often write their own lyrics and music. An artist or band that performs its own material or has its own songwriters is a plus. Your company will not have to do extra work to find good songs or secure rights to music, and you will be able to earn extra income from music publishing.

Does the artist have contracts with any other record labels?

Ideally, you want to sign an artist who has never had a contract with another label. If the artist has a previous contract, ask for a copy and take it to your lawyer. Make certain the artist no longer has any legal obligations under the old contract before you make any investment in him or her. It is not unusual for artists to think they can walk away from an old contract, especially if the label is not working actively with them or if they have already completed a recording. You do not want to produce a record and then have the artist sued for breach of contract by another label. You could be prevented from releasing your record or forced to pay damages, as well as foot the bill for legal expenses.

Is the artist financially solvent?

It is difficult to work with an artist who is desperate for money. Many young artists do not understand that it takes time for a new record to start earning a profit and may have unrealistic expectations. An artist in financial difficulties may turn to you for assistance just because you have signed a contract. You could find yourself in a situation where you are forced to help just to get a recording finished or a promotional tour on the road.

Major records often offer artists an advance, a payment later recovered from sales of the record, when they sign a contract. However, a young independent label might not have the cash reserves to give advances to artists. It is important that the artist clearly understands how he or she will be compensated before the contract is signed to avoid any future financial problems.

Drugs and alcohol

The music industry is notorious for its party culture, and many musicians end up abusing alcohol or drugs. When you sign an artist, his or her alcohol or drug addiction becomes your problem. Even if the artist can manage drug or alcohol use so it does not interfere with recording sessions, sooner or later it will get out of hand. Drug and alcohol abuse often intensifies when an artist is on the road and can lead to erratic and uncontrolled behavior on stage and in public. How many newspaper articles have you read about a musician overdosing on drugs in a hotel room or a band canceling a concert tour because one of its members has checked into a rehabilitation center? Do not sign an artist who has a drug or alcohol problem unless you want to end up as a drug counselor and substitute parent.

Help for musicians with drug or alcohol addictions

The National Academy of Recording Arts and Sciences established the **MusiCares Foundation, Inc.**, in 1989. The MusiCares MAP Fund provides financial and supportive assistance for music people in need of addiction recovery services. If you know of someone in the music industry who is struggling with an addiction issue, please contact MusiCares (**www. grammy.org/musicares/recovery**).

Underage artists

In the U.S., each state's laws regarding contracts for artists under the age of 18 are different. Minors typically are allowed to withdraw from contracts (the legal term is **avoidance**) even after they have signed because of their age and inexperience. Parents or guardians usually must sign the contract and be present at performances and recording sessions. Many states require legal oversight of contracts for performers who are minors; before anyone signs a contract, a court hearing must determine whether it is in the best interests of the minor. If you are considering signing a child or teen artist, know the laws regarding minors in the state where the contract is being signed. You may decide you do not want to pay for the extra legal costs or delay production while you wait for legal proceedings to be completed. Remember when dealing with an underage artist, you will not only have to deal with the artist, you will also have to gain the approval and trust of the parents or guardians. Do not do any work on a recording with an underage artist until you have a legal contract.

You are unlikely to find the ideal artist who meets all the criteria above and is willing to sign with your new and relatively unknown independent label. The first artists you sign will develop alongside your label as you establish a reputation, learn how to engage your audiences, and begin to sell records. Approach a prospective artist with a business-like attitude. Weigh your strengths and weaknesses against those of the artist. Develop a clear plan for accomplishing whatever needs to be done to make your collaboration a success. If your first artist does not work out as expected, apply what you learn from that experience when you select your next artist.

Tales from the Industry

Motown Records: Artist Development Launched the Careers of Many of America's Most Beloved Soul and R&B Singers

Motown Records (now Universal Motown), founded by Berry Gordy in 1960, is famous for creating a unique blend of soul and pop music known as Motown Soul. Gordy made rhythm and blues, soul, and hip-hop popular with a broad international audience by discovering and training talented young African-American artists. Motown stressed artist development as an important part of its operations. Young artists were required to attend Motown's "school," where they were taught to "think, act, walk, and talk like royalty."

Under the tutelage of Charlie Atkins, artists were trained in dance choreography. Private teachers ensured school-aged singers were given a formal education,

and personal trainers and music instructors helped artists develop their voices, instrumental skills, and images. They were also taught life skills, such as etiquette, how to travel by air and pack a wardrobe, and money management. Artists were kept immaculately clean and well groomed, dressed in the most fashionable clothes, and taught sophisticated choreography for live performances. Highly trained musicians were assigned to help individual artists develop their own distinctive sounds with unique guitar riffs and piano structures.

During the 1960s, an annual package tour called the "Motortown Revue" made a circuit of performance venues, first in the deep South, later across the U.S., and eventually overseas. These tours featured most of the artists on the Motown roster, including Smokey Robinson & The Miracles, Mary Wells, The Marvelettes, Barrett Strong, The Contours, Dusty Springfield, The Shirelles and Patti LaBelle & the Bluebelles. Acts such as Marvin Gaye, Martha & The Vandellas, Stevie Wonder, The Supremes, The Four Tops, Gladys Knight & the Pips, and The Temptations were given an opportunity to improve their skills in live performances and learn from experienced artists before they became stars in their own right.

Motown Records remained independent until Gordy sold it to MCA and Boston Ventures in 1988. In 1994, it was sold to The Polygram Group, which was later acquired by Universal Music.

What an Artist Looks for in a Record Label

While you are deciding whether you want to sign a particular artist, that artist is also evaluating your business and deciding whether he or she wants to sign with your record label. The stakes are big; the artist is giving you exclusive rights to a considerable portion of his or her creative output and essentially entrusting your company with the next stage of his or her career. If you do your job well, the artist will become famous and make enough money from sales of records, merchandise, and event tickets to make a living doing what he or she loves best: creating and performing music. If you fail, the artist's record will disappear into obscurity, and the artist will be right back where he or she started — struggling for recognition and looking for another deal with a record label.

An artist might ask you some of these questions:

- What other artists have signed with your label?

- How many successful CDs have you launched, and how successful were they?

- Have you had any notable failures?

- What are your distribution channels? How do your distributors pay you? Do you do any advertising with your distributors?

- What will you do to promote my record and me?

- What is your advertising budget for new releases?

- How much will I get paid from the sale of each record?

- What kinds of Internet promotion do you use, and how do you handle Internet sales?

- Do you have relationships with independent radio stations or promoters?

- How many other artists are you working with now?

- Who will pay for travel expenses when I go on tour?

- Who will select the producer and the recording studio?

- Are you offering an advance?

- What do you expect from me?

As an independent label about to sign your first artist, your answers to these questions probably will not inspire confidence. Instead, impress the artist with what you have to offer: personal attention and complete dedication to the promotion of his or her record. Demonstrate your professionalism by having a thorough knowledge of the music industry and the artist's music. Have all your business tools in place — business cards, website, logo, résumé, letterhead stationery. If you are not able to respond quickly to phone calls, texts, and e-mails, hire someone to do it for you so you do not miss any opportunities. Show the artist a complete marketing plan detailing how the record will be produced, advertised, and promoted. Explain that though your label does not employ a large staff, many important functions are outsourced to competent industry professionals.

A deal with a major record label would probably include a hefty advance payment and a promise of instant international exposure for a new release. But you have your own advantages as an independent label. Here are some points you can use to sell your services to your potential artists:

- You can offer a partnership in which the artist will have a greater degree of control and artistic freedom.

- You will be able to provide a more personal, tailored experience for your artist compared to the all-business approach of major labels.

- You will work side-by-side to craft a marketing strategy that embodies the artist's philosophies and unique qualities, and your success will be shared.

- The artist will have input in the planning of promotional activities and concert tours.

- You are ready to start immediately without the hassle of endless bureaucratic red tape.

- You will be willing to work out an arrangement should the artist attracts the attention of a major record label in the future.

- You genuinely love the music, admire the artist's work, and are concerned about the artist's well-being.

Have a Clear Understanding With the Artist

Many artists, particularly young or inexperienced artists, do not have a good understanding of the legal terminology in a contract, even when they have a lawyer to review it for them. They may unrealistically expect money to come pouring in as soon as their CDs are released, or they might not understand that they are expected to pay part of the production costs. To avoid unpleasantness later on, take the time to explain what each section of the contract means in real terms. Let the artist know what to expect in terms of income after the record is released. Show the artist what the industry standards are for payments and royalties. Explain about copyrights and publishing laws.

Educate the artist about the production and distribution process, and explain the costs involved in each so he or she knows what is going on.

Encourage the artist to ask questions and keep lines of communication open in case doubts or questions come up later on. You need the artist on your side, not continually suspicious of being exploited.

Also, teach your artist(s) about marketing and promotion, and make sure they know what you expect them to do to advertise themselves. The most successful CDs are made by artists who aggressively promote themselves by appearing in the media and in public, blogging and communicating with their fans through Twitter and e-mail, performing live whenever they can, and trying to establish ongoing relationships with their audiences. An artist who understands that continual promotion generates more record sales, and therefore more income, will make a greater effort.

Expectations go both ways. Treat your artist fairly. If you are genuinely concerned about your artist's best interests and well-being, both of you will benefit. Listen carefully to your artist. Try to relate to his or her situation and understand his or her desires and concerns. Identify what is important to your artist and what the artist hopes your collaboration will accomplish. Your artist and his or her fans are on the same wavelength. When you understand how your artist thinks and feels, you will better understand how to appeal to your target audience and market your music.

CHAPTER 6

Contracts and Agreements

A record label's business is founded on legal contracts and agreements that give it the right to record; reproduce; and sell music, art, and film media. Written agreements and contracts are essential tools of the trade. A contract structures the ways in which you will make money through your relationship with an artist. It also attempts to anticipate every circumstance that could possibly affect your business and to protect you from financial loss.

The legal documents a recording label uses range from complex recording contracts to simple receipts acknowledging the delivery of CDs. If you are establishing an independent label solely to produce and promote your own music, you will not need to sign artists' agreements. However, you will still use a variety of written contracts and agreements to define your working relationships with backup musicians, manufacturers, distributors, advertisers, and producers. This chapter covers basic information about the contracts and other legal documents you will use for your record label. Every independent record label is unique, so you will need to customize your contracts, with the help of a lawyer, to fit your particular business model.

Unfamiliar legal terminology may seem bewildering, and you may be tempted to overlook or ignore some parts of a contract, but it is essential for you (or one of your partners) to be familiar and comfortable with the legal aspect of your business. Naïve and inexperienced artists sometimes unwittingly sign away important rights. As a record label owner, you cannot afford to be naïve. A mistake or oversight in a legal contract could cost you an opportunity to earn millions or send your company into bankruptcy. Take time to learn the legal language  and study your contracts carefully. Ask your lawyer to explain the implications of each clause in a contract. If possible, examine contracts other record labels or artists use. You might be able to find examples online, through your lawyer or through your contacts in the music industry.

You can purchase standard contracts and agreements as printed forms or as downloadable templates from the Internet and adapt them to fit your needs. Companies such as 101MusicBiz Contracts (**www.musiccontracts101. com**) and MusicLegalContracts.com (**www.musiclegalcontracts.com**) sell standard contracts for the music business. Never sign any contract, however, without first having your lawyer review it. It might contain an omission or a legal loophole that would allow the other party to break the contract or hold you to a commitment you never intended to make.

Get Everything in Writing

Never rely on a verbal agreement or a handshake to seal a deal. Arrangements that seem perfectly clear during a discussion over lunch or in a club after a performance suddenly become fuzzy when money is involved. Artists, in particular, may be carried away by the excitement of the moment and make promises that are later forgotten. Always carry a notebook and write down the details of any commitments the other party makes. Ask for specifics such as delivery dates and deadlines. When you get back to your computer, type up the information and have the other party sign the document acknowledging that they accept the arrangement. At the very least, get an e-mail confirming the other party has read your notes and agrees with the terms. The state of New York recently ruled that e-mail is legally binding, as of February 2011. According to the verdict, e-mail can carry the same weight as traditional contracts. However, in most states, an e-mail is not legally binding, but it is written evidence that on a specific date the other party acknowledged making certain commitments. Any agreement involving the exchange of money, valuable goods, or labor should be in the form of a signed legal document such as a receipt or a hiring contract.

Enter important dates into a spreadsheet, scheduler, or project management software. This will help you monitor the progress of your projects and ensure that everything is ready for a recording session, promotional event, or record launch.

Finding a Lawyer

A large record label has a business affairs department staffed with lawyers who negotiate the terms of agreements with artists and vendors and then draft legal contracts. At a small record label, the owners typically do much of the negotiation themselves and refer the final drafting and review of contracts and agreements to a lawyer.

Legal rights to copyrighted music and art are the core of your business, so eventually, you will need the services of a lawyer specializing in entertainment or music law. At times, you might also need other types of lawyers — for example, to draw up a partnership agreement, register a copyright, or negotiate the release of one of your artists to a major record label. You might balk at paying a lawyer's fees and be tempted to economize by buying do-it-yourself templates or services instead, but you cannot afford to be an amateur in this area.

Do not wait until you urgently need help with a sudden offer to contact a lawyer. Form a relationship with a lawyer now, and ask him or her to represent you whenever a situation arises in the future. Find one who, ideally, has experience in the music industry and knows about current practices and customary trade-offs. The music business is complex; entire college courses are taught on entertainment contract law. Many types of entertainment lawyers charge a wide range of fees for their services. You do not need an expensive, high-powered specialist to draft a simple two-page contract, just someone with experience in contract law. On the other hand, if you are involved in a dispute that could cause you to lose valuable rights to a recording, you need an experienced lawyer to represent you.

The best way to find a good entertainment lawyer is to ask other record labels and artists for recommendations. You can search local business directories and law directories such as Lawyers by City.com (**www.lawyers-by-city.com**). Schedule an appointment to interview the lawyer by phone or in person. Some lawyers offer a free initial consultation. Prepare a list of questions in advance, and ask the lawyer about his or her experiences, especially pertaining to the music industry. Request references or the names of other clients. If the lawyer makes a good impression but does not seem knowledgeable about your field, or you do not feel satisfied with his or her answers, look for someone else.

What to ask a prospective entertainment lawyer

- What is your experience in the music industry?

- Do you have references or other clients I can contact?

- This is how I plan to fund my business (Explain about any loans from investors or banks, or any distribution arrangements). Does this arrangement put me at risk for losing the rights to the music or create financial liabilities for me?

- What use of my music by another artist would constitute copyright infringement?

Find an affordable lawyer who has a personality with which you are compatible and with whom you can communicate easily. This person may be negotiating with others on your behalf; you need to feel confident he or she can represent you well. A lawyer who takes a personal interest in your projects and believes you have the potential to succeed may be willing to offer free advice on occasion or negotiate lower fees. Highly specialized entertainment lawyers typically are located in large urban centers and can be expensive, but if you find yourself in a complicated contract negotiation, the extra expense is worth it.

Once you have some experience with contracts, you may be able to do much of the work yourself and have your lawyer draw up the final draft, which will save some money. Simple contracts, such as work-for-hire contracts for graphic design, can be easily modified for each new job once you have a customized original. However, any contract involving an artist or recording rights should be reviewed if not written by a lawyer because so much is at stake. An oversight could cause you to lose everything you have invested in making a record or involve you in costly legal proceedings.

Success in the music industry is volatile. When one of your artists reaches the top of the charts, you do not know when, if ever, you will achieve the same level of success again. If a major record label approaches you about releasing that artist from your label, hire or make sure you already have an experienced lawyer to ensure you receive fair compensation for the money and effort you invested in making the artist famous. The same is true for artists — without sound legal advice, an artist might inadvertently sign away rights that would bring in royalties 20 years from now when his or her song is selected for a TV commercial or a video game.

Legal Representation for Artists

It is not unusual for an artist who has begun to receive attention because of your record label's marketing and promotion to try to void your contract in order to sign with a larger label. If the artist finds a legal pretext for declaring your contract invalid, you could lose everything you have invested, revenue from sales of future recordings by the artist and your share of royalties or licensing fees for future use of the artist's music. A common strategy is for the artist to claim the contract is not valid because he or she did not have legal representation when the contract was signed. You do not want the artist to void your contract due to a legal loophole and go on his or her way without a backward glance. For this reason, many recording contracts include a clause stating clearly that the artist chose not to have legal representation. Another option is to have the artist sign a separate letter confirming that he or she has been advised to consult a lawyer before signing the contract and has decided not to. Some record labels offer an advance to pay the artist to hire a lawyer.

Some artists may be so eager to sign with a record label that they waive legal representation or are so naive that they trust the record label's lawyer to draft a fair contract. Even though you know your contract is fair to the artist, encourage him or her to have the contract reviewed by a lawyer for your own protection. Many organizations, such as Volunteer Lawyers for the Arts (**www.vlany.org/aboutus/index.php**) and California Lawyers for the Arts (**www.calawyersforthearts.org**), provide free or low-cost legal advice for artists. In a contract negotiation, the lawyer representing the artist will try to increase the amount the artist receives in royalties, secure at least partial ownership of publishing rights and the master recording, and ensure the artist is not signing away valuable rights. It is to the artist's own advantage to invest in legal representation before signing a contract.

Sometimes the best thing you can do is release one of your artists to a major label because you may not have the financial resources to take the artist's career to a higher level and give him or her international media exposure. Even if you decide to give up one of your artists, your record label will still have a reputation for discovering and promoting great talent. New artists will be eager to sign with you in hopes that you can do the same for them. Distributors and the media will respect your label as a trendsetter. Your name and logo will be forever linked with a famous band or musician, whose biography will read, "after releasing his first CD with YOUR NAME RECORDS in 20XX, the artist went on to…." In order to protect your interests while releasing an artist to a major company, negotiate a legal agreement that allows you to continue receiving compensation for the time and money you invested in the artist's early career and for the income you are forfeiting by not releasing future albums by the artist.

Artists Agreement

An Artists Agreement can be the simple two-page contract independent labels commonly use or a 50-page document like the one major record labels use, outlining complex arrangements and stipulating what will be done in every kind of eventuality. It explains what the artist will do for the record label, what the record label will do for the artist, and what will happen if either party fails to fulfill obligations under the contract. Artists Agreements vary widely in content and form, but all of them contain the same basic elements:

- Term of the contract
- Territory
- Services
- Recording commitment
- Recording procedure
- Recoupable costs
- Advances
- Rights granted to the recording company
- Royalties
- Definitions
- Accounting
- Publishing
- Warranties
- Indemnity
- Suspension or termination
- Group provisions
- Merchandising rights
- Music videos
- Websites and digital rights
- Additional provisions

Term of the contract

The **term** is how long the contract will be in force. It can be expressed as a period of time, but record label contracts typically define the term by the number of songs or albums the artist will record for the label under the contract. Time is not a good measure of achievement in the music world. Any number of factors could delay the release of an album until after a specified time period has expired. A band might be too busy touring to create and record new material, or recording might be disrupted by personal and family problems. The creative process cannot be rushed. Production might be delayed by technical issues or by legal difficulties over the use of certain materials. Delays are not the only time problem to contend with. A band that produces too many recordings in a short time could sabotage its own success by exhausting the record label's promotional budget and saturating the market.

The term usually consists of an **initial period** (also known as initial term or first contract period) followed by several one-sided options for the record label to extend the contract for an additional period. Each option represents another recording.

The initial period begins on the date the contract is signed and can extend for a period of several months after the first album's **street date** (the day the album is officially released) or **delivery date** (the date the master recording is completed and delivered to the record label). At that point, the record label exercises its option to extend the contract or the contract renews automatically (unless the record label indicates it wants to terminate the contract).

Try to get the artist to commit to as many options as you can. That way, if the first album sells well, you can build on that success by releasing additional albums by the artist. If the first album is a failure, you can terminate the contract by not exercising your option to renew it.

Note: Pay attention to renewal dates

Keep track of renewal dates, and note whether your contract renews automatically or whether you must notify the artist that you are exercising a renewal option. If a contract renews automatically, you could be obligated to record another unsuccessful album for an artist whose first album did not sell. If the contract does not renew automatically and you fail to notify the artist before the expiry date, you might lose the opportunity to release another winning album.

Territory

Territory refers to the geographical region where the contract is valid. The territory for a music contract is typically "the world" or "the universe" because music created in one country is often sold in another.

Services

Services refers to the services an artist is promising to the record label. A record label contract usually claims an artist's exclusive services, which means the artist will breach the contract if he or she records for any other company. The contract may make exceptions for certain types of recorded events such as large music festivals and exclude nonmusical performances, such as movie roles or television interviews. Many contracts will permit an artist to act as a producer for another musician. A record label can sign a waiver, called a **side artist agreement**, that allows the artist to perform as a backup singer in another artist's recording.

Recording commitment

The **recording commitment** defines exactly how much material the artist is expected to record during a single contract period. A typical requirement is one full album of new material per contract period, with an album defined as a specified number of minutes. The contract can include clauses allowing the record label to add additional material to the recording commitment, such as a single original song for a charity fund raiser. Usually these additions are limited to no more than the length of one full album. The contract should exclude special recordings such as Christmas albums or compilations of previously released songs, so the record label is guaranteed a regular album with new material during the contract period.

Recording procedure

This section of the contract describes when, where, and how the master will be recorded. It can be as simple as a time and place, or it can outline detailed procedures for every step of the process, such as establishing budgets, selecting producers, and submitting expense reports. The record label typically reserves the right to reject a master recording that does not meet a specified standard of quality and to halt recording if it becomes clear that the resulting master will be substandard.

The recording procedure should give the record label authority to approve a recording budget. The artist should be required to submit a recording budget to the record label several weeks in advance. If the label thinks the budget is excessive, the artist must revise it and resubmit. If the recording goes over budget because of delays in the studio or additional expenses such as equipment rental, the artist will be responsible for the extra cost out of his or her own pocket. Once a budget is approved, the label usually advances the money to pay for recording. The money is not disbursed directly to the artist but put into a special account used to pay bills and make purchases.

The importance of a recording budget

The cost of making the master recording is a large expense your label will not be able to recover for months. After the master is completed, there will be a delay of several weeks before the CD is released and money starts to trickle in from sales. Payments from distributors and retailers may not arrive in your bank account until two or three months after that. A recording budget helps keep your finances under control and ensures you have enough cash on hand to market the CD when it is released.

The recording procedure may also make the artist responsible for collecting tax forms (W-9s or I-9s), Social Security numbers, signed work-for-hire contracts, and other documents from the recording staff and other musicians. If these forms are not submitted in a timely manner, the late penalties the Internal Revenue Service (IRS) assesses could be passed on to the artist.

The recording procedure explains how the producer will be selected and paid. Typically, the artist is responsible for engaging the producer, but in some cases, the record label may have a producer on staff. The contract might specify how the producer's advance and royalties will be paid. If the producer receives a salary from the record label, the contract might specify what portion of that the artist will pay.

Recoupable costs

Many of the expenses incurred in recording and releasing a CD are recoupable, which means the record label pays these expenses initially and is reimbursed out of the artist's royalties. This section of the contract details which expenses the record label will pay outright and which the artist will repay.

Expenses that are always recoupable are:

- Recording costs — Studio rentals, producers, mixers, sound engineers, backup musicians and vocalists, technical staff, travel expenses

- Advances — Money paid directly to the artist as an advance against future earnings

- Tour support — Money paid to the artist to assist with the expenses of going on tour: food and lodging, equipment, bus or van rentals, travel

Expenses that are sometimes recoupable:

- Music videos — The cost of making a music video is typically recoupable from royalties from the video and sometimes the royalties from the album.

- Promotional costs — Some labels will recoup all or part of the cost of any marketing or promotion done specifically for the artist and the artist's albums.

Expenses that are not recoupable:

- Cost of manufacturing and packaging CDs and vinyls

- Distribution costs — Shipping, commissions paid to distributors, promotional materials created for distributors

- Graphics and photography

Non-recoupable expenses are usually subtracted from the money received from CD sales before royalties are calculated, so the record label is still reimbursed. The difference is that the reimbursement does not come out of the artist's royalties.

Because all recoupable costs are taken out of the artist's royalties, it could be a long time before the artist collects. Some artists never collect any royalties because the recoupable costs are never paid off. This can happen when the record label spends a lot to promote an album, when recording costs are high, or when sales volume is low. Although the artist's royalties may never be enough to reimburse the record label for recording costs and advances, the label should still make a profit from CD sales.

Album royalties are not the only income for an artist. An artist who writes his or her own songs also receives a mechanical royalty for each song on the album. **Mechanical royalties** are collected on the use of copyrighted, published material. Mechanical royalties are not subject to recoupable costs. The artist can also earn money from live performances and concerts, merchandise sales, and performance royalties. **Performance royalties** are earned when a song is played on the radio and are collected and distributed by The American Society of Composers, Authors and Publishers (ASCAP) and Broadcast Music, Inc. (BMI).

When negotiating royalties, it does not hurt to grant an artist one or two more percentage points ("points") if you know all of an artist's recoupable costs will never be paid off. Higher royalties mean more money will be available to apply to the recoupable costs.

Advances

An **advance** is any money paid to an artist under a recording contract, usually before the recording has started. It may be designated for a specific purpose such as recording costs or touring expenses, or it may be made available to the artist to use for personal expenses. Advances are recoupable from the artist's royalties.

Large record labels often advance money to artists by setting up a recording fund that is considerably more than the recording budget. The artist gets to keep whatever is left once recording expenses are paid off. The advance helps pay an artist's personal expenses while he or she is touring or composing and recording full time. Small independent labels usually cannot achieve the same level of sales as large labels and will never recoup their recording costs, let alone a large advance, from the artist's royalties. Instead, a small label is likely to pay directly for recording costs and offer the artist a small cash payment, or no payment at all.

This section of the contract may also discuss advances for future albums or advances for expenses other than the cost of recording a master, such as the production of a music video. These other expenses may not be fully recoupable from the artist's royalties.

Rights granted to the recording company

This section explains what rights the record label has to any work the artist produced under the contract. The record label typically acquires copyrights to the master recordings and the right to use the artist's name and likeness to promote the albums.

Even when the rights to a recording have been assigned to a record label, copyright law allows an artist to legally reclaim the copyright after 35 years unless the recording is a work made for hire (work for hire). A sound recording is a work for hire if the artist signs a contract to that effect, and the record label can retain ownership of the master indefinitely. For a record label, copyrights are valuable assets. The label's catalog of old recordings can be sold to another label or reproduced and sold for decades afterward as compilations and greatest hits albums. The record label also benefits when old songs are used in movies or TV commercials. Most artists' agreements are worded as work for hire contracts so the record label can retain ownership of the copyright. *See chapters 7 and 8 for more on copyright law.*

Some independent labels allow the artist to retain ownership of the master recording and license it for exclusive use over a specified period. This arrangement might be appropriate when the artist has already recorded a marketable CD or is doing aggressive self-promotion because the record label's investment in the recording will be smaller.

Owning the copyright to the master recording is not the same as owning the copyright to the composition itself. If your label wants to receive part of the licensing fee when your artist's song is performed on *Glee* or *American Idol*, this should be addressed in a separate section on Publishing Rights. *See the following Publishing Rights section.*

CASE STUDY: MICHAEL JACKSON BROUGHT IN $1 BILLION IN THE YEAR AFTER HIS DEATH

When Michael Jackson announced in March 2009 that he would perform 50 concerts in a comeback tour called "This Is It" at London's O2 Arena, many regarded him as a has-been whose career had peaked 20 years earlier. Although tickets sold out, the tour's promoter, AEG, had to issue a statement saying Jackson had undergone medical tests that proved he was physically capable of performing the shows. Jackson was in serious financial difficulties. Because of his extravagant lifestyle, he was $500 million in debt and could not pay his bills. He owed nearly $9,000 to the Los Angeles Department of Water and Power and $1,300 to

AT&T. His family home in Encino, California, as well as a nearby condo, was on the verge of foreclosure.

Michael Jackson's tragic death on June 25, 2009, awakened a global surge of interest in his music. While the media mulled over the sordid circumstances surrounding his death, Jackson's fans bought every CD and album on music store shelves. Digital downloads made every song in his back catalog instantly accessible. In the week after his death, 422,000 of his recordings sold, and in July 2009, Jackson once again reached the top of the Billboard sales charts. A year later, *Billboard* magazine calculated that Michael Jackson had generated $1 billion of revenue ("How Michael Jackson Made $1 Billion Since His Death." *Billboard*. June 21, 2010). Approximately $200 million of that went to his estate.

Here is a breakdown of where most of that $1 billion came from:

$429 million — Music Sales

- $383 million — Album catalog

  Approximately 9 million albums sold in the U.S.
  800,000 records by the Jackson 5 and the Jacksons in U.S. (Nielsen SoundScan)
  24 million records sold outside the U.S.
  12.9 million digital track downloads in the U.S.
  An estimated 26.5 million digital track downloads worldwide

- $5 million — Ringtone sales

  1.5 million in the U.S.; 3 million worldwide

- $2 million — Subscription services and digital performance royalties in the U.S.

- $4.5 million — Subscription services and digital performance royalties globally

$392 million — Film and TV

- $72 million — U.S. box office earnings for *Michael Jackson: This Is It*, released October 28, 2009, by Sony pictures.

- $188 million — Box office earnings for *Michael Jackson: This Is It* overseas ($56 million of that in Japan)

- $43 million — U.S. sales of the *This Is It* DVD

- $25 million — Revenue from rentals of the *This Is It* DVD in the U.S.

- $25 million — DVD sales in Japan. In Japan the film was also sold as part of a *This Is It* bundle for the PlayStation 3-DVD. Sales on the first day of release topped $18 million; 351,000 Blu-ray copies have been sold.

- $15 million — Estimated value of the exclusive U.S. TV rights for six years, purchased by Viacom

- $24 million — Licensing for showing *This Is It* in airplanes, cruise ships, hotel chains, and other venues outside of traditional theaters, as well as non-theatrical performances

$130 million — Music Publishing

- $50 million — Estimated revenue generated by Michael Jackson's publishing company, Mijac, from June 2009 to June 2010

- $80 million — Revenue from Jackson's half share of Sony/ATV

$35 million — Licensing and Touring

- $6.5 million — Tickets for the "This Is It" tour that were never refunded because fans kept them as souvenirs

- $5 million — Sales of Bravado's "This Is It" concert merchandise

- $3.5 million — Proceeds from an exhibit of Michael Jackson memorabilia in Japan; the exhibit is scheduled to go to China next.

- $10 million — Advance from Bravado for a new merchandising deal

- $10 million — Licensing and retail sales (total retail revenue was much higher)

A dance-oriented videogame by Ubisoft, Michael Jackson: The Experience sold 2 million copies in a month after it was released in the U.S. and Europe in November 2010. Ubisoft expects sales to exceed 4 million when it releases a Japanese version and adds Kinect and PlayStation Move versions (April 2011).

A Cirque du Soleil production, Michael Jackson: The Immortal World Tour, is scheduled for performances in 30 cities during 2011 and 2012.

$31 million — Recording Contract

A contract with Sony Music Entertainment to release ten albums of Michael Jackson's music through 2017, including a collection of previously unreleased tracks.

Michael Jackson featured on Billboard's charts during much of his lifelong career. Thirteen of his singles reached the top of the weekly Billboard Hot 100, a record for male artists, and four songs by the Jackson 5 also reached the top. More than 50 of his singles appeared on the charts.

Royalties

This section of the contract describes in detail how royalties will be calculated. Royalties may be based on wholesale or on retail prices of the record. Before the royalty is calculated, certain costs are deducted from the sale price of a record:

- Packaging (container charge) — The cost of printing labels, inserts, and covers for vinyl and packaging the recordings in CD cases or covers — a standard packaging cost is 25 percent of the list price of the CD.

- Distribution costs — Distribution costs vary depending on how the record label handles its distribution. A distribution company usually places a markup of $2 to $3 on the CDs it delivers to a retailer. Distribution could include the cost of packing and shipping, soliciting and processing orders, or a commission paid to a distribution company.

- Reserves — A certain number of CDs will be returned for refunds after retailers are unable to sell them. A percentage of the sale price (typically 15 to 20 percent) must be held back to cover returns and refunds. The contract may specify the maximum amount that can be held back or leave it up to the record label's discretion. These reserves must be liquidated at regular intervals (three months to one year), and any money not given as refunds to retailers is credited back to the net sales figure.

• Free goods — The record label will not pay royalties on free CDs handed out for publicity purposes to radio stations and retail outlets or given away in promotions. A typical deduction is 15 percent of the list price.

In addition to these deductions, other adjustments might be made to royalty rates. In the U.S., royalties average between 10 and 25 percent, but royalties from sales in some foreign countries are lower. Royalties for CDs sold through record clubs and discount retailers will be based on the lower discounted prices. A deduction might also be taken for taxes.

The artist's royalties are calculated as a percentage of what remains after these items have been subtracted from the retail (or wholesale) price. If there is more than one artist, the royalties may be divided among them according to their level of participation in the band. If an artist performs only one or two tracks on an album, his or her share of the royalties will be a percentage equal to the portion of the album that includes the artist's music.

EXAMPLE OF A ROYALTY CALCULATION		
Retail Price of CD		**$15.00**
Distribution		-$2.00
Packaging	25%	-$3.75
Free goods	15%	-$2.25
Reserves for returns	15%	-$2.25
Royalty Base Price		**$4.75**
Artist's royalties	15%	$0.71
Producer's royalties	2%	$0.10
Net Artist Royalties		**$0.62**

The royalty rate can be tied to the number of CDs sold; for example, it can be raised by half a percentage point when sales exceed 100,000 CDs and raised in increments for larger sales numbers. A high volume of sales will allow the record label to recover production costs and bring in more income. The contract might also start the royalty rate for the second album at the level reached with the sales of the first album.

Note: Royalties should always be based on net sales.

Royalties should always be based on **net sales** — the amount of revenue coming in after you have deducted discounts, shipping costs, and returns — rather than gross receipts (the total amount sold). If royalties are based on gross receipts, once recoupable costs have been paid out of the artist's royalties, you will be paying royalties based on money that is not really income.

Royalties for music videos

Artists are typically paid 50 percent of the net receipts from the commercial use of music videos. The cost of creating and reproducing the videos, as well as a flat percentage of gross sales to cover overhead costs, is subtracted from the artist's share of the net receipts. Music videos sold for private use in the home are treated in the same way as audio recordings.

Royalties for Internet downloads

In the music industry, there is always a possibility that the emergence of new technology will change the way in which recordings are sold within a short time. Examples are the transition from vinyl records to cassette tapes and 8-track tapes, then to CDs, then MP3 players, and now any number of devices that can download, store, and play digital music. Changing to a new method of manufacturing and delivering product typically translates into higher costs per unit for the record label, as it must do research and invest in new technology, often at a time when prices are not competitive. As sales of the new product take over, quantities of the older products may have to be scrapped because there is no longer a market for them. To compensate for the extra expense, the record label usually includes in its contracts a 20 to 50 percent reduction of royalties for albums released using "new media/technology." Many record labels continue to treat digital downloads as "new media" and pay the reduced royalties on them, even though the actual cost of supplying Internet downloads might be much lower than the cost of manufacturing and shipping CDs. Also, although there is no packaging cost for a digital download, some labels continue to deduct 25 percent from the retail price for packaging.

An alternative method some independent labels use to calculate royalties on digital downloads is to split the net sales of digital downloads equally between the artist and the label. A net sales figure is calculated by deducting the cost of selling through an online store, DRM (digital rights management) costs, bandwidth fees, credit card transaction fees, mechanical royalties, and advertising and marketing costs associated with the download from the amount of gross sales.

When are royalties paid?

Royalties are not paid to the artist until the record label has received payment from the retailer or distributor. This could be several months after the records are ordered and shipped, so the amount paid as royalties might not be consistent with the sales figures reported by the record label. The artist does not receive any royalties until all advances have been recouped.

Royalties for producers and mixers

Unless the record label employs a producer or mixer, the artist pays each of them a percentage of his or her royalties. Although the artist is financially responsible, as a courtesy, most record labels do the accounting and send out the paychecks on the artist's behalf. The record label sets aside the producer's share and recoups advances from the artist's portion of the royalties. Although the producer is not responsible for advances to the artist, he or she typically does not receive payment until the hard costs of recording have been recouped from the artist's royalties. When recording costs have been recouped, the producer is paid and continues to receive his or her share of the royalties while promotional expenses are being recouped from the artist's share.

Changing the way royalties are calculated

A record label typically reserves the right to change the way it calculates royalties if its sales strategy changes. For example, a new form of digital technology might arise, or the label might discover that among the artists' fans there is a strong market for vinyl albums. The record label might give away fewer free CDs or downloads than it had originally budgeted for, so the allowance for these items is lower. The contract should explain how these adjustments are made and calculated so the artist continues to receive comparable royalties.

Tales from the Industry

Reprise Records: Frank Sinatra's Label Gave Up Its Rights to Its Artists' Work

The famous Frank Sinatra was enjoying a prosperous career distributing his records through Capitol/EMI. However, when Capitol/EMI would not allow him the artistic freedom he wanted for his recordings, he decided to follow his heart and launch his own label. The result was Reprise Records, created in 1960.

The new "Chairman of the Board," Sinatra appealed to many of his colleagues and friends and wound up signing on big names such as Dean Martin, Sammy Davis, Jr., Bing Crosby, Jo Stafford, Rosemary Clooney, Esquivel, and stand-up comedian Redd Foxx. Each artist was to be given full creative freedom and, eventually, complete ownership of his or her work, including publishing rights.

In 1963, Sinatra sold the label to Warner Brothers because of insufficient sales. Many of the original artists were dropped, and Warner-Reprise began to target teen audiences with a roster of emerging pop artists. Warner Brothers deactivated the label in 1976 but brought it back in 1987. Reprise still issues recordings Sinatra made while on the label and was successful in selling and promoting his greatest hits collections after his death in 1988.

Although it sounded like a beneficial system for artists, the practice of giving artists complete ownership of their works meant that the label did not have a back catalog of its early artists (Dean Martin, Jimi Hendrix, The Kinks). Their records are being distributed today through other labels. Dean Martin's recordings were out of print for nearly 20 years until Capitol Records began distributing them.

Definitions

The terminology in the Royalties section of an Artists Agreement can be bewildering, and the way in which various terms are defined helps determine how much money the artist will eventually be paid. When a word is capitalized in a contract, that word is interpreted according to a definition set out somewhere in the contract. Many contracts have a separate section for definitions, often located near the end of the contract.

Two definitions that are particularly important in calculating royalties are:

Container Charge: An artist is paid royalties on his or her music, not on the plastic container of a CD, the paper and cardboard sleeves of a vinyl record, or the artwork on the cover. The container charge is the amount deducted (usually 15 to 25 percent) from the sale price of an album to pay for its packaging.

Royalty Base Price: The royalty base price is the amount on which the calculation of royalties is based. It is figured by deducting taxes, distribution costs, container charges, and other costs listed in the definition from the retail (or wholesale) price of a record.

Be sure the artist understands the definitions.

When definitions are located separately near the end of a long contract, it is harder for an inexperienced artist to understand exactly what he or she is agreeing to. The artist's lawyer should explain the terms of the contract in detail. If there is still confusion or misunderstanding, explain the definitions to the artist yourself. It is better to establish a clear understanding from the beginning than to have an angry, embittered artist accusing you of deception and treachery later on. An agreement is exactly that — the record label and the artist are agreeing to collaborate in a mutually beneficial business venture. If the first album is a success, you want your artist to be inspired, excited, and willing to cooperate for the second one.

Accounting

This section of the agreement explains how various financial transactions will be handled, what kinds of financial statements the artist will receive, and the procedure for reviewing or contesting these statements. This part of the contract should include a description of how royalty earnings will be applied to advances and promotional costs, and how often **reserves** (money held back to pay refunds for returns from retailers) will be liquidated and added back to net sales figures.

Most record labels send out financial statements every six months. It is not necessary to send out a statement if no records have sold and no royalties have been earned, but providing a simple statement assures the artist you are aware of his or her interest. If royalties have been earned but the artist is not owed royalties yet because of recoupable costs, the statement should show how they have been used to repay advances and other outstanding amounts.

Sales in foreign countries

If you will be marketing the record overseas, this part of the agreement should explain how revenue from sales outside the U.S. will be calculated and reported, what exchange rates will be used, and how often the money will be credited to the artist. Sales in foreign countries are often licensed to companies operating in those countries. You will not be able to provide a statement to the artist until you have received statements from those companies, and there may be occasions when foreign companies cannot obtain U.S. dollars to pay you because of foreign exchange restrictions in their countries. This section should contain a clause stating there could be reporting delays with foreign sales and explaining what will happen if money cannot be converted to U.S. dollars. For example, the company could open an account in the artist's name in the foreign country to hold the foreign royalties.

Procedure for contesting the validity of a statement

There should be a paragraph protecting the record label if the artist wants to contest the validity of a financial statement. For example, the artist could be given two years after the date the statement is received to notify the company that he or she wishes to contest its validity, with an audit to be performed within six months after the notice is given. If that audit uncovers any discrepancies, the artist has one year to take action. If the artist has not filed suit or settled the problem within a year, he or she waives the right to do so. This protects the record label from being hit with a big and unexpected financial settlement for a transaction that occurred a decade earlier. The contract can also specify who will do the audit — a certified third-party accountant or lawyer, not the artist — and restrict the audit to only the financial records pertaining to the artist.

Some contracts stipulate that once the financial records have been audited, they cannot be examined again. This protects the label from having a disgruntled artist come storming into the office at some future date demanding to see the books again because he or she is not pleased with the results of the first audit. Pulling out old financial records and working with an auditor takes time and costs money. If errors are found, you might have to file amended tax returns and adjust the amounts paid to other individuals such as producers. A lawsuit means legal costs. A good contract lays down the rules in case the relationship between the artist and the record company goes sour later on.

Publishing

Artists who write their own songs have another significant source of income for themselves and for the record label — publishing rights. Such an artist is referred to as a performer and a songwriter. Musicians earn royalties each time a song they have recorded is sold as a single or as part of an album. Songwriters earn mechanical royalties every time one of their songs is sold as part of a recording; sold as a ringtone; played over the radio or in a movie or TV commercial; played in a dentist's office, an elevator, or the telephone while someone is on hold; included in a video game; sold as printed sheet music; or performed or recorded by another band (called a **cover**). When a record label makes and sells a recording, it must pay artist royalties and mechanical royalties.

Just as a musician uses a record label to record and sell his or her music, a songwriter uses a music publisher to promote and sell his or her songs. The songwriter assigns the copyright for a song to the music publisher, who acts as the songwriter's agent to sell the song and manage the collection and payment of mechanical royalties to the artist. The publisher receives a portion (usually 50 percent) of the mechanical royalties as compensation. By acquiring all or part of the publishing rights for a song, an independent label becomes the publisher and obtains a share of the income from mechanical royalties. The additional income from publishing rights compensates the record label for the risk of funding a recording for an unknown band that might not bring in much revenue.

Publishing rights are important moneymakers for artists. Recoupable costs are not deducted from mechanical royalties because they are incurred during the recording process, not during songwriting. A singer/songwriter may not receive any artist royalties from an album, but he or she will be paid mechanical royalties from sales of the album, plus any other use of the songs.

If you are signing artists who write their own material, this section of the contract is important. You want at least a portion of the publishing rights, while the artist wants to receive as much income as possible. You will have to offer economic incentives strong enough to motivate the artist to sign over some of the publishing rights.

You will find more information about publishing music in Chapter 7.

Negotiating mechanical royalties

After the first public release of a recording with the permission of the copy-right owner(s), any artist can record a cover of a song by obtaining a compulsory mechanical license. The U.S. Copyright Royalty Board (**www.loc. gov/crb**), a panel of three administrative judges appointed by the Librarian of Congress, determine statutory mechanical royalty rates for compulsory mechanical licenses, which are periodically adjusted for inflation.

Current Mechanical Royalty Rates

CATEGORY	RATE	EFFECTIVE DATE
Physical phonorecords	9.1 cents or 1.75 cents per minute of playing time or fraction thereof, whichever is larger, for physical phonorecord deliveries and permanent digital	March 1, 2009
Permanent downloads	9.1 cents or 1.75 cents per minute of playing time or fraction thereof, whichever is larger, for physical phonorecord deliveries and permanent digital	March 1, 2009
Ringtones	24 cents per ringtone	*
Limited downloads	The formulas for determining rates may be found in the Code of Federal Regulations, TITLE 37 (37 CFR) -- Patents, Trademarks, and Copyrights. §385.10 through §385.17	*
Interactive streaming	The formulas for determining rates may be found in the Code of Federal Regulations, TITLE 37 (37 CFR) -- Patents, Trademarks, and Copyrights. §385.10 through §385.17	*

* Effective date not determined by Copyright Royalty Judges (CRJs). Final rule issued by CRJs; see 74 FR 4510, indicates effective date is governed by 17 U.S. Code 803(d)(2)(B).

Mechanical royalty rates for the first-time release of a song can be negotiated between the record label and the songwriter or music publisher. Record labels typically negotiate a ¾ rate — 75 percent of the statutory rate — for first-time releases of songs written and owned by the artist. Music publishers frequently offer a similar reduced rate to record labels to encourage other labels to use their artist's songs. An artist in great demand might negotiate a higher mechanical royalty for the first release of a new original song, but any rerecording will be subject to the statutory rate.

A Controlled Composition Clause in the contract grants the record label the right to pay lower mechanical royalty rates for songs on the album that are written or composed by the artist or to which the artist holds the copyright.

Limiting mechanical royalties

Record label contracts typically limit the mechanical royalty payments to a maximum of ten songs per album. The artist is free to compose and record additional songs for the album but will not receive additional mechanical royalty payments for them. A capped Controlled Composition Clause sets a limit to the amount of mechanical royalties the artist can collect from an album. If the artist is recording more than ten songs someone else wrote, he or she might be responsible for paying the additional mechanical royalties to the songwriter. These amounts are deducted from the artist's recording royalties.

A contract also can stipulate that mechanical royalties will be paid only for CDs that are sold and paid for, not for those returned by retailers or given away free as promotions. Mechanical royalties can be adjusted or waived for discounted downloads and CDs.

The statutory mechanical royalty rate is raised periodically by the U.S. Copyright Royalty Board to compensate for inflation. If a contract fixes the mechanical royalties at the rate in effect when the album is first released (date of first release), the artist will continue to receive that same amount when the album is sold years later, after the statutory mechanical royalty rates have been increased. Most artists will want to peg mechanical royalties to the rate in effect on the date of manufacture (the date on which the music is downloaded or a CD is made) rather than on the date of first release so that they will be paid the new, higher rate.

Cross-collateralization

Although recording expenses are not recoupable against mechanical royalties, there might be unusual circumstances in which an artist agrees to apply some of his or her mechanical royalties to recording expenses. This might happen if the artist is eager to release an album but the record label is reluctant to undertake the project because it does not believe it will recoup recording expenses. Recouping recording and promotion expenses from income other than artist's royalties, such as mechanical royalties or the artist's royalties from future albums, is referred to as **cross-collateralization**. Cross-collateralization transfers more risk to the artist, who is agreeing to give up his or her income from other sources to cover the cost of recording and promoting an album.

Warranties

Warranties are promises and guarantees the artist makes, assuring the record label that no circumstances exist that could sabotage the recording. If any of these guarantees later prove to be untrue, the label has legal grounds for breaking the contract or seeking compensation for loss. Common warranties are:

- The artist is old enough to legally sign a contract.

- The artist has not signed any other contract that would interfere with this recording agreement.

- The record label will not have to pay additional sums to anyone for any of the rights granted by the contract.

- If a labor union has jurisdiction, the artist is a member in good standing.

- The artist owns the rights to all of the music and other intellectual property he or she is providing for the recording or has acquired a license to record the music.

- The artist has not recorded any unreleased masters the record label is unaware of.

The artist might also make certain promises, such as:

- The artist will be available for interviews and live performances.

- During the term of the contract, the artist will not enter into any obligations that prevent him or her from fulfilling the requirements of the contract.

- During the term of the contract, the artist will not record for any other company or allow any live performances to be recorded without a signed, written agreement that the recording will not be used on a record.

- The artist will not rerecord the songs recorded under this contract for a certain period after the end of the contract.

- The artist will notify the record label if he or she becomes aware of any third party manufacturing or selling unauthorized copies of the record.

Warranty sampling clause

Modern digital compositions often use **samples** — small digital clips such as a beat, vocal line, or **hook** (a musical passage or phrase that catches the listener's attention) — taken from another artist's recording, digitally modified, and placed anywhere and in any amount in the master recording. A **Warranty Sampling Clause** in a contract guarantees that the artist has obtained the necessary permissions and licenses to use a sample in the recording, so the record label retains all the rights granted by the contract. The artist may be required to provide legal copies of documents granting licenses and permissions and is responsible for any payments made to secure the use of the sample.

In 2009, Larrikin Music Publishing filed suit against two members of Men at Work, Colin Hay and Ron Strykert, for using two bars of "The Kookaburra Song" in their 1981 hit, "Down Under." A Melbourne schoolteacher wrote "The Kookaburra Song" in 1932 for the Australian Girl Guides, and it has become a widely known children's campfire song. The lawyer for Larrikin Music Publishing claimed that because "Down Under" incorporated half of the four-bar song in a flute solo, it is entitled to royalties every time "Down Under" is played. Larrikin had acquired the copyright for the song in 2002 and was unaware of the reference to it in "Down Under" until the subject came up in a television quiz show. In February 2010, an Australian court ruled that Men at Work must pay Larrikin 5 percent of their royalties for "Down Under" from 2002 onwards.

Companies such as Sample Clearance Ltd. (**www.sampleclearanceltd. com**) in New York and The Music Bridge (**www.themusicbridge.com**) in California specialize in tracking down copyright holders and negotiating low cost licenses.

Indemnity

An **indemnity clause** makes the artist responsible for paying any expenses resulting from a legal claim made against the company because of the artist's work. It is not uncommon for someone to sue for copyright infringement after an artist has written and recorded a song. When the artist is sued, so does everyone else involved in the recording, including the record label. Even if the lawsuit is thrown out as frivolous or the artist wins, legal costs can run into tens of thousands of dollars. An indemnity clause gives the record label the right to deduct such costs from an artist's royalties.

Suspension or termination

This section of a recording contract describes the circumstances under which the contract might be suspended or terminated and the procedures for doing so. A record label typically reserves the right to terminate or suspend the contract if the artist fails to perform, or becomes unable to perform, by giving written notice to the artist. A contract might be terminated if the artist becomes physically unable to perform or to make public appearances or if the artist ceases to pursue a career as an entertainer. **Suspension** means the artist is given additional time to resolve the problem, and the term of the contract is extended by that amount plus a period of time long enough for the company to determine whether it wants the artist to do a second album (usually four months).

The artist is also given the right to terminate the contract if the record company fails to fulfill its obligations, but not without allowing the record company sufficient time to correct problems and comply with the contract. To terminate it legally, the artist must follow the procedure laid out in the contract, which usually takes several months. This deters an artist from quickly abandoning a contract and jumping to another label. A record label might need time to respond to an artist's demands because it is handling several record contracts at the same time or because it is negotiating with financial backers and cannot get an answer from them right away. Once the record label has signed an artist and planned marketing and promotion for an album, it does not want to lose its rights to that artist.

A typical procedure might go like this:

- Nine months after the date the contract is signed, if the record label has not yet allowed the artist to record an album, the artist has 30 days to send the record label a written notice that he or she wishes to proceed with the recording. If notice is not sent within 30 days, the artist waives the right to take any action.

- The record label has 60 days after it receives this notice to send the artist a written notice initiating the recording of the album.

- If the company has not sent such a written notice by the end of that 60-day period, the artist has 30 days in which to terminate the contract.

- Once the company receives this written notice of the termination, the contract ends except for any ongoing obligations such as warranties and royalties.

Force majeure

"Force majeure" means "superior force." Every contract should include a force majeure clause to prevent termination of the contract if the record label cannot fulfill its obligations due to circumstances beyond its control. These circumstances might include "acts of God" (events beyond human control), natural disasters, civil unrest, government interference, labor union disputes, technical failures, vandalism, transportation delays, and unavoidable accidents. A force majeure clause allows the company to suspend the contract temporarily until it can resume normal business operations or at least for a specified period.

Group provisions

Many artists consist of more than one person. If you are signing an ensemble or a band, the Artists Agreement must be binding for all members of the group. A breach of contract by one member represents a breach of contract by the entire group.

The band must guarantee that it owns the name it is using. Check that the band's name is not being used by anyone else. Just as you do not want your record label to have the same name as another label, you do not want your band to discover someone else is already using its name. *Refer to the section on Selecting a Name for Your Business in Chapter 2*. If it is not already registered as a trademark, do so immediately.

It is common for a band member to leave the group because of a personal disagreement or desire for a career change. Your contract should contain a provision to prevent your record deal from being undermined if a band member suddenly decides to leave the group. The record label should have final approval of any musician who replaces the departing band member, so it can verify the new person is qualified and is not just selected for the job because he or she is a friend or family member of the artist.

The name of the band stays with the remaining group members. If the band dissolves entirely, no one can use the name. The departing band member is not released from the contract and is still the record label's exclusive property even though he or she is no longer recording with the group. Sometimes artists leave a band because they want to record a solo album. A **leaving member option** allows the record label to sign him or her to a solo record deal under terms similar to the original contract.

The record label should also reserve the right to terminate the contract if the departure of a key member makes the band unmarketable. Some bands have one person who is the focal point of their music, or the main composer and vocalist. If that person leaves the band, it will not exist anymore as a highly marketable entity. The remaining band members can sign a new contract as solo artists or under another name.

Merchandising rights

An independent record label typically claims the rights to license the artist's likeness (photos, portraits, and images) and biographical material for use on merchandise such as hats, T-shirts, concert programs, and posters. In return, the artist is given a percentage of the royalties derived from merchandise licensing. An artist may not have the knowledge or the money to take advantage of merchandising opportunities. An independent record label might provide funds so the artist can produce and sell merchandise or produce merchandise itself and wholesale it to the artist who then sells it at live performances.

Music videos

A music video often accompanies the release of a new album. The record label should reserve the right to release a music video without being obligated to do so. Any music video a record label makes is the property of the label. The contract determines the amount of input the artist will have in deciding the concept of the video, the time and location of the filming, and selecting a producer. A production budget should be established in advance, and the artist is responsible for paying for any budget overruns his or her actions cause. The artist is not responsible if the company's actions cause the budget to be exceeded. The contract should list the royalties the artist will receive from use of the music video in various media or its sale as a home video.

In some locations, union contracts may require that the artist be paid for performing in a music video, but the Artists Agreement should limit the artist's payment to only the minimum amount of compensation. The artist will be earning royalties from the music video, and it will be used to promote the artist's music, so he or she will already be making money from it.

Synchronization licenses

A **synchronization license**, obtained from the music publisher, allows a song to be used in a movie, TV commercial, cartoon or film clip, video game, or other visual media not covered by the musical work's copyright. Typically, a flat fee is paid for a license that allows the song to be used for a specified period. The song can only be used in conjunction with the media in which it is integrated, as described in the license. If the record label does not own all the publishing rights to a song, it may be necessary to secure a synchronization license to record a music video.

Websites and digital rights

A band's official website is a crucial element of any music marketing strategy. The official website presents the artist's public persona to the world; carries schedules of events and performances; sells CDs, digital downloads, and merchandise; and acts as a focal point for social media. It is one of the first places where fans from all over the world will look for information. There are many reasons for a record label to retain control of the official website. Its look and feel must support the label's branding of the artist. The website must be professionally maintained and kept up-to-date; an artist may not have the time or resources to do this while traveling and performing. The record label must have the ability to make immediate changes to the site when important news is announced or some kind of negative publicity appears in the media regarding the artist. To capture fans' interest, the website should offer exciting features and the latest technology, which requires access to knowledgeable technicians and sometimes to expensive software and Web hosting. Blogs need to be constantly monitored for abuse. There is also the threat of hackers and malicious cyber attacks.

An Artists Agreement typically gives the record label ownership of the artist's official website. The artist may be allowed to have his or her own website as long as he or she clearly indicates it is not the official site. The contract might contain a provision for sharing any income from ad placements, cross-linking agreements, and sales of merchandise from the official site with the artist. If the artist retains ownership of the official website, there should be provisions for controlling the quality and appearance of the site and making updates. Because the record label owns the master recording, there should also be a provision for allowing the artist to play recordings or show clips of live performances on his or her site.

The contract should indicate who would be responsible for Facebook or MySpace pages and the artist's presence on music promotion sites such as PureVolume™ (**www.purevolume.com**). The contract may also specify which digital distribution channels will be used to sell the artist's recordings and the arrangements for each. This is important because some channels are more vulnerable to illegal downloads than others.

Pink Floyd prevents digital downloads of individual songs.

Digital downloads allow fans to purchase individual songs rather than albums and to create their own playlists and mixes of songs from different artists. Some artists do not want their songs to be sold separately because it violates the artistic concept of their albums. In March 2010, Pink Floyd won a lawsuit against EMI that forbade its longtime label from breaking up its albums and selling individual songs without permission. A clause in Pink Floyd's contract with EMI allows the band to "preserve the artistic integrity" of its albums. Pink Floyd contended that its albums were created to be listened to from beginning to end as single entities.

Additional provisions

An Artists Agreement typically includes additional provisions common to many types of legal contracts:

- Assignment — A provision allowing the record label to assign the contract to a third party, affiliate, subsidiary, or any party who buys a controlling interest in the record company. An assignment provision allows the record label to assign certain rights to licensees.

- Notices — A section describing the manner in which written notice should be given by each party to the other and defines when the notice is considered to have been given (such as the date it is sent by registered mail)

- Confidentiality — A confidentiality agreement preventing the record label and the artist or their agents from showing the contract to anyone else without prior written permission

- Jurisdiction — The state under whose laws the contract will be enforced

- Entire agreement — A clause stating the entire agreement is contained in the contract and that no other written agreements pertaining to the contract exist

- Collective bargaining — A clause incorporating any applicable collective bargaining agreement (with a trade union) in the contract

- A clause stating if any part of the contract is invalid because of a federal, state, or local law, the rest of the contract remains in force

Tales from the Industry

Factory Records: Bankrupted by Top Artists

In 1978, Tony Wilson, a television producer, and Alan Erasmus, an actor and band manager, started a club named The Factory in Manchester, England, as a venue for local bands. Rob Gretton, the manager of the band Joy Division did not want his band to sign with a London record label. Following the example of another local record label, he joined with Erasmus, Wilson, and producer Martin Hannett to found Factory Records. They set up an office in Erasmus's apartment and released their first EP in 1979. In 1981, Hannett left the label, and Erasmus, Wilson, and Gretton formed Factory Communications Ltd.

Factory's creative team gave its artists a recognizable sound and image and shaped the way independent music would be viewed forever. Graphic designer Peter Saville created iconic record sleeves and posters for the label. Fans were intrigued by the label's practice of assigning a unique catalog number starting with the letters FAC to every project, event, and item associated with Factory, including music, videos, its club The Haćienda (FAC 51), the

Peter Hook of Joy Division performs at Sala Apolo in 2010 in Barcelona, Spain

Haćienda cat (FAC 191), a hairdressing salon (FAC 98), a sweater with a picture of a sly fox (FAC 136), a bucket on a restored watermill (FAC 148), a bet between Wilson and Gretton (FAC 253), and a radio advertisement (FAC 294). The catalog numbers were not consecutive, but typically, a specific digit or number sequence was allocated to a particular artist or type of project. Factory artists included Joy Division, OMD, The Durutti Column, New Order, Happy Mondays, and A Certain Ratio.

In 1992, the label experienced serious financial trouble, mainly because of its two most successful bands. New Order is said to have spent £400,000 ($650,362) recording their comeback album *Republic*. For their fourth album *Yes Please!*, the Happy Mondays used a new production team that completely altered their signature sound, a fusion of rock and acid house, and alienated their fans. To try to control band members' drug use, the Happy Mondays was sent to record the album in Barbados, a costly proposition. There, the band members' behavior got out of hand, and Shaun Ryder failed to write any lyrics, so there were no vocals on the resulting master, and the whole recording had to be done again, when the band got back to England. In Barbados, among other misadventures, members of the Happy Mondays wrecked a vehicle and sold the studio owner's furniture to buy drugs. The story of the Happy Mondays and Factory is depicted in the 2002 film *24 Hour Party People*.

London Records expressed an interest in taking over Factory but backed out of the deal when it discovered that due to Factory's early practice of not using contracts, New Order's back catalog was owned by the band instead of by the label. Factory Communications Ltd. declared bankruptcy in November 1992. The artistic freedom and "bad boy" image that appealed to the label's fans resulted in its downfall when the artists could not be controlled.

Other Contracts, Licenses, and Agreements

As you can see, the recording contract you sign with an artist might be supported by a complex hierarchy of licenses, distribution agreements, and sub-contracts with music publishers, producers, backup artists, and technicians. Although the Artists Agreement makes the artist responsible for executing some of these contracts, your lawyer should always review them because your company might become a target of any legal action initiated against the artist.

Contracts used in the music industry

CONTRACT	DESCRIPTION
Artists agreement	A contract between the record label and the artist detailing the obligations of each
Band agreement	A contract signed by all members of a band detailing their duties (and their acceptance of a recording agreement)
Management contract	A contract between a manager and an artist
Record contract	A contract to produce and record a single recording
Producer agreement	A contract between the record label/artist and the producer of a recording
Booking venue agreement	A contract to hire a venue for a live performance or event
Work for Hire agreement	A contract assigning ownership of work produced under the contract to the record label

CONTRACT	DESCRIPTION
Photography or artwork license	A license granting the right to use photographs or artwork
Copyright registration	A form registering a copyright with the U.S. government
Distribution agreement	A contract between a record label or artist and a distributor
Joint venture agreement	An agreement between two parties who agree to pool their resources and share the profits
Recording agreement	Similar to an artist agreement
Side artist agreement	Recording agreement with a backup musician or a secondary artist
Graphic artist agreement	A contract with a graphic artist to design art and graphics
Publishing Agreement	An agreement to assign a songwriter's copyright(s) to a music publisher
Exclusive Songwriter Agreement	An agreement for a songwriter to compose exclusively for a publisher or artist
Nonexclusive Songwriter Agreement	An agreement for a songwriter to compose a specified number of works for a publisher or artist
Mechanical Rights Agreement	An agreement assigning the royalties earned by a songwriter when a song is recorded or performed
Synchronization License	A license allowing music to be used along with a visual presentation in a movie, TV commercial, video game, or music video
Merchandising License	A license to sell merchandise bearing an artist's likeness or biographical material
Coach rental contract	A rental contract for a video
Sampling license	A license allowing a musician to incorporate a small clip of someone else's work in a recording

The contracts you use will depend on the size and complexity of your record label. Some of these contracts will be discussed in later chapters dealing with specific aspects of the music industry.

CHAPTER 7

Music Publishing

*P*ublishing rights to music can be a lucrative source of revenue for a record label. Every recorded song has two copyrights: one for the sound recording of that song and one for the words and music. Music publishing is the business of managing the copyright to the words and music of a song. If you own these rights to a song, you are entitled to a statutory mechanical royalty (in the U.S. in 2011) of 9.1 cents for each physical record or download sold, and 10.5 percent of the revenue from streaming the song over the Internet as part of a subscription or ad-based service. *See Chapter 8 for more information on copyrights.*

The use of music is increasing along with the explosion of new technologies and media formats. Advertising agencies used to compose their own jingles to convey messages about their products on TV commercials; now they frequently employ popular hit songs that evoke specific emotions and associations. Many modern television dramas use well-known songs as their theme songs or play recent hits during the shows. Songs are used in Internet ads and greeting cards, and in video and arcade games. Music is used to create ambience in clothing stores and supermarkets. Callers to business phones listen to appropriate songs while they are on hold. Songs are performed in talent competitions and played on karaoke machines. For any of these uses, a mechanical license must be obtained from the publisher. In addition, publishers sell sheet music and lyrics to performers such as choruses, orchestras, and high school bands.

If your artist records original songs, or gets material from a songwriter, your record label can earn income by claiming all or part of the publishing rights to these songs. Each of the major record labels has a publishing business, and music publishing brings in about one third of its annual revenue. Compared to producing and marketing records, music publishing requires little financial outlay — only administrative costs and the cost of marketing the music catalog.

Music publishing is big business

Bug Music, Inc., an independent music publisher established in 1975, owns and/or manages copyrights for more than 250,000 songs including the songs "Fever," "What a Wonderful World," and "Happy Together." In 2008, the estimated value of its catalog was $300 million. Bug Music collects the standard mechanical royalty of 9.1 cents every time one of its songs is downloaded or sold as part of a CD and 10.5 percent of the revenues from streaming of its songs over the Internet (minus any performance royalties already being paid to labels). The company earns even more revenue by licensing its songs for use in TV commercials, films, video games, and digital greetings cards.

Chapter 6 explained that you could include the assignment of publishing rights in the Artists Agreement signed by the artist and record label. If such an agreement does not exist, the artist is free to manage his or her own publishing rights or assign them to a third-party music publisher. Because of the administrative work involved with registering copyrights, filing with the performance rights societies that collect and pay out the mechanical royalties, and issuing licenses, most songwriters prefer to work with a music publisher. Music publishers actively market their songs by contacting film producers, game designers, and other entities that might be interested in licensing their music. They may recommend specific songs and work with the clients to select the best song for a movie or commercial. It is not fair to the artist or to your record label to acquire the publishing rights to a song and then do nothing to promote it. Some independent labels promote their artists' songs themselves. Others prefer to assign part of their rights to another music publisher and share the mechanical royalties, an arrangement known as **co-publishing**. Co-publishing allows the independent label to still get a portion of the revenue from music publishing, and the copublisher does the marketing. Although the royalty on an individual song is only a few cents, if that song becomes a hit, it can amount to a substantial sum of money.

Nonexclusive Songwriter Agreement

A songwriter can assign the publishing rights to an individual song through a **Nonexclusive Songwriter Agreement**. Conventionally, the publishing royalties for a song are divided evenly between the songwriter and the publisher. Fifty percent goes to the songwriter as the creator of the work, and 50 percent goes to the publisher for promoting the song. In a Nonexclusive Songwriter Agreement, the songwriter assigns all the publishing rights to the publisher and keeps the songwriter royalties. This involves transferring copyright of the song to the publisher. The publisher is granted the right to collect all the royalties but must then pay the songwriter his or her share. The agreement typically gives the publisher the right to use the songwriter's name, photo, and biographical material to promote the music. Income from mechanical licenses (recording) and synchronization licenses (video) is always split 50/50 between publisher and songwriter, but the contract may specify other payment amounts for specific uses of the song such as the sale of sheet music. The songwriter and publisher each collect their own performance royalties for use of the song from one of the performance rights societies, BMI (**www.bmi.com**), ASCAP (**www.ascap.com**), and SESAC (**www.sesac.com**), and the publisher will not owe performance royalties to the songwriter.

An accounting clause in the Nonexclusive Songwriter Agreement sets out the schedule for providing royalty statements and payments to the songwriter. This is often done quarterly and sometimes every six months. Publishers typically do not send a statement if no royalties have accrued during that period to save on administrative expenses. Songwriters are given the right to audit the publisher's accounts, with restrictions similar to those in the Artists Agreement.

An audit can be costly

If the publisher fails to pay the songwriter on time, the songwriter is likely to request an audit. Even though the songwriter is responsible for paying the auditor and for the copying of documents, the publisher will also incur the expense of having its own accountant go over the books to remove confidential information about other songwriters and review the accounts. Without such a review, there is no way of knowing whether the auditor's calculations are accurate, and the publisher could end up overpaying the songwriter.

In the Warranties section of the Nonexclusive Songwriter Agreement, the songwriter must guarantee the song is original and no one else can claim ownership of the copyright to the song. This section makes the songwriter responsible for any legal expenses or penalties incurred if someone sues the publisher for copyright infringement. It is not uncommon for a disgruntled band member to claim later on that he or she wrote part of the lyrics of a hit song. The publisher can claim the right to withhold mechanical royalties in order to build a fund to pay for these legal expenses.

The publisher typically reserves the right to pursue legal action against anyone who infringes on the copyright. Any awards or settlements are split between songwriter and publisher after legal expenses have been deducted. Without a signed Nonexclusive Songwriter Agreement, the publisher cannot prove it holds copyright to the song, and it cannot grant the record label clear rights to reproduce and sell a recording of it. Every song in the publisher's catalog should have a separate Nonexclusive Songwriter Agreement associated with it.

Collecting Mechanical Royalties

In the U.S., the Harry Fox Agency (**www.harryfox.com**), established in 1927 by the National Music Publishers' Association, issues mechanical licenses and collects mechanical royalties on sales of physical records and certain digital formats, including full-track downloads. The music publisher is responsible for receiving the mechanical royalties and paying the songwriter his or her half.

According to an agreement reached in September 2008, by the Digital Media Association (DiMA), the National Music Publishers' Association (NMPA), the Recording Industry Association of America (RIAA), the Nashville Songwriters Association International (NSAI), and the Songwriters Guild of America (SGA), subscription digital download services (limited download) and interactive streaming services such as Napster and

Rhapsody will pay a mechanical royalty of 10.5 percent of revenue, less than any amounts owed for performance royalties. Royalty-free streaming is allowed in some cases for promotional purposes.

Opening a Music Publishing Company

To collect publishing royalties, you must open a publishing company and set up a business bank account to receive the payments. Even a songwriter who is self-publishing must open a publishing company in order to collect the publisher's half of the royalties. To open a publishing company, you first submit three choices of business names to ASCAP, BMI, or SESAC, whichever you or your songwriter is affiliated with. If your songwriters are affiliated with more than one of these agencies, you will have to open a company with each of them. The agency will check your name and make sure someone else is not using it. Once the name has been approved, you will need to get a business license and register your publishing company legally, just as you did when you established your record label. These are the requirements for opening a business bank account into which the royalties can be deposited.

Co-publishing Agreement

A small independent label often wants publishing rights to the artist's songs because it needs the extra income from mechanical royalties to pay its expenses. An unsigned artist may be willing to sign over the copyrights in order to get a record deal, but most artists want to retain at least some of their publishing rights. Often a record label enters into an agreement to share the proceeds from publishing with the artist, known as a **Co-publishing Agreement**. This typically is done by first assigning all rights to the artist's publishing company and then having that company transfer a portion of the rights to the label's publishing company. The two publishers may agree to divide the rights equally, or one may take a larger portion. They are dividing only the publisher's half of the royalties; the songwriter retains all of his or her songwriter royalties. So, a publisher with 50 percent of the publishing royalties is only getting 25 percent of the total royalties.

A co-publishing agreement may exist between two or more songwriters who collaborated on a song but have separate publishers, or between two publishers who wish to share the rights to a song. Both publishers will own a portion of the copyright and promote the song, but only one, known as "the Company," will be responsible for doing the administrative work and collecting and distributing royalties. A co-publishing contract specifies that the copyright will be registered in the name of "the Company" even though both publishers have ownership. The other publisher is known as "the Participant."

The Company is also responsible for issuing licenses because it is managing and collecting royalties. The Company collects mechanical and performance royalties from the appropriate agencies and gives the other publisher, known as "the Participant," its share. The money is divided according to the percentage of the rights each publisher holds. The Company is usually the larger, more experienced of the two and therefore, wants the right to defend against any legal claims. Any awards or settlements will be proportionately divided between the two after expenses have been deducted.

A co-publishing agreement often works well for both parties: the more experienced publisher, usually the record label, makes sure the administration and promotion are done properly, while the less-experienced artist/ songwriter receives compensation and creates a demand for the song by performing it.

Exclusive Songwriter Agreement

In an Exclusive Songwriter Agreement, a songwriter agrees to sign over the rights to all the songs he or she writes during the period covered by the contract in exchange for compensation. It is something like an employment contract and is used mostly for songwriters who are not performers. Rights to the songs belong permanently to the publisher after the contract ends. The publisher usually retains the right to alter the songwriter's compositions or arrange them differently as it sees fit. The songwriter is not permitted to write songs for anyone else during the term of the contract.

Administration Agreement

Instead of handing the copyrights to his or her songs over to the record label's publisher, an artist/songwriter with strong bargaining power might arrange for the publisher to administer the rights in return for a percentage of the royalties. The publisher agrees to handle all the registration and administrative details, issue licenses, collect and pay royalties, and even mount legal defenses on the songwriter's behalf. In essence, the songwriter is paying the publisher to perform all of these tasks.

Licensing

A song belongs to the songwriter or the publisher and cannot be used by anyone without a license. A **license** grants permission to use a song or recording in a particular way — play it, rerecord it, use it in a movie or TV show, print the lyrics in a book, sample it, perform it on stage, or make a music video for it. Each use requires a different type of license.

A **Mechanical License** grants a record label permission to mechanically reproduce a song and distribute it. Under U.S. copyright law, once a song has been published for the first time, Mechanical Licenses are compulsory. Any record company can get a mechanical license, whether the publisher wants to grant it or not, by filing a notice with the U.S. Copyright Office. Most publishers will grant a license willingly.

Each **Mechanical License** is for a specific use of the song. Separate licenses must be obtained for subsequent uses. For example, a mechanical license might be obtained to record a song, and separate licenses obtained to use the recorded song in a video game and a commercial. The compensation is the statutory mechanical royalty rate, unless the publisher and record label negotiate a lower rate.

A **Videogram License** gives permission to make a music video for a song and distribute it to the public. A **Synchronization License** allows that video to be shown on TV or in a movie. Some publishers allow these to be combined in a single license. A **Videogram/Synchronization License** is not compulsory under copyright law. If the publisher refuses to grant the license, the video cannot be filmed.

Any company that wants to use the recorded version of a song needs to obtain the **Master Use License** from the record label. In order to use the song, however, the company must also obtain a mechanical license from the publisher. In this case, the artist will get royalties for the use of the recording, and the songwriter will get mechanical royalties for the use of the song.

CHAPTER 8

Copyrights and Trademarks

The record label business is based on ownership of copyrights to recorded and written songs and of the brands and images associated with a label and its artists. According to the U.S. Copyright Office (**www.copyright.gov**), copyright is a form of legal protection grounded in the U.S. Constitution and granted by law for original works of authorship fixed in a tangible medium of expression. A copyright gives the owner the exclusive right to make copies, license, and otherwise exploit a literary, musical, or artistic work in printed, audio, or video form.

Copyright

Copyright covers published and unpublished works. You do not have to register a copyright to protect your work; it is under copyright protection the moment it is created and fixed in a tangible form that it is perceptible either directly or with the aid of a machine or device. Copyright registration is voluntary, but you will have to register with the U.S. Copyright Office if you wish to bring a lawsuit for infringement of a U.S. work.

In the music industry, there are two types of authors: songwriters and recording artists. A songwriter's work is copyrighted the moment the song is written down or recorded. A recording artist owns a recorded performance as soon as the recording is made. Chapter 5 explained how a songwriter or recording artist could transfer this ownership to a third party, such as a record label.

Copyrights for written songs are separate from copyrights for the recordings of those songs. A publishing company acquires the copyright for a written song through a publishing agreement, and a record label acquires the copyright to a recording of that song through a recording agreement. The songwriter receives a mechanical royalty for each copy of the song sold, and the recording artist receives a performance royalty each time the recording is sold. A third party wishing to use the recording in a movie or a commercial must obtain rights from both the publisher and from the record label.

Duration of copyright

In the U.S., a work that was created (fixed in tangible form for the first time) on or after January 1, 1978 is automatically protected from the moment of its creation and is ordinarily given a term enduring for the author's life plus an additional 70 years after the author's death. In the case of a joint work prepared by two or more authors who did not work for hire, the term lasts for 70 years after the last surviving author's death. Sound recordings created before February 15, 1972 are not subject to federal copyright protection but are protected by common law rights or state statutes where applicable. Federal copyright protection was established in 1978. Before that, state laws and common law determined copyright.

For works made for hire and for anonymous and pseudonymous works (unless the author's identity is revealed in Copyright Office records), the duration of copyright is 95 years from publication or 120 years from creation, whichever is shorter.

In the European Union, the term of copyright for musical compositions in all member states lasts for the life of the author plus 70 years. The term of copyright for sound recordings currently lasts for 50 years from the date of release. In many developing countries, the protection of copyright is inadequate.

Copyright registration

No publication, registration, or other action in the U.S. Copyright Office is required to secure a copyright. Copyright is secured automatically when the work is created, and a work is created when it is fixed in a copy or phonorecord for the first time. Copies are material objects from which a work can be read or visually perceived either directly or with the aid of a machine or device, such as books, manuscripts, sheet music, film, videotape, or microfilm. Phonorecords are material objects embodying fixations of sounds (excluding, by statutory definition, motion picture soundtracks), such as cassette tapes, CDs, or vinyl disks. Thus, for example, a song (the work) can be fixed in sheet music (copies) or in phonograph disks (phonorecords), or both. If a work is prepared over a period of time, the part of the work that is fixed on a particular date constitutes the created work as of that date. For example, each song on an album is copyrighted the first time it is recorded, though the entire album may not be recorded until later.

Copyright registration is not a condition of copyright protection. Registration is a legal formality intended to make a public record of the basic facts of a particular copyright. However, registration provides several legal advantages:

- Registration establishes a public record of the copyright claim.

- Before an infringement suit may be filed in court, registration is necessary for works of U.S. origin.

- If made before or within five years of publication, registration will establish prima facie evidence in court of the validity of the copyright and of the facts stated in the certificate.

- If registration is made within three months after publication of the work or prior to an infringement of the work, statutory damages and attorney's fees will be available to the copyright owner in court actions. Otherwise, only an award of actual damages and profits is available to the copyright owner.

- Registration allows the owner of the copyright to record the registration with the U. S. Customs Service for protection against the importation of infringing copies. To register copyrights, go to the U. S. Customs and Border Protection website at **https://apps.cbp.gov/e-recordations**.

Registration may be made at any time within the life of the copyright. Unlike the law before 1978, when a work has been registered in unpublished form, it is not necessary to make another registration when the work becomes published, though the copyright owner may register the published edition, if desired.

Filing an Original Claim to Copyright with the U.S. Copyright Office

An application for copyright registration contains three essential elements: a completed application form, a nonrefundable filing fee, and a nonreturnable deposit — that is, a copy or copies of the work being registered and "deposited" with the Copyright Office. A copyright registration is effective on the date the Copyright Office receives all required elements in acceptable form, regardless of how long it takes to process the application and mail the certificate of registration. The time needed to process applications varies depending on the amount of material the Office is receiving and the method of application.

Online Registration

Online registration through the electronic Copyright Office (eCO) is the preferred way to register basic claims for literary works; visual arts works; performing arts works, including motion pictures; sound recordings; and single serials. Advantages of online filing include a lower filing fee, fastest processing time; online status tracking; secure payment by credit or debit card; electronic check, or Copyright Office deposit account; and the ability to upload certain categories of deposits directly into eCO as electronic files. You can still register using eCO and save money even if you will submit a hard-copy deposit, which is required under the mandatory deposit requirements for published works. To access eCO, go to the Copyright Office website at **www.copyright.gov** and click on "electronic Copyright Office."

Registration with Fill-In Form CO

The next best option for registering basic claims is the new fill-in Form CO. Complete Form CO on your personal computer, print it out, and mail it along with a check or money order and your deposit. To access Form CO, go the Copyright Office website and click on "Forms." Do not save your filled-out Form CO and reuse it because the information you type into the form generates a unique barcode on the document.

Registration with Paper Forms

Paper versions of Form TX (literary works); Form VA (visual arts works); Form PA (performing arts works, including motion pictures); Form SR (sound recordings); and Form SE (single serials) are still available by postal mail upon request. Online registration through eCO and fill-in Form CO (see above) can be used for the categories of works applicable to Forms TX, VA, PA, SR, and SE.

Copyright Notice

The use of a copyright notice on a work is no longer required under U.S. law, though it is often beneficial. The use of the copyright notice is the responsibility of the copyright owner and does not require advance permission from, or registration with, the Copyright Office.

Form of Notice for Visually Perceptible Copies

The notice for visually perceptible copies should contain all the following three elements:

1. The symbol © (the letter C in a circle), the word "Copyright," or the abbreviation "Copr"

2. The year of first publication of the work. In the case of compilations or derivative works incorporating previously published material, the year date of first publication of the compilation or derivative work is sufficient. The year date may be omitted where a pictorial, graphic, or sculptural work, with accompanying textual matter, if any, is reproduced in or on greeting cards, postcards, stationery, jewelry, dolls, toys, or any useful article.

3. The name of the owner of copyright in the work, an abbreviation by which the name can be recognized, or a generally known alternative designation of the owner

   Example: © 2008 John Doe

The © notice is used only on visually perceptible copies. Certain kinds of works — for example, musical, dramatic, and literary works — may be fixed not in "copies" but by means of sound in an audio recording. Because audio recordings such as audiotapes and phonograph disks are "phonorecords" and not "copies," the © notice is not used to indicate protection of the underlying musical, dramatic, or literary work recorded.

Form of Notice for Phonorecords of Sound Recordings

The notice for phonorecords embodying a sound recording should contain all the following three elements:

1. The symbol of a letter P in a circle

2. The year of first publication of the sound recording

3. The name of the owner of copyright in the sound recording, an abbreviation by which the name can be recognized, or a generally known alternative designation of the owner. If the producer of the sound recording is named on the phonorecord label or container and if no other name appears in conjunction with the notice, the producer's name shall be considered a part of the notice.

Example: P 2008 A.B.C. Records Inc.

Position of Notice

The copyright notice should be affixed to copies or phonorecords in such a way as to "give reasonable notice of the claim of copyright." The three elements of the notice should ordinarily appear together on the copies or phonorecords or on the phonorecord label or container. The Copyright Office has issued regulations concerning the form and position of the copyright notice in the Code of Federal Regulations (37 CFR 201.20).

Tales from the Industry

99 Records (pronounced Nine Nine) 1980-1984

Ed Bahlman started 99 Records started. It got its name from its location in the basement of 99 MacDougal Street, off Bleeker Street in New York's West Village, a shop that sold imports of releases on many UK indie labels. Bahlman was involved in the music scene in New York; he routinely put on shows and did production. In the early 1980s, UK labels Y Records, On U Sound, and Rough Trade inspired him, and he thought the New York music scene would benefit from something similar. Glen Branca, a legendary music figure in New York during that time, was a frequent patron of the 99 shop. He would complain to Ed about the lack of independent labels in the U.S., compared to the explosion of small indies in the U.K. Branca had already recorded some music and persuaded Ed that it would cost very little to start a label and release it.

Fortuitously, this was an active period for independent music in New York. Ed knew clearly the sound he was seeking and actively participated in the mixing and production of many of the 99 releases.

A 3-track EP by Bush Tetras, an (almost) all-girl New York band started by Pat Place, quickly became 99 Record's biggest hit. "Too Many Creeps" was played in new wave clubs around the U.S. and made *Billboard*'s dance charts. The record sold 30,000 copies, giving 99 Records the cash to record new bands and release its next few records.

While judging a talent show, Ed's attention was caught by ESG (Emerald Sapphire Gold), a group of sisters (the Scroggins). He became their unofficial manager and got them bookings in new clubs such as Hurrah's and Danceteria. "Moody" and "UFO" from their EP are two of the most sampled records of all time.

Other artists released on 99 Records included Y Pants; Congo Ashanti; Singers and Players; Liquid Liquid, led by bassist Richard McGuire; and Vivian Goldman, a London journalist who released a version of her 7 inch called "The Dirty Washing EP."

Liquid Liquid - Optimo / Cavern / Scraper / Out, a 12 inch released in 1983, ended up destroying 99 Records. "Optimo" and "Cavern" became big hits in the clubs. "Cavern" was a particular hit among hip-hop fans, and they flocked to the 99 shop asking for the record with that bassline. It sold almost 30,000 copies. At that time, sampling was a new concept, and the legal ramifications of sampling other people's records were unclear. Sugarhill Records, the first commercial hip-hop label, soon appropriated the bassline from "Cavern" for the backing to Grand Master Flash's "White Lines." At first, Liquid Liquid, who admired Flash, were pleased the group had used 'Cavern,' but that changed when the song became a global hit. An outraged Ed contacted Sugarhill to demand payment. Sugarhill had not sampled "Cavern" literally; instead, the

Sugarhill Band had replayed the bassline and appropriated other elements of the song.

Sugarhill was renowned for its shady business practices: its first hit release, "Rappers Delight," contained material stolen from other rappers, and it was notorious for not paying anyone. Despite intimidation, Bahlman pursued Sugarhill through legal channels and eventually, brought the matter to court. In a case that set precedents for sampling rights, the judge ruled in favor of 99 and ordered Sugarhill to pay compensation. Instead of paying up, Sugarhill filed for bankruptcy. In frustration, Ed, who had invested all his energy and money in the case, got out of the music business and urged all the artists on 99 to do the same.

Ironically, Liquid Liquid eventually got a payout when Duran Duran covered Sugarhill's "White Lines."

"Cavern" became a hip-hop classic and was used in several films. Its bassline is possibly one of the most famous and instantly recognizable in the history of popular music.

99 Records represents a brief era in New York's musical history and is known only to a small coterie of fans. Since its demise, the reputation of the label and of its groups has steadily grown. Its original heavy U.S. vinyls with their thick card sleeves now sell for high prices on auction sites such as Ebay.

Trademarks

Your record label name, logo, and motto, as well as the names and logos (if any) of your artists are valuable trademarks. A **trademark** is a word, phrase, symbol, or design, or a combination of words, phrases, symbols, and designs, that identifies and distinguishes the source of the goods of one party from those of others. It is not necessary to register a trademark; you can establish rights in a mark based on legitimate use of the mark. Because you will be making a considerable financial investment in promoting the reputation of your label and your artists, it is wise to register your trademarks in the Principal Register of the U.S. Patent and Trademark Office

(USPTO). You do not want a copycat band stealing your artist's name after you have made it famous. Someone else inadvertently could choose words and phrases associated with a particular genre of music for the name of a record label or music company.

As with registering a copyright, owning a federal trademark registration provides several advantages:

- Registration notifies the public that you claim ownership of the mark and provides legal grounds for your ownership and your exclusive right to use the mark nationwide.

- You cannot bring an action concerning the mark in federal court unless you register the trademark.

- You can use the U.S. registration as a basis to obtain registration in foreign countries.

- You can file the U.S. registration with the U.S. Customs Service to prevent importation of infringing foreign goods, such as pirated CDs.

Any time you claim rights in a mark, you may use the TM (trademark) or SM (service mark) designation to alert the public to your claim, regardless of whether you have filed an application with the USPTO. However, you may use the federal registration symbol ® only after the USPTO actually registers a mark and not while an application is pending. Also, you may use the registration symbol with the mark only on or in connection with the goods and/or services listed in the federal trademark registration. You can learn more about registering a trademark or a service mark on the USPTO website (**www.uspto.gov/trademarks/basics/Basic_Facts_Trademarks.jsp**).

CHAPTER 9

Setting Up a Website

Your website is the public "face" of your record label. It will be the first contact you have with many of your customers, prospective artists, fans, and vendors, so you want it to deliver just the right first impression. A well-designed website can streamline many of your business activities, including collecting personal information from your contacts, directing enquiries to the appropriate staff members, managing sales, organizing financial data, advertising upcoming tours and new releases, and gathering demos from prospective artists. Youthful audiences in particular are increasingly tuned in to social media and the Internet, but middle-aged music lovers also are likely to look up your website on their cell phones, iPads, and laptops when they want information about you or your artists.

According to the Recording Industry Association of America (RIAA), between 2004 and 2010, revenues from digital music downloads increased by
1,000 percent. The Digital Music Report 2011 of the IFPI (International
Federation of the Phonographic Industry) found that sales of digital music
in 2010 equaled $4.6 billion, amounting to 29 percent of record compa-
nies' total revenues — an increase of 6 percent from 2009. There are currently more than 400 legal digital music services globally, and these digital
retailers now account for more than 35 percent of all music sales. In February 2010, iTunes, the current leader in digital music sales, served its 10
billionth music download. As digital sales increase, so will the importance
of your website. Fans who purchase digital downloads will look at your
website to learn more about your artists, find out when new releases will
become available, and buy merchandise and tickets for live performances.

It costs very little to purchase a domain name and set up your own website
using a template and the free design software available from companies
such as GoDaddy.com (**www.godaddy.com**), Wix.com® (**www.wix.com**),
Buildfree.org (**www.buildfree.org**), and Weebly.com (**www.weebly.com**).
A simple website might be all you need if you are setting up a record label to
sell your own CD and promote yourself or your band, but because a website
is a central element of a record label business, consider your needs carefully.
Unless you are already a skilled Web designer, or you have hours of time to
invest in research and experimentation, consider paying a professional to
design your website. Large Web design companies may charge thousands of
dollars for their services, but you should be able to find a smaller company
or individual who will design your website for $300 to $400.

Look for a company that has experience with music sites. An experienced
Web designer will already know which software programs are most compatible and offer the best value and how to solve glitches that might keep
your website from running smoothly. He or she will also know how to
optimize your website so it appears near the top of search engines' result
pages (using SEO — search engine optimization). Look at other record

labels' websites. When you come across a website you particularly like, make a note of the URL, and look at the bottom of the home page for the designer's name and copyright. Contact that designer, and request a quote for designing your site. When you are talking to Web designers, show them examples of sites you like and features you want to include on your website.

Selling music and merchandise online

Many distributors will allow you to link to your own sales page on their site where customers can purchase music downloads and order CDs. The distributor handles all the financial transactions and takes a commission from your sales. *See Chapter 11 for more information on online distribution.*

An online shopping cart gathers and processes information for customers making purchases. Most website design programs include a shopping cart template so you can add an online store to your site. If you are selling merchandise, you can use shopping cart software that calculates sales tax for online sales and processes orders for as little as $30 per month.

You will also need a payment gateway, a service that takes credit card information and validates it before transferring funds to your bank account. Popular payment gateways include Flagship Merchant Services®, GoEmerchant (**www.goemerchant.com**), FastCharge™ (**www.fastcharge.com**), Merchant Warehouse (**http://merchantwarehouse.com**), Instamerchant (**www.instamerchant.com**), or Durango Merchant Services (**http://durangomerchantservices.com**). Consider paying extra for chargeback insurance to protect you from losses due to purchases made with stolen credit card numbers.

You can open a merchant account to receive the funds from online purchases with almost any bank. All of these services charge various service fees, transaction fees, and/or monthly subscriptions. Shop carefully and purchase only the services you need. Make sure your shopping cart software, payment gateway, and merchant account are compatible before you make any commitments.

If you are not ready to set up a full-fledged e-commerce system and commit to monthly subscription payments, you can use a third-party payment system such as PayPal™ (**www.paypal.com**), 2Checkout (**www.2checkout.com**) or ClickBank® (**www.clickbank.com**). These companies act as payment gateway and merchant account rolled into one. Instead of monthly subscriptions or service fees, they take a commission from each transaction. These commissions are higher than the transaction fees merchant accounts charge, but you only have to pay when you make a sale. Many third-party payment systems also process payments from customers in foreign countries.

Selecting a Name for Your Record Label in Chapter 2 recommended choosing a name that was available as an Internet domain. Protect your website and your marketing efforts by registering your URL with all the appropriate endings: .net, .info, .org, .mobi, etc. Also, register alternative spellings and possible typos — you can redirect these other domain names to your website. Many spam merchandisers and ad sites attempt to capitalize on legitimate website addresses by registering misspellings of popular URLs. Any fan who looks at your website is a potential customer. You do not want to lose even one opportunity because someone misspelled or mistyped your name. You can reserve a domain name for $6 to $10 per year, a small price to pay to protect your name. Domain name registrations must be renewed every year. Ensure you do not lose your domain name by setting up automatic registration with your vendor.

Planning Your Website

Before you begin speaking with website designers, have a clear concept of how you want your website to look and function. A website designer will be guided by your vision — his or her job is to provide the technical and artistic expertise. Spend some time exploring the websites of other record labels and artists. You can find thousands of record label website links on sites such as AllRecordLabels.com (**http://allrecordlabels.com**) and A2G

Music.com (**http://a2gmusic.com/content/record_label**). Observe how each website is organized, where the navigation menus are located, and the ease with which you can find information. Note the way in which artists are presented, the use of music videos, and the color schemes. Look for features and functions you want to include in your own website.

The overall design of your website should reflect the genre of music you are promoting and the unique qualities of your label. Your input is important, but your personal tastes and preferences might not be the most effective. For example, you might want to your website to open with an impressive animation using Adobe® Flash®, a multimedia platform that allows streaming of audio and video. However, visitors to your site probably want to access information as quickly as possible and may not be able to view the Flash presentation clearly on a handheld device or an older computer. A montage of CD cover images, publicity photos, and information links may produce better sales results and encourage visitors to view more pages on your website. An experienced website designer knows how to appeal to an audience and how to make the website easy for visitors to use. Listen to the suggestions of the website designer before you decide on a final design.

Your website should be created so you or someone on your staff can add new pages, edit text, update each section, maintain blogs and newsletters, change photos, and manage sales and reports without having to rely on the Web designer. Make this clear in your Web design contract, and define exactly what kind of ongoing maintenance the Web designer will provide and the procedures for making changes to the website design.

If you will own and manage the official websites of your artists, have these sites designed so they are compatible with your record label website and carry out a similar theme and look. Website maintenance can take up a lot of time; streamline the process by making all your websites consistent and easily accessible to the staff member who will be updating them.

Elements of a record label website

Make a list of all the things you want your website to do — known as the scope of your project. A website designer needs this list to prepare a proposal and a price quote. Your primary purpose is to promote your artists and your record label. To accomplish this, you must provide photos, samples of music, videos of performances, tour schedules, and biographical information. You will probably want to sell downloads, CDs and merchandise, and possibly tickets for live events. In addition, you might use your website to solicit new artists, disseminate press releases, communicate with retailers, organize street teams, build a community of fans, and gather names and e-mail addresses for a monthly newsletter. Your plans for maintaining your website and responding to inquiries are also part of its scope.

Below are elements commonly found in record label websites. You do not have to include all of them in your site. The sections and pages you need for your website will depend on its purpose and the business activities for which it will be used.

Home page

Your home page is a snapshot of your entire website and a statement about your record label. In a few seconds, someone who opens your home page will understand what kind of music you are promoting and what information is available on your website. Your home page should be exciting and informative. The top portion of your home page, which appears in the browser screen when someone opens your website, is the most important because many readers do not stay on your website if they do not see something that interests them right away. According to Nielsen Online, the average time spent looking at a Web page is 56 seconds. You have less than a minute to grab a fan's attention.

At a glance, a visitor to your home page should see your name and logo, a captivating image of at least one of your artists, and a list of the sections of your website. Most record label home pages have a permanent portion that displays their name and navigation menu and an area with images and/or text that is changed at frequent intervals to keep fans coming back. Music fans respond quickly to visual images, names of artists, songs and albums, and important dates. Detailed information, biographical material, and mission statements can be placed on other pages or in a lower section of the home page and linked to an introductory sentence or navigation bar at the top of the home page.

Navigation

Navigation refers to the way in which visitors to your website move from one page to another. Website designers know that a certain percentage of visitors leave a site each time they are required to click on a button or link to open an additional page. It is important to organize your website so your visitors quickly find what they are looking for and are able to return easily to pages they have already looked at. For example, you can place a button (a small image that can be clicked on to open a new page) for buying your newest CD near the top right-hand corner of your home page. Divide the functions of your website into distinct sections: an area for fans, an area for sales, an area for media and business contacts, and so on. A navigation menu across the top or down the side of your home page links your visitors to the various sections of your website: a list of your artists, your online store, press releases for the media, contact information, music downloads, and maybe a page where aspiring artists can submit their demos.

Artists

Your artists are the main feature of your website. Music, photos, biographical material, concert schedules, and video clips for all of your artists should appear somewhere on your website. This is an opportunity for the artists to deepen their connections with their fans. You can include links to the artists' own websites, and sign-ups for e-mail newsletters, Twitter, Facebook, and other social media.

News

Your website should have a section with regularly updated news about your artists and your record label, such as new releases, tour dates, and clips of newspaper articles. This helps to engage your fans, but more important, it attracts attention from search engines such as Google and draws traffic to your website.

Photo gallery

Photos of recent live events and artists can be posted in a photo gallery. Make sure to include copyright information concerning how the photos can be used.

Premieres and new releases

As part of your marketing strategy, your website can be used to build up anticipation for upcoming releases, tours, and the debuts of new artists. This information typically is located prominently on the home page and is updated frequently to keep fans interested.

Store

A store displays information for items sold on the website, including CDs and downloads, and includes a shopping cart so customers can place orders and pay for purchases. If you are selling music downloads through an online distribution channel or an affiliate, you can link to their Web pages from your store.

About Us

Most record label websites have an "About Us" section with information about the label, the history of the company, a mission statement, and anything else the company wants to officially communicate to the public. This is a good place to put your résumé and the skills and qualifications of your record label staff. This section might include links to your contact information or media press kits.

Community

You might want to encourage your fans to become involved in an online community by posting comments in a blog or message board and signing up for social media. A community section can contain information about charities and benefit performances or general news items about the music industry. When visitors to your website are allowed to contribute to an online community and interact with other fans, they develop a stronger loyalty to your label and your artists.

E-mail Newsletter

E-mail is a powerful way to communicate with loyal fans. Encourage them to add their e-mail addresses to your list, and send out e-newsletters at regular intervals informing them about your artists' touring schedules and upcoming releases. E-mail recipients often forward interesting newsletters to their friends and family. You can use your e-mail list to learn about your fans by documenting their responses to special offers and their use of coupons and promotional offers.

Tours

Tour schedules and dates of live performances should be updated frequently. This section can also help to build enthusiasm for a concert tour and link to merchandise and ticket sales.

A&R and Demos

Some independent labels actively solicit new artists on their websites by explaining what their policies toward new artists are and offering a link to upload a demo.

Media and Press Kits

Create a section specifically for the news media where you can post press releases, announcements, and official photos for use in newspapers, magazines, and newsletters. If you do not want to make this material available to the public, put a request form on this page so journalists can contact you and get a special login to download photos and documents. When you send out e-mail notifications or press releases, you can refer journalists to this area of your site to get photos and additional information.

Contact Us

This is an important page; it gives addresses, telephone numbers, and e-mail addresses for the various departments of your company. If you do not want to receive phone calls, you can supply visitors with a form for submitting e-mail inquiries. You or someone on your staff should check inquiries every day. You do not want to miss an opportunity for publicity.

Advertising

Although most record label websites do not carry advertising, you can make extra income by selling advertising space on your site. The ads should be for products and services relevant to your music. You can also advertise your own music or merchandise in a space along the side of each page.

Business and Distribution

Depending on your distribution channels, you may need an area on your site where distributors can place orders for CDs and merchandise, make payments, and print out invoices.

Website Analytics

Once your website goes live, monitor it regularly to see how many fans are coming to your site and which areas attract the most attention. The analysis of website traffic is a science in itself. You probably do not need to go into it in depth, but a few simple observations can be useful. **Page views** refers to the number of times someone opens a page on a website. **Click-through paths** show how visitors to your site move from your home page to the other areas of the site. A **click-through rate** is the percentage of visitors who click a link on one page to open and view another page. If one page or area of your site is receiving a large number of page views, it might indicate that your fans are especially interested in that artist or topic. It could also mean you are receiving attention in a news article or another website that is directing readers to your website. You may be able to capitalize on this interest by giving the artist additional exposure or making this part of your website more prominent.

Low click-through rates from your home page to other areas of your site could indicate that fans are losing interest after they see your home page and that you need to try a different look or approach. Low click-through rates could also indicate technical problems, such as a page that takes too long to load in a browser. Test this by trying to open the page in other browsers and on other computers with different operating systems and software. When visitors enter your shopping cart and then fail to complete orders, they might be having difficulty with their credit card payments, or your prices might be too high.

Most website design software includes some reporting and traffic analysis features. Google Analytics (**http://www.google.com/support/analytics**) allows you to track conversion data, analyze the flow of visitors through your site, and identify elements of your site that could be changed to improve visitor retention, and it is free for websites with fewer than 5 million page views per month. If you decide you need a detailed, in-depth analysis of traffic through your website, you can purchase a website analysis software program or service from a company such as Webtrends™ (**www.web trends.com**) or Alexa® (**www.alexa.com**) or Adobe Web analytics powered by Omniture™ (**www.omniture.com/en/products/online_analytics**).

Your website is a central focus of your marketing strategy, but it is only one component. It will not make your record label successful all by itself. A website is a tool that can be used, together with aggressive media promotion and live appearances by your artists, to gain recognition for your record label in the music industry. Schedule regular website maintenance on your calendar so that your website remains up-to-date and attracts visitors with fresh information that corresponds to your most recent press releases.

CHAPTER 10

Recording and Production

Your business as a record label is to make good music into a marketable product and sell it. Your artist is depending on you to showcase his or her creativity and talent to the world. Success depends on making a top-quality recording with the resources at your disposal. If the recording is mediocre, a good band and a great song may slip unnoticed into obscurity. A mediocre song, on the other hand, can become a hit if it is well recorded. A good-quality first record will establish your label's reputation with DJs, distributors, retailers, and fans. For these reasons, devote considerable time to doing research and learning as much as you can before you make your first record. Employ professionals who compensate for the knowledge and experience you lack, and study what they do. Everything you learn from making your first record will help you to make your future records even better.

As you will see in this chapter, a number of factors contribute to the quality of a record: the recording studio; the expertise of the producer and the sound engineers who record, mix, and master the record; the artwork and packaging; and, of course, the music itself.

The production of a record goes something like this:

- The artist assembles enough songs for an album (or an EP) and practices them until they are perfect and ready to be recorded in a studio.

- The record label makes arrangements for the recording session: locates and books a studio; assembles a staff of producers, engineers, and assistants; hires additional vocal or instrumental backup; gathers all the necessary equipment; and arranges accommodations and catering for the staff if needed. The artist may be responsible for some of these arrangements as specified in the recording contract.

- The artist, sound engineer, and producer record the songs in the studio. Each song is "mixed" by an engineer who puts the tracks together. Everyone reviews and critiques the songs, and the recordings are tested on various types of sound equipment.

- The album is "mastered" to create the final recording: the songs are equalized to compensate for acoustic effects in the studio, regular intervals are inserted between the songs, and songs recorded in different surroundings are balanced so that the whole album plays at a similar volume.

- In the meantime, a label for the CD cover or vinyl album cover is designed and printed.

- The master recording, CD labels, and packaging are delivered to the manufacturer, who replicates the album on CDs and packages them. The master recording is delivered to digital distribution channels along with graphic images to be used on Web pages.

- The packaged CDs are delivered to distributors and retailers. The record label simultaneously launches a publicity campaign for the new release.

As you will see later in this chapter, the actual recording process is much more complex and will be influenced by the genre of music and the expertise of the artist and staff. Some studios and manufacturers offer turnkey (all-in-one) packages that combine several services and present you with a finished product. An artist or producer may have multiple skills and be involved in several aspects of the recording process. At each step, you will be faced with choices and decisions. Your priority is always to produce the best quality you can, while ensuring that you have enough financial reserves to market and promote the record when it is released.

Your Production Budget

Major record labels have financial backing, a large staff of music professionals, and access to the best recording studios. You will have to do the best you can on a limited budget. Unlike an artist, who might make recordings as money becomes available, a record label must complete an entire album and begin marketing it in the shortest possible time. Artists will not want to work with a label that drags out a first release because it lacks funding, and the label needs to make sales in order to recoup its investment and work on new projects. Chapter 4 mentioned that money would not immediately start pouring in, even if an album is an instant success. It might be weeks and even months before you receive payments from your distributors. When the record is released, you will need money to promote it — otherwise, fans may never be aware of its existence. To protect your business and assure the success of your record, you need a production budget. An accurate **production budget** will show you where you stand

and help you make difficult decisions. A budget also removes some of the uncertainty from your business venture; when you see you are exceeding projected costs, you will be able to make adjustments to compensate and still achieve your goals.

Make a list of everything you will have to do to produce the record and promote it for the first few months, along with the estimated cost of each activity. Sum up these costs, and add another 30 percent to that amount for emergencies and unexpected overruns. If you do not have this amount of capital available, you need to find additional funding, reduce the scale of your project, or find ways to economize. Do not proceed with a vague hope that everything will work out; make a concrete plan for every eventuality.

PRODUCTION BUDGET FOR ALBUM	
Your production budget will be determined by the type of recording, the number of artists, prices in the city where the studio is located, the instruments and equipment you need, the number of days in the studio, and the additional staff that must be hired. Fill in this worksheet as you research your recording project.	
Recording	
Rehearsal space rental	
Studio fee X number of days	
Drum amp, mic and phase	
Recording tape	
Equipment rental	
Transportation	
Lodgings while in studio	
Catering	
Mixing	
Mastering	
Tape copies, reference CDs	
Instruments	
Shipping	
Fee for sound engineer	

PRODUCTION BUDGET FOR ALBUM	
Fees for side artists, backup vocalists	
Fee for producer	

Music Video (to be recouped from Artist Royalties)

Camera rental	
Crew	
Processing and transfers	
Off-line	
On-line editing	
Catering	
Stage and construction	
Transportation	
Director's fee	
Support staff	

Manufacturing

Album artwork	
Deposit or advance	
Printing labels	
UPC code	
Shipping	

Promotional Expenses

Promotional photo shoot and duplication	
Events	
Posters	
Advertising	
Launch party	
Internet ads	

PRODUCTION BUDGET FOR ALBUM	
Press kits, sample CDs	
Postage	
Tour Expenses (to be recouped from Artist Royalties)	
Bus	
Crew	
Food and lodging	
Fuel	
Consumable supplies	
Wardrobe	
Promotion	
Agent's cut	
Manager's cut	
TOTAL	
Plus 30% for unexpected expenses, overruns, and emergencies	

Preproduction

The recording session in the studio is not the first step in making an album, but the culmination of a great deal of preparation. Preproduction refers to all the administrative work, scheduling, planning, and organizing that goes on before the artist arrives in the studio. Well-organized preproduction can make the difference between a superlative and a mediocre recording and between financial success and disaster due to unanticipated budget over-runs. You are paying for every hour spent in the studio. To make the most of those hours, you want to make sure that the artist and staff members show up prepared and ready to go to work with all the equipment they need and that everything runs smoothly.

Administrative

The record label is responsible for locating and booking a studio and a sound engineer, engaging a producer (sometimes the recording contract makes the artist responsible for this), and executing a signed written agreement with each entity involved in the recording. This includes contracts with the recording studio and with any side artists or technicians. Collect and file required employment documents such as W-9 forms, copies of Social Security cards, or proof of union membership (if your musicians belong to a musician's union). Licenses must be obtained to use any copyrighted music or lyrics.

Musician's Unions

Musicians, sound engineers, and other technicians may belong to a trade union that sets compensation guidelines and imposes standards for working conditions. Add the following checkbox to your hiring agreements:

____ I AM NOT a member of a union/organization. I am a free agent with no representation except my own.

_____ I AM a member of a musician's union/organization. I belong to _____, and I am bound by its performance guidelines.

If the employee is a union member, contact the union to learn about pay, working hours, and other requirements. Add a copy of the union membership card to the employee's file.

Read over the Artists Agreement carefully, make sure each person understands his or her responsibilities, and that all the requirements of the contract are being fulfilled. The artist or the record label might have to get sampling licenses. Arrange for purchase or rental of equipment and supplies, and for transportation, lodging, and catering during the recording session. Try not to overlook any detail. Set up a production calendar and make sure everyone has a copy. Schedule rehearsal times and at least one meeting with the artist, producer, engineer, and record label staff.

Artist preparation

Work with the artist to select and review the songs for the album. The artist should practice as much as possible. If backup musicians or side artists will be used in the recording, hold rehearsals to work out their parts in advance. Have the artist practice performing while standing still because movement in the recording studio will interfere with the recording.

Confirm that the artist has the musical instruments he or she needs, extra guitar strings, backup equipment, etc. If sampling or prerecorded tracks will be used, make sure these are ready. Urge the artist to get plenty of rest the night before the recording session.

Meeting with producer, engineer, and artist

Hold an advance meeting with the recording engineer, producer, artist, and anyone else directly involved to discuss what will take place during the recording session. Give the engineer a preliminary recording of the album so he or she will know what to expect. If possible, take the engineer to a live performance of the artist. Make sure the studio has all the equipment needed to record the artist's music.

Communication

Communicate openly with the artist and producer about your plans, expectations, and financial resources. They know you are a small, independent label with limited finances; it is best to be honest and enlist their cooperation in keeping costs down. For example, you might set a goal of recording three songs per day for four days. Make it clear that money saved during the recording session can go toward promoting the new record. The better you understand each other, the more smoothly you will be able to collaborate.

Establish rules to minimize distractions (such as phone calls and friends stopping by the recording session) during the recording session, and make sure everyone understands them. Ask everyone to be on time for the start of the recording session, and limit coffee breaks and lunch breaks. Do not allow family or friends to be present during recording sessions because they will draw the artist's attention away from the music. Discuss whether to allow consumption of alcohol during recording sessions because an inebriated band member may not be able to perform well.

Selecting a Studio

Recording studios are everywhere. A recording studio can be anything from a modified garage or bedroom in someone's house to a specially designed complex with multiple sound rooms. Equipment, services, and prices vary

widely from one studio to another. With modern equipment and computer software, a good sound engineer can record a good-quality album for $10,000 to $20,000. A recording session at one of the top studios in New York or California could cost more than $100,000. The recording studio will significantly affect the quality of your final product, so it is worth investing time and effort to find the one that best fits your project and your budget. You are looking for a studio and staff that can help you succeed not only with your current project, but also with your label's future records.

Find local recording studios by looking through telephone directories and on the Internet; talking with local musicians, music stores, DJs, and entertainment lawyers; and reading through the ads in music publications and fan magazines. When you contact a studio and learn that it does not suit your purpose because it is the wrong size, lacks equipment or is already booked, ask the person to suggest other studios. Place a classified ad on Craigslist (**www.craigslist.org**). Contact local universities and technical schools that teach media classes. Look in directories such as the Musicians Atlas Online (**www.musiciansatlas.com**) or RecordProduction.com (**www.recordproduction.com/usa_studio_website_directory.htm**). If you like the quality of your artist's demo, ask where it was recorded. Make a list of the best prospects, the services offered, and the prices.

Visit the studios on your list, talk to the owners and engineers, and ask to see their equipment. Bring along your producer or someone with experience recording to help you evaluate the studio. Most studios include the services of an engineer in their pricing. Ask to hear samples of the engineer's work and, if possible, watch a recording session in progress and observe how the engineer interacts with the musicians. Find out how many microphones are used and whether there are any amplifiers or instruments (such as synthesizers, keyboards, or drum consoles) available in the studio. Learn whether the studio has mastering equipment to produce a final master recording. Ask what musicians have recorded at the studio, and listen to their records. Contact them to learn how they feel about their experience recording in that studio.

When you have narrowed down your list to three or four possible studios, weigh the advantages and disadvantages of each. The main considerations are:

- Do you feel comfortable in the studio environment?

If the studio or the engineer intimidates you or makes you feel nervous, follow your intuition, and walk away. To make a successful recording, you need to feel confident that the engineer will cooperate with the artist and follow the direction of the producer. This is your recording, and you do not want the engineer to dominate it or get into arguments with the artist. Is the recording area large enough to accommodate the artist and backup musicians comfortably? Do you like the acoustics? Bring the artist to visit the studio and get his or her opinion. The final decision is yours, but it is a good idea to get input from everyone involved.

- Does the studio have the equipment you need?

Every style of music uses different instruments and equipment. Make sure the studio has the right equipment for your artist and that the engineer is experienced with your genre.

- Does the price fit your budget?

The cost of renting the studio takes up a large part of your budget, but it is not your only expense. If you spend more than you budgeted for the recording, you may not have enough money to promote your new album when it hits the market. You can try to negotiate a lower price with the studio. Some studios give discounts if you book for 24-hour blocks or for "graveyard" blocks (during the night and early morning hours — keep in mind that no one is at their best when they are tired). You can also limit time spent in the recording studio by rehearsing in another location and having the songs perfected beforehand.

Try out studios with individual recordings

If you are undecided about your choice of studios, arrange to have your artist record a single in each and compare the results. The recordings will probably be good enough to be used on the final album with a little adjustment, and you will be able to see which studio produces the best results for the artist.

Hiring a Producer

A producer oversees the recording process and directs the artist, musicians, and technicians to create the sound and arrangements the artist and re-

cord label want. The role of the producer depends on the scope of the project and may include selecting songs and side artists, coaching the artist in the studio, controlling recording sessions, overseeing the budget, and supervising mixing and mastering. Many producers are musicians and may participate in the recording or contribute to the musical arrangements. Often a producer is hired to create a particular "sound" with the artist's music. Some producers double as recording engineers (see below). On a small project, the artist, recording engineer, or record label owner may take on the role of producer.

An experienced producer is an invaluable asset to a recording and can make the difference between a mediocre album and an exciting, innovative hit. The producer supplies a vision of the finished product and knows the steps necessary to fulfill it. He or she might have useful contacts in the music business and know where to find the right backup musicians, studio, and equipment for the recording. A producer with technical skills can understand what the artist and engineer want to achieve and show them how to accomplish it. The producer provides additional creative input and knows what will appeal to the artist's audience. Unlike the artist, the producer is actively involved in recording music every day and knows about the latest trends and techniques.

The producer also helps enforce the recording schedule, keep everyone focused, solve problems, and smooth over disputes. A good producer understands the music business and the label's priorities, as well as the artist's needs. The producer decides when songs need to be rerecorded and when the recording session is over.

Some studios provide a producer as part of their overall pricing package, and some producers own recording studios. A producer-owned studio has a vested interest in creating a successful record that will enhance its reputation. Because the producer owns the equipment, you may be able to negotiate a flat rate for production and recording combined.

A producer sometimes serves as the sound engineer during the recording. This arrangement can work well, particularly with an individual artist or a small group, or when there is an assistant engineer present to take care of setup and technical details. A producer who is also doing the engineering will not be able to devote as much attention to other aspects of the recording session.

How a producer is paid

A producer is typically paid a flat fee, an hourly salary, or a fee for each song recorded. A producer might charge anything from $250 to $10,000 per song, depending on his or her experience and the artist's reputation. In addition, the producer receives a record royalty, usually 3 percent of the sales price of each album sold. In modern genres such as rap, techno, and hip-hop, producers are artists in their own right, creating digital tracks over which the artist's vocals are inserted. In cases like this, the producer receives an additional royalty for the music he or she created.

The section on Royalties in Chapter 5 described the typical arrangement for producer's royalties: the producer's points (percentage of record sales price) are subtracted from the artist's royalties and set aside. The producer is paid when the record label has recouped the hard costs of recording the album. The record label provides an accounting of royalties to the producer as well as to the artist and usually takes responsibility for making the payout.

Producer's contract

The Artists Agreement should specify that the record label will hire a producer on the artist's behalf (sometimes subject to the artist's approval) and that the producer's royalties will be paid out of the artist's royalties. In addition, because the producer is involved to some degree in the creative process, have an attorney draft a contract specifying what services the producer will provide to your label and what compensation the producer will receive. All issues pertaining to your label's rights to the recording should be clarified in a written, signed contract before the producer begins work.

Everyone involved in making a recording shares the copyright to that recording. The contract should transfer the producer's recording copyrights to the record label. Otherwise, the producer is considered a coauthor of the recording and is legally entitled to a share of all the profits, not just royalties or a flat fee. A standard producer contract transfers all rights to the recording to the record label as a work made for hire. If the producer creates tracks to accompany the artist's vocals, you will need a separate Producer of Tracks Agreement to secure your label's ownership of each musical track.

A producer who composes and records tracks to accompany an artist's vocals has ownership rights to the written song, which he or she will keep. The producer is entitled to a credit in the song (his or her name is given as a coauthor) and half the songwriting royalties. (*See Chapter 7 for information on songwriting royalties.*) Sometimes a producer makes a substantial change by rewriting or arranging a song originally written by the artist. In that case, the producer legally may be considered a coauthor of the song and co-owner of the publishing rights.

The producer's contract should clarify whether the record label has the right to use the producer's name in promoting the record.

The contract should also include a detailed plan for paying the producer. Failure to include a payment schedule in the producer's contract could become legal grounds for voiding the contract in the future, which would allow the producer to claim rights to the recordings and additional compensation from the record label. The contract should explain how the record label would provide accounting of royalties or other payment to the producer.

Recording Engineer

The recording engineer operates the sound equipment during the recording sessions. He or she listens to the audio and adjusts the equipment and recording levels, and sometimes he or she coaches the artist, so the recording sounds clean and perfect. The engineer is responsible for ensuring that all the studio equipment is set up, is working properly, and is ready to go when the recording session begins. He or she helps the artist set up instruments and equipment in the studio.

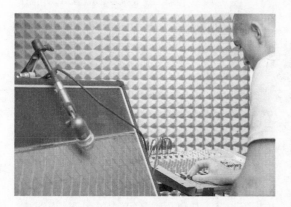

The engineer provides technical expertise. He or she should have expert knowledge of microphones, musical instruments, and amplifiers, as well as a thorough familiarity with all of the recording equipment in the studio and its effects on the sound of the recorded audio. Most studios provide an engineer who is experienced using their equipment. If you are using a producer/engineer or supplying your own engineer, make sure he or she has time to practice with the studio equipment before the recording session begins.

Many recording engineers are musicians themselves. A good recording engineer is familiar with the sounds and techniques used in a particular genre of music and knows how to reproduce them in the studio. He or she should prepare by studying your artist's songs in advance. An experienced recording engineer, like a good producer, will be able to help the artist achieve the desired outcome.

Technically, the engineer has rights to the recording because he or she participated in it. These rights are typically addressed in your contract with the studio that employs the engineer. If you are working with an independent engineer, you will need a written contract assigning the engineer's rights to the recording to the record label in exchange for compensation.

Mixing

During the recording session, the sounds of musical instruments and vocals are recorded, either one at a time or simultaneously, onto multiple individual tracks that can each be accessed, processed, and manipulated to produce the desired results. The sound from each microphone or input line is record-

ed on a separate track. The recording engineer is often able to make mechanical corrections to individual tracks, such as adjusting off-pitch notes. Any track, such as a guitar part, that contains errors or needs to be changed can be replaced

with a rerecording. After all the tracks have been recorded, they must be **mixed** — combined so that all of the tracks are heard at the right volume.

Mixing is just as important to the quality of a record as the recording of the music itself. It is a process of fine-tuning each component of the sound until the desired effect is achieved. Sometimes, when the recording session has run for longer than expected, you might be tempted to rush the mixing. This is a mistake. Mixing should be done with great care and reviewed numerous times. Often, several mixes are created before the recording is finalized.

Mixing requires special skills. A large professional studio has one or more mixing engineers. In a smaller studio, the mixing is often done by the recording engineer or by the producer, but in a larger studio, there is a specialized mixing engineer. The artist may want to sit in on the initial mixing, but it is more efficient to allow the engineer and producer to create a rough mix first and then call in the artist and other musicians to review it and make suggestions.

The mix may sound different on the studio's high-quality speakers than it does on other sound systems. Make copies of the mix and play it on computers, boom boxes, MP3 players, and car stereos to see how it sounds. After listening to music for hours on end, you may lose the ability to discern subtle imbalances. Take a break to rest your ears, and then listen again. Play the music for other people and note their reactions. When the producer approves the final mix, the tracks are all combined into a single recording, and the record is ready for mastering.

Mastering

Mastering is the process of enhancing the recording and transferring it to a data storage device (the master) from which all copies of the record will be produced. The recording studio may be able to master your record, but in many cases, you will have to send it to a separate mastering studio. A small mastering studio should be able to master your record for $500 to $1,500.

The mastering studio is different from the recording studio. The room contains a minimum of furniture and equipment, and speakers are arranged so the mastering engineer can listen without acoustic interference. During the mastering process, the songs are placed in order with uniform spacing in between; volume is adjusted; clicks and buzzes are eliminated with noise reduction; stereo widths are adjusted; audio is equalized for all the songs; and the sound quality is optimized for the medium that will be used to reproduce the record (CD, digital download, or vinyl). The mastering engineer cannot make changes to the individual tracks because they have already been combined into one recording. For CDs and digital files, the beginning and end of each song and an album index are defined. The record is then transferred to its final master format — a high-quality CD-R, files on a flash drive or external hard drive, or digital master tapes in Digital Audio Tape (R-DAT), Exabyte, or Umatic formats.

CASE STUDY: WHAT DOES IT TAKE TO MAKE A GOOD RECORDING?

Josh Jones is an experienced sound engineer who has helped several up-and-coming bands record their first CDs.

What advice would you give an amateur musician or band that wants to make an album and sell it?

Make sure everyone, especially the drummer, can play to a click track. Missing takes costs money!

Know what you want before going into the studio. It is best to talk about the sound and feel of an album you are going for before you start.

Most important, BE REALISTIC about your expectations. Albums are not worth their price in gold like they used to be. The industry is changing... use your album more as a marketing tool, and get the fans on your side and out to your shows.

What does it take to make a good recording?

There are many aspects to making a good recording:

• The size and acoustic treatment of the room you are recording in. Walk around and listen to the room. Where does the sound start to liven up, where are all the low ends? Ultimately you need to rely on your ears... they will not lie to you.

• Obviously the higher end the gear you can afford, the better. High-end converters, pre-amps, clocks, and mics always help. Ultimately, a lot of a good recording lies with the engineer.

• Are you micing the sweet spot of the instrument? (Placing the mic in the best location to capture the sound of the instrument.) If you are using more than one mic, are you phasing? Are you in tune and do you have the right tone?

• Always use a DI (Direct Input) in line with stringed instruments. (A cable that feeds the sound from an electric guitar directly into the recording device.) I cannot tell you how important this can be in the mixing process. If the take is good but the recording just does not cut it, you saved the mix just by doing this simple step.

• Create samples of your drums for mixing later.

• Take your time and get a usable take. Unless you are going for an effect, Autotune cannot fix slop. Get the take as close as possible and use Autotool as a tweaking tool to make it right.

• Editing is probably the most overlooked aspect of a good recording. Make sure everything is on time. If you double your guitars, make sure they are in time with each other. Cut out excess noise...

• Sound replacing your drums is common. Using the samples you created in tracking will give you your clean, realistic drum sound.

• Getting a good mix and mastering engineer is priceless. Knowing what frequencies to cut, how to niche your instruments to sit in the mix, and how to pan everything to get a good stereo image, is priceless. These steps are an art that takes many engineers years to master.

How much would you estimate it would cost (minimum) to record an album and have it mixed and mastered?

This really does vary. I suppose with the bare minimum, the artist could buy his or her own interface and mics, and record relatively cheaply. This is perfectly fine, but do not expect to get the same result as having high end converters, pres, and mics in line, not to mention the knowledge of an experienced engineer. This is a tough question to answer just because of the vast number of routes one could take. There are many small pro-sumer grade studios popping up just because of how cheap some gear has become. Also, with plug-ins, you can avoid buying high-end outboard gear, again cutting the costs.

What is the best way for a musician to locate an affordable recording studio?

Call around and ask your fellow musicians where they recorded. Many studios offer deals from time to time when they are slow. Just keep a look out. Remember going cheap is not always the best way either. Do your research... find out what kind of gear they have, who the engineer has worked with (ask for a sample), and weigh the costs.

What have you learned from your own experiences in the studio?

Being patient goes a long way. When you get nervous or agitated, so does the artist. If you make it a relaxed environment, the artist will get to the end much faster, and will be more prone to want to work with you again.

Always back up your files, and keep the raw takes until you are sure they are no longer needed.

Every engineer hears differently. Do not be afraid to try new things and create your own sound. Again, your ears will not lie to you.

Over the last few years, social networking sites like Facebook and YouTube have made it easier for new artists to get exposure to potential audiences. Do you think that increases artists' chances of making a profit from selling their records?

I would say it depends greatly on the artist. I think the opportunity is definitely there. The infrastructure is in place. With iTunes you can buy per track, anyone with an account can log in and download your music. So talking distribution, you can get your music out to a large audience. However, this does not change the fact that you still have to do your marketing. Be unique with your marketing, use tools like YouTube; see if you can get a video to go viral.

As I mentioned before, give your music away, and get the fans to your shows. The industry is changing, the days of sitting back and selling albums is long gone. Be proactive, be unique, and please have a live presence to back it up!

Manufacturing

Once your recording is finalized, you are ready to sell your record as a CD, vinyl record, or digital download. To sell digital downloads, all you have to

do is upload the files through the Internet to a digital distribution channel. CDs and vinyl records must be physically replicated, packaged, and shipped to retailers and individual customers. There are numerous manufacturing options from small, specialized local factories to global all-in-one companies that provide multiple services including printing of labels and posters, accounting, and the management of royalties and publishing rights.

Part of your preproduction work should be researching and selecting a manufacturer for hard product and a distributor for digital downloads. It takes time to manufacture CDs once the master has been delivered to the company; you need to make certain the CDs will be available when you need them to launch your new release. The manufacturer needs advance notice to schedule production of your CDs. It will request the audio files in a particular format, and your producer and recording engineer might adjust the mix if you are planning to produce a vinyl record. Knowing the cost of manufacturing CDs and vinyls and the pricing and commissions for digital downloads will help you price the finished product and calculate how much revenue you can expect from sales. It also takes time to have artwork designed and printed.

The best place to look for a manufacturer is on the Internet because you quickly can compare prices and services. Talk to other artists, DJs, and record store employees. Find CDs that you feel are good quality, and see what company made them. When you have located two or three companies that seem to fit your requirements, call them, and ask for a quote. Question them about the manufacturing process, how long it will take to deliver your order, and the formats for artwork and audio files. Some companies do all the work themselves, including labels, on the premises, while others act as brokers and outsource various functions.

Select a manufacturer and a process that suits your business model. Several companies, such as CDBaby (**http://members.cdbaby.com**) and CreateSpace (**www.createspace.com**), allow you to manufacture and sell CDs and vinyl records on demand; each time a customer orders a CD, it is created, packaged, and shipped. If you are a solo artist or a new band testing the waters with a limited budget, an all-in-one company might be the best solution. You will pay more for each CD, but many of the details including printing and shipping are taken care of for you. You can order a small number of CDs to begin with and get larger quantities later to place in retail outlets. Your CD will be made available immediately for sale online, and you will be given a Web page you can link to your website and a discount code for wholesale orders. Some of these companies will create a free sample of your CD so you can examine the quality.

If you need boxes of CDs to sell at live events or sign up with a distributor who wants hundreds of CDs or vinyls to place in retail outlets, find a CD manufacturer who will replicate and package them for you at a lower price. You can have CDs manufactured for less than $1 each. Bulk CDs without packaging cost even less.

Some manufacturers will give you a check CD to review and approve before running your full order. Others charge extra for sample CDs. It is important to get samples and listen to your CD several times before you proceed with the manufacturing. Ask the artist and producer to listen, too. You will lose money if you manufacture 1,000 CDs and then discover an error or flaw.

Duplication and replication

Duplication is the reproduction of CDs using CD burners similar to the one in your personal computer. Hundreds of CDs are duplicated simultaneously on multiple linked computers, each with several CD/DVD trays. Replication is done using a **glass master** — a circular block (typically 240 mm in diameter and 6 mm deep) of highly polished glass with a special chemical coating. The information on the master recording is engraved on the face of the glass master, which is then used to press the recording into the plastic CDs as they are manufactured. The artwork on duplicated CDs is usually not as good as the silk-screening on replicated CDs. Both processes produce high-quality records, but the quality of replicated discs is higher.

If your first run will be 1,000 copies or fewer, you will probably have them duplicated. Most manufacturers will not accept a replication order for fewer than 1,000 CDs. Because of the cost of making the glass master and preparing the material for manufacturing, duplication is more economical for smaller orders. Some companies require a minimum order of 500 CDs for duplication.

Artwork and labels

Whether you are selling digital downloads or CDs and vinyl records, your record needs a graphic image for its label. That image will appear on the CD case, the cover of the vinyl record, and the sales page for the digital download. The visual impression your album cover makes is just as important as the album's name. Fans will automatically associate that image with the songs on the album. Put careful thought into your graphics and get a graphic designer to create the final layout. If you do not have a talented friend, hire a professional or an art student. When someone is deciding whether to buy your CD or choosing between two CDs, the visual appeal of your label might be the deciding factor. You can use a well-chosen photo of the artist as the image on the label, but if the artist is not already famous, the photo could be a turn-off for some potential buyers. A good image can sell the CD, but if the photo somehow does not appeal to the fans because of the artist's dress, image, physical appearance, or poor photography, or if the image does not fit the genre, a potential fan might choose to buy another artist's CD. It is safer to use the name of the album and the name of the artist with some kind of artistic background. The colors, the font, and the images should fit with the genre and convey something about the music.

You can decide what text to put on the CD or record label: a list of the songs, biographical material, a statement from the artist, or nothing at all. Be sure to include the name of your record label, your logo, and contact information such as your website or address. The contact information on one of your CDs might be your connection to an overseas licensing deal or your next successful artist. Also, include the © symbol and the words "Copyrighted 20__."

Make your packaging fit your market.

Keep your marketing strategy in mind when designing your labels and packaging. Some independent labels try to attract attention with a package that is an unusual shape or odd size. If you are planning to sell through retail outlets, this kind of packaging can make it difficult for a store to fit the CDs in a regular display rack or put your CDs in standard plastic cases to prevent theft. (More than two-thirds of all music stores use some kind of security tag or case.) Labels without bar codes cannot be scanned at the register. If you plan to display your CD in a store, the album's title or band's name should be printed on the top half of the label so it will be easily visible to customers browsing through the racks. Fans of ethnic or classical music might be attracted to a package that includes a booklet or insert with historical information and photos. Unique packaging might be appropriate for albums sold mostly at live performances.

The artwork for your CD label or vinyl record cover should be created and submitted according to the requirements of the printing company. Most printing companies include downloadable templates and instructions on their websites. The artwork should be proportioned to fit the correct trim size (the exact dimensions of the label), with an extra $1/8$ inch of bleed allowance. **Bleed allowance** extends the colors beyond the borders of the label so that no white edges show when the labels are cropped in bulk by a machine. Most printers ask that your full-sized image have a resolution of 300 dpi (dots per inch) and will specify the file formats compatible with their printing equipment. Your artist should communicate with the printing company in advance to avoid errors that might cause delays or mistakes. Review the finished artwork carefully for spelling errors and omissions; ask two or three people to look at it in case you miss something.

The artwork printed directly onto a CD typically is screen printed and has a coarser resolution. A design that is too complicated or elaborate may not show up clearly when it is printed on the CD. Create a simpler design in one or two colors that carries out the same theme as your CD label.

Some CD manufacturers arrange to have your labels printed as part of the job. If you are using a separate company for printing, plan ahead so the labels are shipped to the CD manufacturer on time. You can find a printer in a local business directory or by searching on the Internet. Ask the printer how long it will take to have your labels delivered. You must give your graphic artist enough time to create a design, submit it, and make any corrections before the deadline for the printed labels.

UPC Bar Code

If you want sales of your record to be tracked or you plan to sell your product through a distributor, your CD label or vinyl record cover will

need a UPC bar code, the series of black lines and numbers scanned at the cash register when someone purchases an item. Bar codes allow retailers to keep track of merchandise and automatically enter prices into their cash registers. In the music industry, bar codes are particularly important because Nielsen SoundScan,

Sample UPC bar code

the official method of tracking sales of music and music video products, uses them. Nielsen SoundScan collects sales data from the cash registers of 14,000 retail, mass merchant, and nontraditional (online stores, venues, digital music services) outlets in the U.S., Canada, and the U.K. Every Wednesday, this information is reported to SoundScan subscribers, which include record company executives, publishing firms, music retailers, independent promoters, film and TV, and artist management agencies. SoundScan is the data source for the *Billboard* music charts; without a bar code, your record will never appear on the charts.

A bar code consists of a unique number assigned to a company, followed by whatever ID number the company assigns to each of its products. The cost of registering for a bar code ID is about $750 for an independent record label, plus an annual renewal of $150. You can register online at GS1 (**www.gs1us.org**). (GS1 is the international not-for-profit association that provides bar codes.) Allow a few weeks for the registration to be processed. Once you obtain your unique company ID, you can use a software program such as SmartCode (**www.technoriversoft.com/products.html**) to generate bar codes for your products and insert these in your artwork. If you are not ready to register for your own bar code, you can obtain one through a third party. Some CD manufacturers will assign you a free bar code for your CD using their own registration ID numbers; others charge a fee of $25 to $50.

Each of your records should be given a **catalog number,** a unique ID number assigned by the record label to each of its records. This is typically three letters followed by three numbers: for example, XYZ123. Distributors and retail stores use the catalog number on orders and invoices. It should be included somewhere on your printed CD label so employees who are pulling orders or stocking shelves can see it.

Bar codes can be added later

If you choose not to have a bar code on your CDs at first and later decide you need one, you can always register later on. The bar code can be printed on stickers to be affixed to your CD covers.

Quantities

The size of your first order of CDs is determined by several factors, including your marketing plan and your budget. A distributor that is going to place CDs in multiple retail outlets may require a specific number. If you are planning to sell CDs from a box at live performances, a few hundred will be enough. The manufacturing cost per CD may be lower if you order a larger quantity; in that case, buy as many as you can afford because your profit on each one will be higher. Ask your manufacturer how long it would take to fill a second order. If the manufacturer is able to supply more CDs within a few days, you can order a smaller quantity at first and later order more if you start to sell out.

Overruns

You will not always get the exact quantity of CDs or vinyl records that you order from a manufacturer. A certain number of the finished CDs will be substandard and will not pass quality control. Rather than purchasing small quantities of additional materials and setting up the manufacturing run a second time, manufacturers' contracts usually allow them to supply you with 5 percent more or less than the quantity you ordered. A manufacturer will always order slightly more material than is required for your job to allow for damage and error. You will pay for the quantity you receive, not the quantity you ordered. Always be aware of your manufacturer's policy regarding overruns and be prepared to budget a little extra for manufacturing costs.

Promotional CDs or vinyls

You will be giving away a certain number of free promotional CDs to DJs, radio stations, music critics, distributors, and fans. Calculate how many you need, and ask the manufacturer not to shrink-wrap them in plastic; you can save a little money that way. Promotional copies should be marked as "promos" in some way. Otherwise, there is always a possibility someone will return one to a distributor or music store for credit, and you will end up refunding them for a CD you gave away. Write "Promo" across the label, punch a hole in the bar code, or cut corners off the label to indicate they are not cleans — the name for product sold in stores.

Vinyl is back

Cassette tapes all but disappeared from store shelves in 2007, and sales of digital downloads are outpacing CDs, but vinyl records are making a comeback. Although vinyl records will never dominate the music industry again, the market for them is growing. According to a report released by Nielsen SoundScan in January 2011, sales of vinyl records in 2010 increased by 14 percent over the previous year to 2.8 billion units, even while overall album sales dropped by 13 percent during the same period. This is the highest number since Nielsen began tracking vinyl record sales in 1991. Rainbo Records (**www.rainborecords.com**), which has been pressing vinyl LPs since 1955, currently presses more than 25,000 albums a day, compared to about 6,000 to 8,000 a day in the late 1980s through the late 1990s.

Independent record stores sell the majority of vinyl albums (71 percent in 2010). Although owners of fine stereo systems insist the sound of a vinyl album is far superior to that of a CD or digital file, the market for vinyl records seems to be primarily high school- and college-age people who grew up with MP3 players and CD players. They appear to be attracted by the packaging, accompanying literature, and by the collectibility of vinyl albums. Popular vinyl albums are mostly re-issued classics and indies. The top-selling artists of 2010 were the Beatles, the Black Keys, Radiohead, Arcade Fire, Jimi Hendrix, the National, Pavement, Pink Floyd, Metallica, and Bob Dylan. The best-selling albums were the Beatles' *Abbey Road* and Arcade Fire's *The Suburbs*. A variety of new designs for turntables that play vinyl records were displayed at the 2011 International Consumer Electronics Show in Las Vegas.

Recordings have to be mastered differently for vinyl records because too much bass can cause the phonograph needle to jump out of the groove on the record. If you want to produce a vinyl record, you will probably have to pay for two mastering sessions.

CHAPTER 11

Distribution

istribution is the process of getting your album out into the marketplace where fans can buy it. Music sold as digital downloads or MP3 files is distributed through music sales websites on the Internet. CDs and vinyl records must be physically shipped from the manufacturer to record stores and retail outlets. There are many levels of distribution in the music world. Major labels have their own global distribution networks that place their products in stores all over the world, timed to coincide with their promotional and marketing activities. Regional, state, and local distributors act as middlemen, buying records from multiple record labels and placing them in retail stores in their geographic areas. Subdistributors called rack jobbers buy CDs, DVDs, and music merchandise from wholesale distributors and lease shelf space in drugstores, bookstores, department stores, and other retailers whose primary businesses are not selling music. **One-stops** are subdistributors that wholesale a wide selection of CDs, movies, games, and other entertainment media to smaller independent retail stores. These independent stores, known as mom-and-pop stores, often cater to more specialized markets and are better equipped to generate grassroots interest in a new artist.

Some turnkey CD manufacturers offer distribution as part of their packages, and you will also encounter distribution services that offer to take over all aspects of distribution for you, including placing your CD in retail outlets, packing, shipping, and invoicing and processing payments (for a fee). As a new record label, you will probably start by distributing your own CDs, of-

fering them for sale at live performances, and visiting retail stores in your area.

Simply getting your CD on a shelf in a retail store or listed on a website does not guarantee fans will buy it.

Distribution companies get a commission or a percentage markup for each record sold. Neither you nor your distributor will make money unless an effective marketing and promotion strategy creates a demand for your music. Distributors work closely with record labels and retailers to coordinate marketing efforts and make sure records are available where and when fans want to purchase them.

Most distribution is done on consignment. The distributor places the product in a retail store and is paid only when the product sells. Whether you leave some of your CDs at a local record store, or a distribution company puts them in a chain of retail outlets, you will not get any money until fans buy your records. Remember that you are competing for shelf space with thousands of other CDs. After a few weeks or months, if your records are not selling, the record store will return them to make room on its shelves for other artists. A distribution company typically delays payment on a consignment of records until the retailer has been sold them.

Your record label relies on income from record sales to pay for promotion and fund new projects. You cannot expect money to come pouring in right away from your distribution channels. Instead, it will trickle in gradually as retail outlets sell CDs and payments are processed. Even when your record becomes an immediate hit, it will be weeks and even months before you receive payment from your retail outlets or distributors. When you are creating your budget for marketing and promotion, you must plan to sustain an active marketing campaign for several months before you can expect record sales to pay your expenses. You might receive income during this time from other sources, such as ticket sales for live performances or sales of merchandise, but without aggressive marketing, your record will not sell through retail outlets; without retail sales your distributor will not pay you. Your distribution method must tie in closely with your marketing plan and your genre of music.

Self-distribution

When you first start out as a record label, you will probably do the distribution yourself. A large distributor will not be interested in a new record by an unknown artist or an unfamiliar record label with no track record. Distribution companies have to pay their own expenses, including salaries of sales representatives and shipping and warehousing costs, and they need to make a profit that makes their investment worthwhile. Distributors are looking for records they know will sell. Until you have demonstrated that your record label has steady sales and your artists have an established fan base, you cannot expect a distribution company to accept your records.

There are several reasons why a large distribution company is not the best choice for a newly established record label. National distribution in retail stores must be supported by a nationwide marketing campaign; it is unlikely that your new record label has the resources and staff to execute a campaign on this scale. Employing an agency to do this kind of marketing is expensive, and you may never recoup your costs. In addition, you must manufacture a large quantity of CDs or vinyl records to supply the distributor. Whether they are selling or not, these CDs and records, and the money you invested in manufacturing them, will be sitting on store shelves for months. A large distributor already is involved in promoting the new releases of lucrative artists and may not devote much attention to getting your record recognized.

When your first shipment of 1,000 CDs arrives on your doorstep, how are you going to sell them? Begin by selling CDs at your artists' live performances. Start with a launch party *(see Chapter 12 for more information about launch parties),* and take boxes of CDs to every venue where the artist performs. Set up a merchandise table by the door or near the stage. If you are not able to be on hand yourself for every performance, make the artist responsible for selling CDs. Perhaps the artist can find a friend or family member to supervise the merchandise table. Make sure the artist announces during the performance that CDs are available for sale. If possible, have the artist sit nearby during breaks to chat with fans and sign CDs or posters. Personal contact is powerful. Fans who are moved by the performance or want to support the artist will be inspired to purchase a CD on the spot. For those who do not make a purchase right away, have a supply of one-sheets (see below) to hand out with information about the CD and where it can be purchased, for example, a website address or local retail outlet.

Be sure to keep track of the CDs sold at live performances; it is very easy for some to "disappear" during the excitement. Count CDs before and after each performance. Keep a tally sheet and mark down each sale, or have a receipt book with carbon copies, and give a receipt for each purchase. If you are giving CDs to the artist to sell, consider selling them directly to the artist at a wholesale price. Then, the artist can keep the profit from the

CDs he or she sells, and you will not have to worry about trying to get your money or paying sales tax. Remember that you are supposed to charge and pay the applicable sales tax for the geographical area where you sell the CDs. If you are making cash sales, consider adjusting the retail price so the total comes out to an even dollar amount, such as $10 or $15.

Distribute locally by taking your CDs to any retail store that might sell them: local record stores, bookstores, coffee shops, and art galleries. Ask the manager if he or she would be willing to take some CDs on consignment. Try to develop a personal relationship with managers and staff at these stores. Play your CD for them, and see if they like it. Listen to their advice and suggestions. You might learn about a local distributor or network or about other local artists. Salespeople in record stores often direct their customers to purchase music they themselves find exciting. Look for opportunities to book a live performance in a store for your artist. If a store does not immediately accept your CDs, do not give up. You might be more successful on a return visit or with your label's future CDs. Once you have left a consignment, contact the store at regular intervals to see if any CDs have been sold and if the store needs additional supplies.

Make a spreadsheet listing all the retail outlets where you have left consignments of CDs or vinyl records, and keep a record of each store with contact information, dates of your visits, dates and amounts of payment, and notes about the staff and management. Consider purchasing CRM (Customer Relations Management) software to automate your sales and ordering process and help you keep track of your customers. CRM software can be integrated with your website and your accounting software to allow retail outlets and individual customers to place orders and process payments online.

Customer Relations Management (CRM) Software

CRM software uses a database of linked tables to organize client information, keep in contact with clients, and produce reports for them. You can send out automated e-mail and statements, maintain notes about each client, pull up reports with a click of your mouse, and keep a calendar of scheduled meetings and deliveries. These are the most popular CRM software programs:

ACT!	www.act.com
Junxure	www.junxure.com
Redtail CRM	www.redtailtechnology.com
Web IS Pocket Informant	www.pocketinformant.com

Whenever you leave a consignment of records in a store, take along a receipt, and get the record store manager's signature acknowledging receipt of a certain number of CDs. *You will find a sample receipt on the companion CD.* The receipt will prove invaluable when you are asking the store for payment later on.

Some on-demand manufacturers allow you to place orders online and have them shipped directly to the address you specify. You can give retailers a login and a discount code to purchase CDs directly at wholesale prices. A manufacturer who handles packing and shipping for you saves you a lot of work, so you will have more time and energy to devote to marketing.

Your one-sheet

A one-sheet is a vital sales tool. It is a single page containing all the important information about the CD and the artist. You can create a glossy, full-color one-sheet and have it reproduced by a printer or an office supply store, but a black-and-white photocopy is just as effective. The one-sheet should include the album name and the record label name, a short description of the music, biographical information about members of the band, and contact information for the record label. Most include an image of the album cover and/or the artist. In addition, the one-sheet can include press reviews, the artist's touring schedule, and other information to generate excitement about the album. One-sheets for distributors and retail stores should also include the UPC code, release date, order information, catalog number, and suggested retail price. Often, the store uses the one-sheet to enter information about the CD into its point-of-sales (POS) system.

Supply stores with enough one-sheets to hand out to interested customers. If you are using a distributor, it will also need a generous supply for its retailers. You can create a special one-sheet to hand out to fans at live performances, music festivals, and clubs, with information about how they can purchase the album online. *(The Companion CD includes templates for one-sheets.)*

When your self-distribution system is bringing in steady sales, it is time to expand your model to a broader market. You might contact retailers outside your region or in other areas where your genre of music is popular. If your online sales are doing well, you may be able to place your album with some of the more selective distributors, such as iTunes, that might not have been interested in your label before. By this time, you might have attracted the interest of a regional distribution company. Whatever distribution method you choose, always make sure it fits well with your marketing strategy and your available resources.

Online Distribution

Online distribution takes two forms: the sale of CDs and vinyl records through online stores and the sale of digital music downloads. Digital downloads accounted for more than a third of all music sales in 2010, and that market share is sure to increase as new sales models are developed and new technologies further integrate music downloads into more types of electronic devices. There is no denying, however, that there is a continuing demand for hard copies of records, as evidenced by the growing popularity of vinyl records. Music fans not only enjoy listening to music; they apparently like to have CDs they can hold in their hands, give as gifts, buy as souvenirs, and add to collections. Sales of CDs at live performances are an important source of revenue for a young record label and a relatively unknown artist who might not otherwise attract buyers.

No one can predict exactly what direction the music industry will take, but it is clear the Internet has changed not only the way in which music is shared, but also the way in which retail sales of CDs and vinyl records are conducted. Virgin Megastore closed its doors in 2009, following the ex-

ample of numerous other large record stores. Consumers no longer go to large stores to look for a particular CD; they do a quick online search and order it by mail from the cheapest source. Small record stores, which have knowledgeable staff that introduces customers to new artists and offer an enjoyable shopping experience to their clients, are still doing well.

Online sales present marketing opportunities that never existed before. Geographical location is no longer an important factor; fans anywhere in the world can listen to and buy your music. All you have to do is get their attention. You can attract listeners through online communities and social networks, and friends can introduce each other to new artists from the comfort of their sofas without ever meeting face-to-face or popping a

CD into a CD player. A record label's or artist's website serves as a central source of information and as a store for selling merchandise, 24 hours a day, without the need to answer telephones or maintain an office staff.

To sell music downloads, you do not have to invest any money in manufacturing, storing, packing, or shipping a physical product. There are no consignments, no unsold returns, no stolen or damaged CDs. The buyer downloads a file onto a computer, MP3 player, or other listening device, and the distributor takes its cut when a sale is made. Just like sales in record stores, however, aggressive marketing must support online distribution. Buyers tend to purchase one song at a time rather than an entire album. You are competing with millions of other songs and hundreds of thousands of artists; you must find a way to reach your target audience and to stand out from the crowd. You have to build an active fan base through promotional tours and live performances, as well as through online videos, marketing, and social networking. After your artist visits a university campus or a club or gets some exposure on local radio, the audience will go online to look at your website and perhaps make a purchase. Fans want to interact with artists and take "ownership" of new music, which they then introduce to their friends.

Online music retail sites offer additional features not available to buyers of CDs. Many offer short or low-quality music samples that customers can listen to before buying; free streaming of extra content such as interviews and live performances; free promotional downloads; and ringtone sales. Some artists offer free downloads of alternative versions of their songs. Customers can also link directly to the artists' websites and purchase a full line of merchandise.

Digital music downloads are sold in physical locations, such as the kiosks in record stores where you can compile a customized playlist and burn it to a CD or upload it on to an MP3 player. Digital music also is sold in coin-operated jukeboxes and as part of video arcade games.

Digital music sales

Digital music files are sold through online retail music services using a variety of business models. Prices differ to reflect the extent to which the listener is buying rights to listen to the music. Individual songs and albums are sold outright as permanent digital downloads (Digital Phonorecord Deliveries, or DPDs) for a one-time fee. The buyer then owns the music much as he or she would own a CD purchased in a record store. The sale of full-quality tracks of individual songs is sometimes called á la carte because the buyer picks and chooses only the songs he or she likes, rather than purchasing a whole album. Listening devices and audio software allow listeners to create playlists of their favorite songs or songs tied together by a particular theme or mood.

Some music downloads are tethered or captive, locked in to a single listening device such as a computer or MP3 player. Recent developments in DRM (digital rights management) allow the buyer to make limited copies of the purchased songs on additional devices ("to go" services), for example, on a laptop and an MP3 player. Files that can be listened to when devices are not linked to the Internet are called **untethered files**.

Subscription services such as eMusic (**www.emusic.com**) charge a monthly fee for a specific number of permanent downloads per month. Every month the subscriber can add new songs to his or her playlist. The price of individual songs is lower if the buyer downloads the full number every month, but many buyers do not. Some subscription downloads are conditional; they expire when the subscriber stops making monthly payments.

Tales from the Industry

Upbeat Records: Response to a "Greatest Hits" Compilation

In an era when music fans can create their own playlists and easily download the songs they want to listen to, albums compiled of a band's most popular songs still sell well. At least half of the 50 top-selling catalog albums in recent Nielsen SoundScan sales charts are compilations of "greatest hits" from other albums. Catalog sales of old material make up approximately 40 to 50 percent

of a label's annual gross sales. The Eagles' *Their Greatest Hits (1971-1975)* is the best-selling album in U.S. history. Bob Marley's *Legend* was at the top of the Nielsen SoundScan catalog chart for 106 weeks straight. To appeal to fans, labels often include rare unreleased material or create unique packaging for these albums. Greatest-hits albums also help to introduce new audiences to unfamiliar artists.

Because greatest hits albums are so lucrative, labels are pushing artists to make these compilations relatively early in their careers. Britney Spears, Hilary Duff, and Sugar Ray have already released "greatest hits" albums. Some artists, however, strongly object to the concept. AC/DC, Radiohead, Phish, Pink Floyd, and Metallica are among the groups who refuse to break up their prior albums into individual "hits." They consider each of their albums as an integrated work of art to be listened to as a whole.

Whether a label must have the consent of an artist to issue a compilation depends on the contract between them. A legal battle ensued when Cake ("The Distance," "Short Skirt, Long Jacket") refused to make a greatest-hits album for Columbia Records. The band thought it was too early for a "Best of Cake" compilation because they had released only a few albums. Cake lead singer and guitarist John McCrea said the idea was a commercial ploy that "reeks of desperation." Cake left Columbia to form its own label, Upbeat Records, and in 2007, instead of a greatest-hits album, it released "B-Sides and Rarities," a collection of covers including Black Sabbath's "War Pigs," Kenny Rogers' "Ruby, Don't Take Your Love To Town," and Barry White's "Never, Never Gonna Give You Up."

Over its 20-year history, Cake has emphasized its independence from the trends and pressures of the commercial music industry. The band thrives by pursuing its ideals, which include a democratic process in composing and recording music and an appreciation for diverse styles and sounds. The band has recently built its own environmentally friendly studio and declares that being free from the demands of a large label gives it the time to refine its music and produce good-quality recordings.

Digital Rights Management (DRM)

Digital Rights Management (DRM) technology allows control of the use and distribution of music files and protects the revenue stream of artists and record labels. The digital file provider sets policies regulating the use of the music file, such as its price, how a consumer will be allowed to access it, how many times it can be played, whether it can be saved or copied, and the time frame in which it can be played. The music file is meta tagged with these rules, then sealed and encrypted. A third-party clearinghouse sells and manages individual licenses for each consumer who buys the music file. When a consumer pays for the download, or is identified as a subscriber, he or she is given a **license** — a key to unlock the encryption and use the file. The license can be delivered to a computer or listening device without the consumer being aware of it. It may be delivered when the consumer makes a payment, when the consumer first tries to listen to the music file, or each time the music is accessed. The consumer is then able to listen to the music file according to the rules in the file's meta tag. In addition to ensuring that consumers pay for the music they listen to, DRM technology tracks information such as how many times a particular song is listened to.

Streaming music services, such as RealNetworks' Rhapsody (**www.rhapsody.com**), MediaNet (**www.mndigital.com**), and Pandora (**www.pandora.com**) play music on demand directly from the Internet. Music files are stored in "the cloud," on the Internet rather than in individual listening devices, and accessed by the listening devices through an Internet connection. Subscribers pay a monthly fee to listen to songs that they select and place on a playlist online. Some streaming services let fans listen to music free and pay record labels a portion of the money they make by selling advertising and commercials on their sites. YouTube (**www.youtube.com**), Playlist.com (**www.playlist.com**) and MySpace (**www.myspace.com**), as well as by dedicated music streaming services that offer free music, follow this model. Noninteractive services, such as Pandora, Last.fm (**www.last.fm/music**), betterPropaganda (**www.betterpropaganda.com**), and Epitonic (**www.epitonic.com**), where the listener does not select the songs on the playlist, are treated as online radio stations. Some sites, such as Pandora, incorporate a discovery feature that searches for songs and genres similar to the songs the listener selects and presents them randomly. Listeners have the option to purchase each song through a link that takes them to the iTunes or Amazon websites. Pandora also offers a paid subscription for listeners who do not want to be interrupted by commercials.

The royalties and licensing fees paid to the artist and record label for online music sales are determined by the type and method of delivery. Streaming companies must sign license agreements with the music performance rights societies, BMI (**www.bmi.com**), ASCAP (**www.ascap.com**), and

SESAC (**www.sesac.com**), for the performance of the music embodied on the sound recordings. The payment of royalties for digital music sales is determined by the U.S. Copyright Office and by Congressional law, and the payment to record labels for sales of their music is negotiated with online distributors. Revisions are constantly being made; you can find the latest information on the SoundExchange website (**www.soundexchange. com**), the Digital Media Association website (**www.digmedia.org**), and the Copyright Royalty Board (**www.loc.gov/crb**).

Payment for the delivery of ringtones to cell phones, digital downloads, and over-the-air soundtracks (OTAs) and audio streaming to mobile devices, such as the Android and iPhone, is even more complicated because a third party, the phone or wireless service carrier, is involved.

Aggregators

There are more than 400 online retail music services; the largest are iTunes, Amazon, eMusic, Napster, and Rhapsody. Many of the smaller services cater to niche markets or specific geographical areas. These services do not have the administrative resources to negotiate complicated licensing deals with thousands of independent record labels and artists, many of whom have only one or two albums in their catalogs, or to do the work involved in uploading, updating, and formatting music files for a variety of delivery methods. Instead, retail services purchase independent music from aggregators, middlemen who compile digital warehouses and license the content for retail sale.

An aggregator can get your label's music into many retail outlets at once, including the major music services, smaller retail outlets, kiosks, streaming services, wireless and phone providers, and manufacturers who preload music into their video games, cell phones, and MP3 players. The major aggregators include IODA (**www.iodalliance.com**), The Orchard (**www.the orchard.com**), CD Baby (**www.cdbaby.com**), TuneCore® (**www. tunecore.com**), BFM Digital (**www.bfmdigital.com**), and Iris (**www.

irisdistribution.com). You typically sign an exclusive deal with an aggregator for a term of one to three years. For about 15 percent of the total sales revenue, an aggregator will encode and format your music files, deliver them to music service providers, collect receipts, and pay you at regular intervals. Many aggregators provide multiple services, including the manufacturing, distribution and online sale of CDs, graphic design, personalized Web pages for labels and artists, marketing, and printing of posters and promotional materials. Because payment for online purchases is made immediately and all the data concerning sales is automatically logged and analyzed by computer software, aggregators are much more efficient at paying you and providing sales reports than physical distribution companies (see below). You will, on the average, be paid within two months of the time when a download was sold.

Mobile aggregators such as Skyrockit (**www.skyrockit.com**), Mobile Streams® (**www.mobilestreams.com**), and Jamster™ (**www.jamster.com**) license the rights for mastertones (digital sound recordings of the original master recording), OTAs, and video to sell as downloads to cell phones and other mobile devices.

Major Digital Music Aggregators

COMPANY	URL	PRICING	DELIVERY	PAYMENT	NOTES
CD Baby	**http://members. cdbaby.com**	Setup for digital and physical sales costs $35 per album.	Digital files and physical CDs	Payment is made weekly. Labels get a larger percentage than through most distribution deals.	CD Baby is a well-known online record store that attracts fans looking for new albums. The staff listens to every album they sell and advises customers. You must promote your music to attract attention.

COMPANY	URL	PRICING	DELIVERY	PAYMENT	NOTES
The Orchard	www.theorchard.com		Digital files and physical CDs		
AUK Ltd.	www.andrewsuk.com/music/about.html		Digital files and physical CDs	50% of net profits	
Iris	www.iris distribution.com		Digital only	Monthly	Special marketing programs with digital music retailers
Tunecore	www.tunecore.com	Based on size of upload, choice of stores	Digital only		Free UPC; graphic design available
IODA	www.iodalliance.com		Digital only		Label storefronts
Catapult™	www.catapult distribution.com	$25 for album, $9 for single	Digital only	91%–95% of profits	UPC, barcode, graphic design, SoundScan registration are additional services.
SongCast™	www.songcast music.com	$5.99 per month. One time set-up fee of $19.99 per album or $9.99 per single	Digital only	Monthly	Tools for linking social networking into the retailers make it easy for consumers to find and purchase your music online.
INgrooves	www.ingrooves.com		Digital only		Digital distribution to more than 400 online and mobile destinations worldwide

Each aggregator has a different payment program based on the way the music is delivered and the services offered. Whatever arrangements you make with a digital music aggregator, be sure you do not sign away the rights to your music.

Finding a Distributor

Once your label is growing steadily through self-distribution, you will need a distributor to expand your business to the next level. A distributor buys CDs (and vinyl records) from your record label and wholesales them to retail stores. Distributors work with a broad network of retail outlets and are specialists in selling records. They know all the finer points of retail sales, which seasons have the strongest sales, how to attract customers' attention in stores, and how to engage store employees in promoting and selling records. Distributors make money by buying CDs from you at about 50 percent of the retail list price and charging the record stores a markup of $2 to $6 on each CD.

Aligning yourself with a reputable distributor is the fastest way to get your CD on store shelves, but as mentioned in the beginning of this chapter, it is important to choose a distributor that fits with your marketing plan and the scale of your promotional activities. The distributor, record label, and artist work together to promote and sell a record. By taking care of the physical aspects of selling records, the distributor frees you to spend more time on marketing and drawing public attention to your artist. The artist attracts customers through performances, social media campaigns, and exposure in the media. When you arrange an interview on the radio for your artist, the distributor makes sure that listeners will be able to find the CD in stores.

Distribution companies operate on local, regional, and national levels. Some offer better services than others. A distribution company might stock your CD in its warehouse, list it in its catalog, and supply any orders that happen to come in from retail stores, or it may actively promote your record to retail outlets and collaborate in advertising and marketing activities. Some distributors are highly organized, efficient, and pay invoices in a timely manner. Others may disappoint you. Start looking for a distributor by talking to the staff at stores where you sell your CDs on commission and to other local artists. Once you have located a prospective distributor, ask exactly what services they provide, and talk to some of their clients and retail outlets. You can also do a background check on the Internet by typing the distributor's name in a search engine to see if they are named in any lawsuits or if anyone is blogging complaints about them. You can check for complaints with the Better Business Bureau in the area where the distributor is based or with the state Department of Consumer Affairs.

A distributor is not going to be interested in your label unless you can demonstrate that your records are already selling and that you have a solid marketing plan that will continue to build a fan base for your artists. When you meet with a representative from a distributor, take a detailed marketing plan and recent financial statements, along with copies of your records and promotional packages for each of your artists. Show the distributors which outlets and retail stores are bringing you the most sales. You must convince the distributor it will be able to make a reasonable profit by distributing your record.

Distributors have long-term relationships with their retailers and know how to interest them in stocking your records. Cultivate personal relationships with the staff at your distributor so they remember who you are and are familiar with your music. A sales representative from the distributor might take along copies of your CD to a retail outlet and play it for the buyer while explaining why the record is likely to sell. The distributor gives its retail outlets information about your label and your artists. It will supply record stores with your one-sheet and list your records in its sales catalog. It may feature your record in its bulletins and e-mails to retailers.

These are some of the things distributors do:

- Make sure your record is in stores in time for a planned release, promotional campaign, or a concert in the area.

- Resupply record stores when they start to run out of your records.

- Suggest promotional opportunities, such as payment for placement on an endcap (the display shelf at the end of an aisle) at a listening station in record stores or an in-store appearance by your artist.

- Supply record stores with point-of-purchase items (POPs) such as one-sheets, cardboard stands to be placed near the register, posters, and fliers advertising live performances by your artist.

- Include your label in its catalog and its newsletters to retail outlets.

- Organize co-op advertising in magazines and newspapers with other record labels or with retail outlets.

- Collect money from retailers for you.

Major record labels have their own national and international distribution networks and entire departments devoted to coordinating distribution with promotional campaigns. Major independent distributors include Caroline Distribution/EMI Label Services (**www.carolinedist.com**) and Select-O-Hits (**www.selectohits.com**). These companies have been distributing independent labels for decades, and sometimes they have distribution arrangements with the distribution arms of major labels or with overseas distributors. Most independent distributors work on a regional level. All distribution companies are affiliated in some way with online retail outlets. Some of the digital music distribution companies also offer distribution of CDs to retail stores. When you are comparing distributors, find out what this means. Many distributors ask you to sign an exclusive contract to sell your CDs only through them.

Tales from the Industry

STAX: Survived a Bad Distribution Deal and made Rock and Roll History

Stax Records, founded by Jim Stewart and Estelle Axton, his sister, as Satellite Records in 1957, played a major role in creating the Southern soul and Memphis soul music styles and released recordings of gospel, funk, jazz, and blues. The label changed its name to Stax Records (**ST**ewart – **AX**ton) in 1961 to avoid confusion with another "Satellite Records" company in California.

The company's location in an old movie theater, the Capitol Theatre, at 926 East McLemore Avenue in South Memphis, gave it some unique advantages. The recording studio was situated in the old theater, where the sloping floor created an acoustic anomaly that gave many recordings a deep yet raw sound. To protect this signature sound, Stax later refused to allow non-label artists to record in its studio. The staff of the Satellite record store, located in the old refreshment stand area of the theater, was able to observe what type of music was selling and to test audience reaction to new releases by playing them while shoppers were in the store. Stax had a multitalented house band, including pianist Booker T. Jones, bassist Lewie Steinberg, and drummer Curtis Green, that backed up almost every recording from 1962 through 1970. Steve Cropper, Stewart's assistant and official A&R director, was himself a gifted songwriter, producer, and session guitarist. Isaac Hayes and David Porter wrote and produced many hits for Stax. Along with Motown and

Atlantic Records, Stax became a national powerhouse, launching the careers of many R&B stars.

Stax had contracted with Atlantic Records to distribute some of its records. In 1967, Warner Bros.-Seven Arts bought Atlantic Records. When the distribution deal was being renegotiated, Stewart found he had unwittingly signed away rights to the original master recordings for all of Stax's Atlantic-distributed recordings. Warner executives refused to give up their new ownership. A week later, Stewart sold Stax to Paramount Pictures (a unit of Gulf+Western) but stayed on with the company. Deprived of the most lucrative portion of its back catalog and devastated by the death of its star Otis Redding in 1967, Stax rallied, regrouped, and went on to release successful recordings by a number of artists including Isaac Hayes, Johnnie Taylor, and Elvis Presley, who gave Stax Records an eternal place in rock and roll history.

In 1972, vice president Al Bell purchased Stewart's interest in the company and negotiated a distribution deal with CBS Records, whose president Clive Davis was looking for a way to tap into the African-American market. However, CBS lost interest when Davis was no longer president. Sales plummeted because the distribution agents gave priority to other CBS releases in large retailers and bypassed the mom-and-pop stores that had traditionally sold Stax music. Stores in cities where Stax music was in demand complained they had no records to sell, but CBS refused to release Stax from the distribution contract. At the end of 1975, Stax was forced into Chapter 11 bankruptcy. Jim Stewart, who had mortgaged his home to try to keep Stax afloat, lost everything. Stax owed Isaac Hayes more than $5 million in royalties, which it could not pay. Hayes also had to declare bankruptcy and consequently lost the rights to all of his future royalties from the music he had recorded with Stax.

The label did not die, however. In 1977, Fantasy records purchased the Stax-owned master recordings and the name "Stax Records." Fantasy re-launched the label under David Porter, and it enjoyed a number of hits with new artists and compilations of previously unreleased material by its top artists. From 1982 to 2003, the company focused on re-issues. Concord Records purchased Stax in 2004 and began releasing newly recorded music under the label once again. In 2003, the Stax Museum of American Soul Music was opened on the site of the original Stax studio.

Always question a distributor about its distribution channels, which retail outlets it services, and how it interacts with them. You do not want to sign an exclusive deal with a digital distribution company and then find out you are shut out of the very stores where your fans shop. Gain a thorough understanding of how the distribution process works so you can coordinate your marketing campaigns effectively. You need to know how much time it takes a distributor to get your CD into stores, how quickly it can resupply its retail outlets, whether it is proactive in introducing and promoting new records to record stores, and what promotional opportunities it offers.

You will be expected to supply a distributor with:

- Distributor one-sheets that include promotion and marketing plans, price information, tour schedules, release dates, and other pertinent information

- A certain number of free CDs to be used as incentives for retailers and promotional copies to be used by sales staff and handed out to the media

- One-sheets and promo packages for retail outlets and press kits for the media

- A minimum number of CDs to sell

- Some distributors require you to pay for an ad in their catalog or monthly newsletters. This payment may be deducted from one of your invoices or may be required outright.

Getting paid

Distributors do not pay you immediately when they buy your records. They take your records on consignment or use a **purchase order (PO)**, a document requesting goods to be supplied and promising payment. *There* *is a sample purchase order on the companion CD.* It then places your record in retail stores, also on a consignment basis. At regular intervals, the distributor collects payment from the record stores for any records that have been sold. Eventually, the distributor passes on your share of that payment. Several months may pass from the time you deliver a shipment of CDs to a distributor until you receive payment for it. You might have to pressure the distributor for payment by sending invoices or statements after a certain amount of time has passed.

Distributors typically accept your CDs with the understanding that the payment on the invoice will not be due for 60 to 120 days. Most contracts make this arrangement negotiable, which means it can be changed if both parties agree. When the 60 or 120 days have passed, the distributor will not necessarily pay the full amount of the invoice. It will pay only for the number of CDs placed in retail stores, not for the CDs still sitting in its warehouse.

As standard practice, record stores eventually return all damaged or unsold records to the distributor, who returns them to the label. If the distributor has already paid the label for those unsold CDs, it could have a difficult time getting its money back. The record company might have gone out of business in the meantime or be having financial difficulties. To protect itself from losses, a distributor holds back (reserves) 15 to 20 percent of the amount owed on an invoice until all the records in retail stores have either been paid for or returned. In some cases, a distributor payment holds back payment on the most recent invoice until all the records are sold or until it receives a consignment of new records to sell from the record label. This practice is called **open invoice**.

TIP: Consign as few records as possible to your distributor.

Most distributors require you to place a minimum number of CDs or vinyls with them. Do not push them to take a larger order because you will not be paid for those CDs until they are sold. If the distributor takes more CDs than it is able to place in record stores, the rest (and the money you invested in making them) will sit gathering dust for months in a warehouse. If the distributor is about to sell out of your CDs, you can always supply more. One-stops often are willing to accept smaller quantities because the retail stores they service select only a few of each item.

Documents

The documents you use when consigning your CDs or records to a distributor and requesting payment contain important details. The record label usually is responsible for the cost of shipping product to the distributor and any insurance. Here are the documents used for shipping and invoicing:

- **Packing slip** — After a distributor places an order using a purchase order, you must prepare a packing slip to include with the shipment. The packing slip includes the PO number, record label's contact information, details of the order, what is in the shipment, and the number of boxes being shipped. All CDs intended for retail sale should be shrink wrapped (sealed in plastic film) to protect them from tampering and damage.

- **Invoice** — After the shipment has been sent, the distributor should be sent a separate invoice through the mail. The invoice includes a unique invoice number, date, the record company's contact information, distributor's PO number, a detailed list of what was included in the order, the unit price of each item sent, the total amount due, and instructions for payment.

- **Statement** — When the payment is due, or on a monthly basis, the distributor should be sent a statement requesting payment by a certain date. The statement should include the names and addresses of the distributor and record label and a list of all outstanding invoices with the invoice numbers, PO numbers, and amounts owed on each, along with the previous account balances and any payments made since the last statement.

Most accounting software includes templates for all of these documents and generates them automatically from the data stored in the accounting system. *You will also find templates on the companion CD.*

Pressing and Distribution (P&D)

Some distributors arrange to pay for manufacturing your CDs and then wholesale them to record stores. The cost of manufacturing is deducted from the wholesale price of the CDs as they are sold until manufacturing is paid for. This is referred to as a **Pressing and Distribution (P&D) Deal**. Some P&D deals include an advance to the record label to pay for promoting the record. Although this seems like a good way to get a record on the market when finances are tight, it is risky. If your record does not sell, you will be forced to pay the manufacturing cost of all the unsold records out of your own pocket, and you may be charged a distribution fee for each unsold record. Even when the record is selling, you might not receive any money until the distributor has recouped its manufacturing costs and advances. In the meantime, you still are obligated to pay the artist royalties for every record sold. This could leave you short of cash to pay for marketing.

Many distributors give precedence to other clients from whom they can make more money and devote little or no effort to promoting a P&D record. The marketing is completely up to you, and if you fail to generate interest in your record, you will suffer financial losses.

CHAPTER 12

Promotion and Marketing

A record label has two primary functions: to create top-quality recordings and to make money for itself and its artists by selling those recordings. You have discovered a talented artist, hired a good recording studio and an experienced producer, recording engineer, and mixer to create a top-quality recording. Your new record is unique and captivating. Now it is time to get out and sell your product. Marketing and promotion are the things you do to attract the attention of music fans and inspire them to buy your music.

From the moment you first considered starting a record label, you have probably been thinking about who will buy your music and how you will reach them. A **marketing plan** is a detailed, written document setting out these goals and the practical steps you will take to achieve them. Like a business plan, a marketing plan helps you identify your label's strengths and weaknesses, make a budget, and schedule the activities necessary to realize your goals. It also serves as a yardstick to measure your progress and a guide to keep you on track when you encounter obstacles or distractions.

Marketing entertainment is different from marketing goods or services. You will succeed when you connect with the emotions, hopes, dreams, and desires of your target audience. Success in the music industry is volatile — media gives you access to millions of potential listeners whose acceptance can boost you to success in just a few days or weeks, but who are always moving on to something new. You must be able to adapt quickly to fresh developments while finding ways to retain the interest of loyal fans. Be prepared to exercise creativity and innovation and, at the same time, carry on traditional marketing methods that bring proven results.

As a one-man record label, or a small company with a handful of staff, you will have to select the promotional activities that use your time and resources most effectively, find ways to outsource work, and recruit volunteers among your family members and fans that want to support you. Major labels have the financial resources to conduct massive advertising campaigns in multiple locations. You will have to tailor your marketing to reach as much of your audience as you can with a small marketing budget.

Music sales absolutely depend on publicity. When the publicity stops, the sales stop. For independent labels, sales traditionally have been driven by the artists' live performances in clubs, coffee shops, and theaters; at concerts, parties, and festivals; on tours; and whenever possible, on television, the stage, and in movies. The Internet presents some new opportunities, including the ability to stream videos of artists' performances 24 hours a day to anywhere in the world and vast social networks through which music fans recommend artists to each other.

Learning About Your Target Market

To create an effective marketing plan, you must study your fans — the people who make up your target market. You probably already know something about the people who enjoy the music you want to sell. Begin by looking around at the audiences who come to your artist's performances, and write down everything you observe: their ages, styles of dress, apparent level of income and education, and the types of venues where they come to hear the music.

Make up a simple marketing survey with questions about gender, age group, town or city of residence, profession, education level, favorite genres of music, preferred foods and beverages, favorite music and social networking websites, and preferred devices on which to listen to music (MP3 player, computer, iPhone, stereo system, boombox, car stereo). Make the survey easy to complete by using checkboxes, but leave a few blanks to fill in. Ask how the person heard about this show, and where and how often he or she goes to hear live music. Finally, ask the person to sign up for your e-mail list or newsletter. Leave space at the end for comments. *You will find a sample survey on the companion CD.* Set up a table near the entrance of clubs or venues where your artist is performing, and invite people to fill out the survey as they go in or out. Thank them and reward them with a giveaway, a coupon for a free drink, or a free ticket to an upcoming show. Be sure to hand participants a schedule of your upcoming performances, a one-sheet, or a flier promoting your new album as they leave.

Study the surveys and create a profile of your fans. This profile will help you decide where to place ads and campaigns and what kind of advertising will appeal most to your fans. You may discover some surprises — for example, that your fans are older or younger than you thought or that a rough-looking audience in a club is actually composed of computer programmers and other professionals. A local crowd might not be local after all; people may be driving an hour or two from surrounding towns and cities to come and hear the music.

Do not overlook potential fans who are not showing up in your live audiences. High school students and underage young people cannot get into bars and clubs, but they are a large fan base for many types of music. Release a single or put some free music on your website, and use website analytics to see the geographic areas where your music is being downloaded or listened to. *See Chapter 6 for more information.* Some types of American music, such as hip-hop and rap, are popular overseas. In 2009, a 9.5 percent decline in WMG's U.S. sales was offset by a 12.7 percent increase in international sales, driven largely by digital downloads. If you discover that you have a substantial number of fans in Brazil or the Czech Republic, your marketing plan should include online advertising or an Internet promotion in that region and perhaps a tour.

Creating Your Marketing Plan

Start your marketing plan by holding informal brainstorming sessions with your artist, staff, and interested friends and family. Talk over your plans with the professionals who work with you: your producer, recording engineer, studio owner, DJs, promoters, and other artists. Write down every idea, no matter how crazy it sounds. Review and add to the list from time to time

Simply looking at the profile of your fans should suggest obvious strategies for marketing your music. If they frequent certain clubs and venues, work on establishing a personal relationship with the owners and DJs, give them promotional CDs to play, and try to arrange live performances there. Look for similar clubs and venues in nearby towns and cities. If your fans listen to a local college radio station, try to get radio play, arrange a live interview with your artist, and look for similar radio stations on other campuses. If a friend on Facebook introduced them to your band, step up your Internet presence by posting more videos of live performances.

Study other artists with a similar style of music. Look at their touring schedules to see the types of venues where they are performing. Check out their websites and social networking sites. Watch their music videos and listen to their free downloads. See what kind of merchandise they sell. Type their names in top commercial search engines, such as Google, Bing™, Yahoo!, Ask, and AOL Search, to see what kind of Internet ads they are running and where news articles and reviews about them are appearing. Set up Google Alerts (go to **www.Google.com** and select "more" and "even more" in the drop-down menu at the top of the screen) to send you e-mails whenever they show up in the news. The strategies that work for those artists will work for you, too. Once you begin marketing, you can set up Google Alerts to send you all the articles that mention your artist.

Some conventional marketing strategies, such as buying print ads in newspapers and magazines, may be too expensive for your label, or beyond the scope of your distribution network. Concentrate your marketing strategy in areas where you can have personal contact with the people promoting your music, such as the local club scene, local journalists, radio hosts, or music festivals specializing in your genre. Your personal influence and the influence of your artists carries more weight than a classified ad listing or a glossy photo in a national magazine. When you are ready to move on to regional or national distribution, you can invest more in print ads and other conventional marketing channels.

Fill in the details

From your list of marketing ideas, select those that fit best with your label's current distribution network and promotional budget. Identify the activities you believe will bring the greatest results, and prioritize them by importance. When your money, time, and available staff are limited, you might have to sacrifice some activities in order to do other activities well.

Assign a start date for each activity. For example, you can start pursuing performance bookings and promoting your artist through social networking right away; send out press kits three months before the planned release of a new CD; and put up posters three weeks before a concert.

Make a detailed list of the materials you will need and the steps you will follow for each marketing activity, along with the estimated cost and lead time (the time it will take to get prepared). Use this list to prepare a checklist. This checklist will not only help you organize your work for your current campaign, but also it can be used for future campaigns and handed off to staff members as your label grows so they can repeat the activity successfully.

Add up your cost estimates, compare them to your budget, and make adjustments to reduce costs if needed. When you get quotes and invoices from vendors, update your estimates and review your budget to see if you are on track.

Schedule each detail of your marketing campaign on a calendar. For example, if you plan to send out press kits on a certain date, you will need to schedule a photography session, have someone write press releases, buy folders, compile a list of publications and addresses, and stuff the envelopes (or put together an e-mail press release) before that date. Posters must be designed, printed, and shipped before the distribution date. All the artist's performances should be on the calendar along with the activities done to promote them. The success of your marketing campaigns depends on having all the elements in place at the right time.

You may need a copy of your marketing plan when you approach a distributor, a venue, a potential investor, or a store owner. A concise and detailed marketing plan shows that you know what you are doing and that you are working hard to attract buyers for your music. For some purposes, you will need to create a simplified marketing plan. For a distributor one-sheet, for example, a schedule of tour dates and a brief description of your other promotions is enough.

Marketing plan software

Get help writing a detailed marketing plan with software that walks you through the process. You can download a free template for creating a marketing plan in Microsoft Office from the Microsoft Startup Center website (**www.microsoft. com/smallbusiness/startup-toolkit/marketing-plan-for-startups. aspx**). Palo Alto Software (**www.paloalto.com**) offers free sample marketing plans on its Mplans website (**www.mplans.com**), along with its marketing plan software. Other companies selling marketing plan software include Business Resources Software (**www.brs-inc.com/marketing_plan.asp**) and Planware (**www.planware.org/salepwm.htm**).

Alternative Marketing

Independent labels and artists are associated with innovative grassroots (individual-level) marketing techniques that are so effective they have now been adopted by major labels and entertainment companies and even by manufacturers of brand-name products. Word-of-mouth advertising by **street teams**, groups of supporters who hand out fliers and spread information before a concert or a new release, is a good way to reach the people who are interested in your music. Social networking through online communities also boosts music sales and attendance at live events.

Remember that your goal is not just to sell thousands of copies of a single album or hit song, but also to create a reputation and an image for your label and your artists that will make people want to buy concert tickets and future albums. Some of your marketing activities might not result in immediate sales, but they will familiarize the public with the artist's name and music. In the music industry, swag (Stuff We Always Get) is the term for giveaway items with the band or label's name and URL printed on them. Pens, bottle openers, bags, stickers, posters, transparencies for car windows, T-shirts, and CDs or flash drives with free music can be handed out in strategic locations to create interest in your artist. Distribute these items to stores where your target audience shops and offer the stores free music and free event tickets in exchange for handing them out. You might be able to do a contest with stores in the areas where you are performing by giving away free tickets to their winning customers and allowing the store to have a display at your event.

Use creativity to get the attention of your target audience. Every genre has unique characteristics that make it suitable for certain types of venues. Stage live performances in bookstores, libraries, museums, churches, schools, on college campuses, at festivals, conventions, music conferences, public parks, private parties, and at mall and store openings. Hold a charity fund raiser for a good cause, donate the proceeds from ticket sales, and sell CDs at the event. People who see your artist at these events will go home and look up your website.

Viral marketing through interactive games: Nine Inch Nails

For the release of the 2007 album *Year Zero* by the group Nine Inch Nails, singer-songwriter Trent Reznor collaborated with Jordan Weisman of 42 Entertainment, a pioneer of alternative reality games (ARGs), to create a tantalizing trail of clues and puzzles that could only be figured out by thousands of fans pooling their resources on the Internet. The game started with cryptic clues hidden in the text printed on T-shirts at a February concert. The clues led fans to mysterious telephone numbers and hidden websites hinting at the theme of the upcoming album. Internet communities buzzed over the meaning of clues and new Nine Inch Nail songs found on flash drives left in the public bathrooms at concert venues. The uploaded songs spread quickly through the Internet. By the time the album was released in April 2007, 3.5 million fans had become involved in the game.

Street teams

Street teams are groups of volunteer fans or hired employees who publicize artists and events through personal contact with potential fans and customers. They can hand out fliers, stickers, or free music to people on the street or at other concerts and events; wear your T-shirts and walk around at music festivals and concert venues; put up posters; and visit local music stores to distribute one-sheets and talk up your artist's upcoming performance. At performances, they staff your merchandise tables, sell CDs, and help with the crowds. Give the members of your street team free music to hand out to their friends and acquaintances.

You can hire a company to organize and manage a street team for you, but the most effective teams are made up of fans that are genuinely enthusiastic about your music. Start with friends and existing fans, and invite people to sign up on your website and your artist's website. If you are having a performance in a city where you do not have a street team, advertise the creation of one on your website, Craigslist, and Twitter. You can offer to pay each person for a few hours' work or reward them with free event tickets, free music, or special privileges such as admission to a private performance or backstage party. Have them RSVP by e-mail, and tell them when and where to meet. Create an area on your website where street team members can log in and communicate with each other and where you can post information not available to the general public.

Live Performances

Live performances drive music sales and help build a fan base, but it is often difficult for an unknown artist to get gigs. Start locally, where your artist may already have a reputation in the music scene. Identify the clubs and venues that play your genre of music. Call the booking manager to set up an appointment, introduce yourself, and give him or her a promo package with a CD. Follow up a few days later with another phone call.

A live performance draws customers to a club or bar, which makes the venue money by selling drinks. Offer to perform on a weeknight when the club or bar is quiet. Invite family and friends to come and hear your band or artist. The owner will be motivated to ask you back if you demonstrate you can attract a small crowd. Offer to give a free performance on the same night every week; your artist will gain a regular following while rehearsing on a sound stage.

Get to know local bands that play regularly and might need an opening act. Find the venues where bands on tour perform, and inquire if they need a local act to open for them. If you book a venue for yourself, remember that you will have to pay the rent and do all the promotion for your performance. You should not have to pay anything if you are invited to open for another artist.

Build up an e-mail list of local venues and booking agents. When your artist performs, notify them of the location so they can come and observe if they want to. Contact promoters and introduce your artist. A promoter might be willing to book the venue and promote your show or to schedule your artist as an opener for another band. You can find promoters by talking to other artists and by seeing who is organizing events for other artists in your genre. You also can search on the Internet and in business telephone directories.

Do not focus on making money at first. The important thing is to be noticed by your audience and to build up a fan base. Some arrangements pay you a specified fee no matter how many people show up. Door split deals give the artists a percentage of the admission fees collected during the event. You may not earn any money from some shows and might even end up paying out of your own pocket. It does not matter. Club owners and promoters are taking a risk by allowing a new artist to perform; be grateful and make the most of every opportunity. When an audience responds well at one venue, look for similar clubs. Chances are that they will already have heard about you and will be willing to try you.

Always show up on time and ready to perform for every booking. Ask the artist to respect the venue, take breaks when scheduled, and avoid drinking alcohol. The patrons are there to relax and be entertained, but the artist is there on professional business.

Be sure to update your websites with the dates, times, and locations of all your artist's performances. Publicize performances well in advance with listings in events calendars, posters on bulletin boards, and newspaper ads. Supply local music stores and bookstores with fliers advertising the upcoming performance.

Tales from the Industry

Jet Records: Founder's Personality Hurt the Business

Don Arden, father of Sharon Osbourne and David Levy, was an agent, manager, and businessman whose best-known clients were rock groups Small Faces, Electric Light Orchestra, and Black Sabbath. He was notorious for his aggressive and occasionally illegal business tactics, which earned him the UK nicknames "Mr. Big," "The English Godfather" and "The Al Capone of

Pop." In 1974, he set up a small British label, Jet Records. Its first release, "No Honestly," a single by Lynsey De Paul, reached the UK top 10. In 1975, ELO and Wizzard, a band formed by Roy Wood after he left ELO, moved to Jet and brought their recent Warner Bros. material to Jet's catalog.

Island Records (1974-75) first distributed Jet Records, then Polydor Records (1975 to 1976), then United Artists (1976 to 1978). When album sales of ELO's newly released *Out of the Blue* were hurt by the sale of defective copies at discounted prices in record shops in the U.S. and Canada, Jet switched its distribution to CBS Records. By the end of the 1970s, ELO had become extremely popular, and Jet began reissuing ELO's albums and some new singles in vinyl records of many different colors. Don Arden lived the opulent lifestyle of a music mogul; his extravagant purchases included Howard Hughes' former house in Beverly Hills. He brought his daughter, Sharon, and his son, David, into the business with the hope of establishing a family dynasty.

Ultimately, though, it was Arden's abrasive, controlling personality and cutthroat attitude that undermined his initially successful business. After producing two hit singles and a popular album (*Love Bomb*), Lynsey De Paul left Jet and brought legal action against Arden for nonpayment. Ozzy Osbourne, who signed with Jet and released three albums after leaving Black Sabbath, began dating Arden's daughter Sharon and eventually married her. Arden became furious when Sharon took over management of Osbourne's career. As a result, she was estranged from her father for 20 years, and Osbourne left Jet and moved to CBS's Epic label. Osbourne's departure and the diminishing popularity of ELO in the early 1980s further added to Jet's financial difficulties. In the mid-1980s, Don Arden bought the outdated Portland Recording Studios and installed David as manager. To make ends meet, he sold ELO's recording contract and back catalog to CBS in 1985. In 1986, David was arrested, tried, and eventually sentenced to several months in prison for allegedly assaulting an accountant employed by Jet Records. Arden was tried on related charges and acquitted. The protracted legal proceedings distracted the two from managing the business, and the legal fees proved too much for Jet. The landlord evicted the label from its studios at 35 Portland Place for unpaid rent.

Jet struggled on until 1991 and released a single, "1-2-3," by Roy Wood in 1987. In September of 1990, the label recorded *Live at Fairfield Halls* by Bucks Fizz. The release of the album in April of 1991 coincided with the closure of Jet Records. Consequently, the album was barely promoted and failed to chart.

In 1991, Arden sold the production company offices and holdings to Bagdasarian Productions, which reopened the label under the new name Chipmunk Records.

Publicity

Publicity draws public attention to your artists and your label and supports the other elements of your marketing strategy. Remember that a positive newspaper article or review is desirable but remains in the public eye for only a short time. You constantly must look for ways to spark renewed interest in your artists, your music, your albums, and your label. If you can afford it, hire a publicist to create press releases, submit stories to newspapers and magazines, and maintain your public profile. You might be able to hire a recent graduate or a freelancer to work part-time for you. An experienced publicist has personal contacts that can help to get the word out.

There are many ways to get free publicity. Research all kinds of news media, trade magazines, online publications, local newspapers, and local radio stations for opportunities to submit articles and music for review. Create a press kit to send out initially, and follow up with timely press releases when your artist does something interesting. It is much easier to generate a buzz around a specific event, such as an upcoming concert, a new release, or even a personal event in the artist's life like an awards ceremony, a marriage, or the birth of a child.

Select publications and news outlets that are likely to be interested in your music and sympathetic to your artist, and tailor your press releases to match their interests. For example, a local newspaper might run an article about an artist who is a local resident. A jazz magazine would like to tell readers about a jazz artist's novel use of traditional instruments.

Generate a media contact list of journalists, music critics, writers, radio hosts, and PR representatives, and send them invitations to your live performances. Ask if the person would like to be added to your guest list and request an RSVP. If a media representative comes to listen to your artist, be sure to greet him or her and make a personal introduction. Send out holiday cards, free music, and occasionally, a small gift of appreciation.

One of the best ways to get free publicity is to submit information about upcoming performances to local events calendars online and in newspapers and magazines. You can start submitting several weeks in advance. Every time people look at the events calendar, they will see the listing for your artist.

Press kits and promo packages

Press kits and promo packages are essential marketing tools. Assemble a collection of images, press clippings, and background information that can be put together and sent out at a moment's notice whenever someone asks for information. Hire a good professional photographer to do a photo shoot with your artist, and pick out a selection of top-quality photos that convey the right image and personality. Newspapers and magazines like to publish images along with their stories; if you supply some striking photos they will be more likely to take notice of you.

Begin collecting press clippings, reviews, quotes from radio interviews, and any news videos about your artist. Make a promo package for the artist with a photo, short bio or one-sheet, and the press clippings. As time passes and your artist's career develops, update the promo package to reflect his or her latest achievements. Your press kit should include your contact information, a short history of your label, the artists' promo packages, a press release with information about an upcoming event or release of an album, and relevant press clippings.

Your press kit and promo package should not be large or bulky. Journalists do not want to sift through stacks of papers. Present the important information in a concise format, preferably in a presentation folder with two pockets. You can have a folder printed with your logo and your artists' names, or use a plain folder with a printed adhesive label. Always include your business card.

If you are sending your press kit or promo package by e-mail, copy and paste the information into the e-mail, and provide a link to your website. Do not attach anything to the e-mail. It might not get through the company's spam filter, and journalists are not likely to open attachments anyway. The e-mail always should be accompanied by a personal phone call; otherwise, you have no assurance that the journalist saw it.

Create a media section on your website where you can post photos, the items from your press kit and promo package, and press releases. If there are items that you do not want the public to access, create a special login, and give out the password only to the people you approve. A media section allows anyone who is interested in your label to get information without having to contact you.

Submitting your CD for review

Music reviewers who write for magazines, newspapers, and the Internet are bombarded with submissions, so you need to make your submission stand out. The best way to do this is to contact the reviewer personally and ask how you can send a submission for review. Follow his or her instructions. Send a CD, the artist's one-sheet, and a press release about the album, accompanied by a personal note thanking the reviewer for his or her time. Because there is so much competition for attention from national news media, look for reviewers who write for local newspapers or genre magazines. A regional newspaper might be interested in a local artist. A good local review might be picked up by other media and lead to further reviews. It might show up in Internet search engine results when people are looking for information on your artist.

Do not attempt to exert any pressure on the reviewer because harassment is likely to result in a negative review. Wait for your other marketing efforts to catch the reviewer's notice.

Advertising

A newspaper or magazine article will be before the readers' eyes for week or a month and then subside into the past. You need repeated exposure in the media, and that can be achieved only through paid advertising. To get the most out of your advertising dollar, you need to find the most effective places to run your ads. Study the kinds of advertising done by artists similar to yours. Find out what publications they run ads in. If you see several bands advertising themselves there, it must be because the ads bring results.

A full-page ad can be costly, but there are many ways to cut costs on advertising. Run a half-page or a quarter-page ad instead. Choose monthly or bimonthly publications over weeklies because your ad will be on display longer. Ads in some specialty magazines continue to bring results for months after publication. Do a co-op ad with a record store, a club, or other artists: you share the cost of an ad that promotes both the club and your performance there or the music store and the CD you are selling there. You might be able to get a record store to trade advertising for free product: the store pays to run the ad and then deducts your share of the cost when it pays the distributor for your CDs. The distributor deducts its markup on the CDs from the money it owes you. You can also offer to stage an in-store performance for a store if it will pay to advertise it. Double up on your ads by promoting a tour schedule and a new release in the same ad.

Planning Publicity Around a New Release

Publicity for your artist is most effective when it is focused around a particular event such as a new release or a concert tour. The element of time gives fans a sense of urgency and excitement. Think of the hundreds of people camping out to attend a theater's first showing of a new *Star Wars, Lord of the Rings,* or *Twilight* movie, even though it is having "first showings" in numerous other locations. The release date of a new record provides an occasion to send out press releases, invite media and fans to hear the artist at a special event, put posters up in music stores, and advertise on the Internet.

All this activity takes months of advance planning and preparation. All the elements must be in place for your publicity campaign to succeed. The first priority is to make sure that your CD will be in your hands, ready to sell, on the release date. Most of your efforts will be wasted if you book a venue, invite hundreds of guests, pay for food and drinks, and then do not have CDs to sell at your launch party. Advertising has to be scheduled, posters printed, and CDs delivered to retail stores. Magazines often have lead times of several months before they print a review or an article. Fix on a specific release date for your record, then create a detailed schedule for everything that has to be done along with due dates. If something is not ready by the due date, adjust your plans to compensate. Working toward a release date will help you to focus your activities and stay on track. *You will find a checklist for promoting a new release on the companion CD.*

Organize a launch party for your new CD. Find a venue that is the right size for the number of guests you want to invite. A local club might be willing to host your party free if your artist performs afterward for regular patrons. Invite everyone on your contact list: media, promoters, club owners, DJs, retailers, other musicians, family, and friends. Follow up with a phone call to confirm they will attend; nothing is worse than a half-empty room at a media event. Provide food and drinks. If your budget allows it, offer an open bar for an hour. If your artist is already well known locally, you may be able to get a sponsorship from a beer or liquor distributor. At a typical launch party, the entire album is played for the guests over the sound system, followed by a live performance. Sell CDs, hand out one-sheets, and collect e-mail addresses. For a new artist, the launch party may be your label's first opportunity to sell a quantity of CDs.

The timing of your release is also important. More than a third of all music sales occur during November and December when people are shopping for the holidays. Major labels time their big releases to come out at that time to maximize sales. With CDs from big-name artists crowding the shelves and dominating the endcaps in retail stores, you will face additional challenges trying to get attention. By releasing your CD during a quieter season, you will have a better chance of being noticed.

Social Media and Networking

Social media and networking on the Internet are essential marketing tools for independent artists and labels. Major labels and well-known artists orchestrate extensive marketing campaigns on social media to publicize upcoming releases and concert tours. Many independents rely on social media to drive sales of music downloads and CDs and to boost ticket sales and attendance at events.

Social networking takes place through online communities of people who connect and communicate with each other via blogs, e-mail, instant messaging, forums, video, or chat rooms. The largest social networking sites, Facebook and MySpace, have hundreds of millions of members, but there are thousands of smaller sites focused on specific interests or age groups. Many allow users to share favorite music, videos, and photos with the click of a button.

The appeal of social networking sites is that users feel in control of their Internet experiences. They are able to craft their own elaborate networks of friends and contacts, selected websites, and collections of music and photos. Interactive communication on the Internet is deeply engaging, and for some people, even addictive. Members of some online communities that are fiercely loyal to a celebrity, artist, or cause voluntarily commit their time, money, and influence to supporting them.

If your record label or artist can gain the attention of an Internet community, its members will tell their friends, who tell their friends, and your fame will quickly spread across nations and continents. This phenomenon, called **viral marketing**, can be extremely effective, but it does not happen by chance. Social networking, like any public relations effort, requires hours of work, regular updates, constant monitoring, and ongoing research into the latest trends and technologies. Major corporations that have recognized the potential impact of viral marketing are investing millions in developing a presence on social networks. Firms such as Quantcast (**www.quantcast.com**), Bridge Ratings (**www.bridgeratings.com**), Comscore (**www.comscore.com**) and Visible Measures (**http://corp.visiblemeasures.com**) monitor activity on social networks, provide detailed analyses to help companies target specific markets, and hire staffs of experts to manage Internet activities. You or your artist may have the know-how and interest to do this work yourselves; if not, pay someone else to do it for you. Social networking is an opportunity that you cannot afford to neglect. Numerous companies offer social networking services especially for musicians, or you can hire a local fan or college student well-versed in social and music media to manage your presence on social networks.

Susan Boyle: a Viral Marketing Superstar

Scottish singer Susan Boyle achieved international fame through social media after she stunned the judges on a TV talent show, *Britain's Got Talent*, on April 11, 2009, with her rendition of "I Dreamed a Dream" from *Les Misérables*. According to Visible Measures, a U.S. Web video tracking firm, within a week, 850 video clips of her on the Internet had received more than 100 million views and 290,000 comments. The firm identified more than 200 unique videos related to her performance. The official *Britain's Got Talent* video clip had been viewed more than 35 million times within a week of April 11, making it the 48th most viewed YouTube video of all time. Ten of the top 20 videos on YouTube's Most Watched Videos for the week of April 22, 2009, featured Susan Boyle.

Susan Boyle's first album, *I Dreamed a Dream*, released on November 23, 2009, was Amazon's best-selling album in presales. *Billboard* reported that the album experienced "the best opening week for a female artist's debut album since SoundScan began tracking sales in 1991." In six weeks of sales, it sold 9 million copies and became the biggest selling album in the world for 2009. She was #36 in Billboard magazine's list of music *Top Money Makers 2011*, netting $4.77 million in royalties during 2010.

In September 2010, Boyle was recognized in the Guinness Book of World Records three times for:

- Having the fastest selling debut album by a female artist in the U.K.

- Having the most successful first week sales of a debut album in the U.K. It sold 411,820 copies in its first week in the U.K., almost 50,000 more than the Arctic Monkeys.

- Being the oldest person (48 years old) to reach No. 1 with a debut album in the UK

One of the advantages of social networking is that it is free. Although social networking can be as simple as putting up a profile on a social networking site, linking it to your website, posting a video of your artist, and telling your friends, marketing successfully through the Internet is a complex science. Your social networking efforts will be much more successful if they are targeted to appeal to a specific audience. Everyone does not use social networking in the same way. Determine who your potential fans are — their ages, gender, and musical interests. Sign up as a "follower" on the social networks of artists similar to yours, and observe the methods they use to promote themselves, and then try similar methods yourself. A recent study by Bridge Ratings found that as users age and as they become more familiar with social networking, their behaviors change, and they begin to move on to new communities and different forms of networking. You must be prepared to adapt your social networking strategy to keep up with your fans.

Social networking sites are constantly evolving, adding new technologies, and changing their policies, especially concerning online sales, copyright protection and the ways music can be downloaded and shared. Larger companies frequently buy smaller sites, and alliances are formed with other companies to offer additional features. Keep abreast of new developments by reading news articles and blogs about the music industry, and by watching the activities of your fans. For example, from 2009 to 2011, years, MySpace lost millions of members while Facebook expanded exponentially, but music lovers continued to remain loyal to MySpace Music.

Begin by creating an account and a profile for your artist and/or your label on the social networking sites (Orkut, Facebook, MySpace, YouTube, Digg™, Twitter) and on the music websites (thesixtyone, Bandcamp, SoundCloud, RootMusic®, Last Fm, Jango Music Network, ToneFuse Music Network, MSN® Music) listed in this section. Each site has customizable templates for designing your profile page, and many allow you to include photos, videos, streaming music or music downloads. Link these profiles to your official website. Many social networking sites have **widgets** — small graphic symbols that you can place on your websites, blogs, and articles to link readers to your profile page in that social network. For example, a Twitter widget on your official website would allow fans to sign up to follow you on Twitter, or to tweet their friends about your site. When creating these profiles, be conscious of the image you want to project. You might choose to use the same photos and graphics on all your profiles for a consistent image, or you might use different images and songs to appeal to a different segment of your fan base. Some sites have e-commerce features that allow you to sell your CDs and downloads directly; others link to a sales page in Amazon.com or iTunes. If you have signed a contract with an online distributor, check the contract for any restrictions on selling your music independently. Online distributors typically have arrangements with major social networking sites to sell your music.

Popular social networking sites

Orkut is a popular social networking site owned by Google with millions of users; 63 percent of Orkut traffic originates from Brazil, followed by India with 19.2 percent. Like other sites such as Facebook, Orkut permits the creation of groups known as "communities," based on a designated subject, and allows other people to join the communities.

Facebook is the leading social networking site. It has more than 500 million active users at the time of publication, half of whom log on to Facebook on any given day. Initially, Facebook was developed as a network for university students, but when the site became available publicly, its popularity exploded. On Facebook, it is easy to add friends, send messages, and create communities or event invitations. More than 2.5 million websites have integrated with Facebook, and more than 200 million active users currently access Facebook through their mobile devices.

MySpace (www.myspace.com) is a social networking website offering an interactive platform for all its users. It allows the sharing of files, pictures, and even music videos. You can view the profiles of your friends, relatives, and any other users; you can also create and share blogs with each other. Usage of MySpace declined drastically during the last half of 2010, perhaps because visitors did not like the heavy advertising component.

YouTube (www.youtube.com), owned by Google, is the largest video sharing network site in the world, and it is a good place to do video marketing. Members can create playlists by selecting music videos of songs they want to listen to. To become a member of YouTube, go to the "Signup" page, choose a username and password, enter your information, and click the "Signup" button.

Digg (www.digg.com) is a place to unearth and share content retrieved from anywhere on the Web. Digg is unique compared to other social networking sites because it allows you to directly network with people and sell your products. Once a post is submitted, it appears on a list in the selected category. From there, it will either fall or rise in rank, depending on how people vote. Digg is a "social bookmarking" site, where users can share, organize, and search bookmarks of Web pages or articles in an online, public forum instead of simply on their browsers. Other Digg users — known as Diggers —review and rate your content. Highly rated content gets posted on the Digg home page, which gets thousands of visitors a day and can drive traffic to your website or blog.

Twitter (www.twitter.com) is a microblogging service that allows users to broadcast short messages — in Twitter's case 140 characters or fewer — to other users. With Twitter, you can let your friends know what you are doing throughout the day from your phone or computer. When you sign up with Twitter, you can post and receive messages (known as tweets) with your Twitter account. The site sends your tweets out to your friends and subscribers, and you receive messages sent from those you wish to follow, including friends, family, and celebrities. It is so effective that it has been credited with helping to bring down the regime of Egyptian ex-president Mubarak.

Flickr (www.flickr.com) is Yahoo's photo and video sharing site. You can upload photos and videos from your desktop, send them by e-mail, or use your camera phone and organize and store them online. It has editing features to eliminate red-eye, crop a photo, or add fonts and effects.

Google Picasa® (http://picasa.google.com) is a similar photo sharing and storing application.

Once you have established profiles on the social networking sites, here are some ways to increase your presence on the Internet:

- Link from your website to your social network profiles. Put a widget on the side or bottom of each page or a link saying something like, "Follow me on Twitter."

- Use social bookmarking to increase your website's exposure on social networking sites. Social bookmarking includes creating playlists or lists of favorite websites that can be shared with friends on a social network. It also includes tagging — clicking a small symbol such as a heart or box to show that the reader "likes" or "recommends" this site to others. For example, Pandora recently began sharing individuals' playlists with their Facebook friends.

- Create and share music videos and photos on Flickr and YouTube. Upload film clips from recent concerts, live interviews, rehearsals, jam sessions, and photo shoots. New and interesting content keeps fans coming back for more.

- Use social networking forums to promote your artist, website, and blog. Forums are message boards and chat rooms where you can exchange comments with an online community and post announcements.

- Promote your music through your profile on social networking and music sites such as Facebook and MySpace, with links to your home page and a sales page.

- Set up a Twitter account and send out communications whenever you have news for your fans, such as a concert or a new song or video available on the Internet.

- Invite fans to sign up for your e-mail list to receive announcements and special offers.

You cannot expect your fans to do all the work for you. Part of the appeal of social networking is a personalized experience in which the person feels he or she is contributing something and receiving individual attention. Communication is important. Your website and profiles should allow users to sign up for Twitter and interface with other social networking sites. The artist or someone on your staff must respond quickly to e-mails and messages. Find ways to reward fans that participate in your social networks with invitations to impromptu performances or meet-and-greet opportunities after concerts, exclusive access to video clips, and free music.

Internet users like to see something new once or twice a week. Someone on your team should be constantly updating blogs, uploading video clips of recent performances, posting news, and dropping hints about new songs and upcoming releases. Major labels and artists make a lot of effort to appear as though they are on the same level as their fans, doing everything personally, but they cannot avoid stereotypes because of the sheer scale of their activities. As a small independent label, you have the advantage of truly being close to your fans — in age, geographical location, musical tastes, and attitude toward life — and therefore, are better able to engage them in an online relationship.

The Internet presents some exciting marketing opportunities, but do not forget that you are competing with thousands of other labels and artists for fans' attention. In 2010, MySpace alone carried 13 million music profiles worldwide. Among these are more than 2.5 million registered hip-hop acts, 1.8 million rock acts, 720,000 pop acts, and 470,000 punk acts. The quality of your music alone will not be enough to make you stand out. Your marketing and your ability to expand your fan base by coming up with new music and new ideas will make the difference.

Music websites that interact with social networking media

Amazon (www.amazon.com)

If you have exclusive rights to your CDs, you can sell your CDs on Amazon. com by producing them on-demand through CreateSpace (www.createspace. com) or selling physical inventory on consignment through Amazon Advantage (you will have to send enough copies of your CD to meet customer demand for several weeks). In order to sell MP3 files as downloads on Amazon, you must go through one of these distributors:

- CD Baby (**www.cdbaby.com**)
- Createspace (**www.createspace.com**)

- Eone Distribution (**www.e1distribution.com**)

- InGrooves (**www.ingrooves.com**)

- Iodalliance (**www.iodalliance.com**)

- Iris Distribution (**www.irisdistribution.com**)

- Red Eye (**www.redeyeusa.com**)

- The Orchard (**www.theorchard.com**)

- Tunecore (**www.tunecore.com**)

- Virtual Label® (**www.virtuallabel.biz**)

Amazon allows artists and labels to create online artist stores free. Photos, artwork, music, and content to enhance these sites can be uploaded through Artist Central (**https://artistcentral.amazon.com**).

Bandcamp (http://bandcamp.com)
Bandcamp allows you to distribute your music free, charge a set price for it, or let fans name their own price, with the minimum set by you. You can sell both physical merchandise and digital music from Bandcamp and create combination packages such as a vinyl record, poster, and download package in which fans receive the digital files immediately and the merchandise through the mail. Each account gets 200 free downloads to give away to fans each month.

Jango Music Network (www.jango.com)
Jango is an ad-funded social music service that lets listeners create and share custom radio stations. Its unique "Jango Airplay" music promotion service gives emerging artists guaranteed airplay as similar artists alongside the popular artists chosen by listeners. Packages start at as little as $10 for 250 plays.

Last Fm (www.last.fm)
Last Fm is a music recommendation service that delivers personalized recommendations to each of its listeners every day. It maintains online communities, encourages social tagging, and allows listeners to connect their playlists through Twitter. It gives you exposure to new fans. You can give your listeners free downloads, stream your music, or sell downloads.

MySpace Music (www.myspace.com/music/artisthq)

Myspace Music is highly rated for its artist profile pages and playlist features. The site tracks the most popular music with charts similar to Billboard charts and enables users to view music popular in other countries. You can sell music on MySpace either through an arrangement with an online distributor, or by placing a link to another sales page on your profile.

Pandora (www.pandora.com)

Pandora is an ad-funded Internet music recommendation service based on the Music Genome Project®, a database built from more than ten years of analysis by a trained team of musicologists using up to 400 distinct musical characteristics. The database spans everything from new releases to Renaissance and Classical music. Listeners can build playlists based on their favorite music. The Music Genome Project continually updated with the latest releases, emerging artists, and an ever-deepening collection of catalogue titles. You can submit music for consideration by e-mailing suggest-music@pandora.com.

ReverbNation (www.reverbnation.com)

Allows artists to create profile and use free viral marketing tools for MySpace, Facebook, Twitter, blogs, and websites. Develop a mailing list and send e-mail newsletters with the free version of FanReach™, the e-mail system more than 100,000 artists use.

RootMusic (www.rootmusic.com)

A RootMusic BandPage™ lets fans listen to new tracks while reading more about your artist and looking at your upcoming event schedule. Tracks play through a special, Facebook-share enabled SoundCloud music player. Fans can purchase or download music through links on SoundCloud. Fans can easily share and send music through their Facebook networks.

SoundCloud (www.soundcloud.com)

SoundCloud allows artists to upload or record originally created sounds and share them via social networking sites, along with a visual representation of the music. Timed comments let friends and fans give feedback at specific moments throughout the soundtrack.

thesixtyone.com (www.thesixtyone.com/)

On thesixtyone, artists can sign up to sell songs and merchandise directly to fans. Artists make at least $7 per album and are paid every 30 days.

YouTube (www.youtube.com)

Artists can create a profile and upload music videos, which their fans share through social media. A link on the profile can connect the listener to a sales page.

CASE STUDY: COMMUNICATION IS THE KEY

Daniel Ennis is a student at the University of Florida who is double majoring in advertising and English.

I have played in several bands over the last seven years and before coming to college, I used to set up shows for other musicians to play, too. We recorded a lot of music in those bands but did not have much interest in making money from it. We mostly just ended up handing CDs out at cost or giving free downloads to people. We did not make money, but we had a reputation in our hometown.

With websites such as Bandcamp, MySpace, Facebook, and other social media channels, music can be spread with the click of a button. This can be advantageous for do-it-yourself types because relatively unknown bands can easily attract fans all over the world, but at the same time, it is detrimental to the record label system that has been in place since music has been recorded. Anybody can download anything. Social media and the Internet perpetuate this spread of information and give opportunities to bands that would not ordinarily get attention. The notoriety of bands that became known on e-zine and music community websites such as Pitchfork[SM] Media (**http://pitchfork. com**) or Stereogum (**www.stereogum.com**) has a shorter shelf life. Bands come and go as frequently as the seasons, and trends in styles come and go at the same time. It is a very interesting time, with a lot of opportunity for the early adaptors that are willing to take a little risk and play the game.

If you have a DIY label, one of the biggest difficulties is creating interest. If the music is good enough, then it will speak for itself, so to speak. But it is not always that easy. When the label promotes its artists through shows to create a grassroots feel, while at the same time using new forms of social media such as YouTube, it is easier for the listener to participate in generating interest, which makes it easier for the DIY label to exist.

Communication with potential fans is also a key. Communication, always seeming "new" and in the moment, always creating new things, or giving the impression that new things are always coming out is really important. But at the same time, you do not want to saturate your audience with too much all at the same time. If the band can find the right balance between saturation and silence, they are likely to be able to get interest and notoriety enough to build a network of fans that come back for more.

The best way to succeed on Twitter is to be interactive. If you are talking a lot, responding quickly to anyone's retweets and mentions, they are more likely to have a conversation with you. Conversation is a big way to get attention that can then promote music.

Social media is moving very fast all the time that it is hard to predict which direction will be next. I would like to be able to say that Facebook will be around forever, but I know that is not true — not by a long shot. Commercialization takes away the appeal of many sites such as Twitter, Facebook, and Tumblr, so people are more likely to abandon one social medium in search for another that does not disrupt their day-to-day socializing as much.

People will want to keep finding ways to communicate on the Internet and find new ways to interact so they can find new music (and other things such as news and videos). Still, it is hard to say what is next. Maybe Xanga will make a revival, but for the sake of people on the Internet everywhere, I hope it does not. (Xanga was notorious for illegal file sharing and pornography.)

Music Videos

A report released by the International Federation of the Phonographic Industry in March 2010 estimated that a major label typically spends $200,000 to produce a package of three videos for a new artist breaking in a major market. These videos are major productions that are shown on television and sold on their own as product.

For independent labels, the role of music videos has changed. Instead of seeing an artist for the first time in a music video on television, most potential fans are exposed to a new artist online through video clips. Fans search for videos of the artists they want to see. The photographic quality of the video is no longer as important because it will probably be viewed on a computer screen or even a phone. With so many video clips available, it is important to have interesting videos and get the viewer involved with the artist.

With today's digital cameras and editing software, it is possible to make your own good-quality videos. Fans like variety; they like to see different versions of individual songs and videos of live performances. Each time you upload a new video, your fans will share it with others, increasing your exposure and the traffic to your websites. You can also make DVDs of your lower-quality videos to hand out to fans at concerts and give away in record stores.

CONCLUSION

What Does the Future Hold?

The rapid development of digital recording and of new technologies for listening to music have drastically changed the music industry over the last decade, eroding traditional business models and causing real concern over whether the recording industry can remain viable. An artist can gain a global audience more rapidly and effectively than ever before, but the revenue from music sales is declining, raising the question of whether record labels can afford to continue investing in new artists. In its 2010 report, *Investing in Music: How Music Companies Discover, Develop & Promote Talent*, the International Federation of the Phonographic Industry (IFPI) calculated the music industry as a whole invests $5 billion annually in musical talent. Almost 30 percent of its total revenue is invested in A&R and marketing. This is high when compared to the amount invested in research and development by other industries. The same report estimated that a major label typically invests about $1 million to develop and promote a new group or artist. The music business is risky; the estimated success rate for new artists varies, from one out of five artists to one out of ten artists. The revenue realized by record companies is invested in developing new artists. If record companies cannot make enough profit, new artists will never have a chance.

Another serious threat to the music industry is digital piracy through illegal file-sharing on peer-to-peer networks and illegal streaming sites and forums. According to the IFPI's Digital Music Report 2011, research by The Nielsen Company indicated that 45 percent of Internet users in Spain and 44 percent in Brazil use unlicensed digital music services every month. The top five EU markets averaged 23 percent of users. The effect on new artists is measurable: Spain had no new local artists in its top-50 album chart, compared with ten in 2003. There are two reasons for this. Because charts rank artists by tracking sales of their records, the artists do not get on the charts if their audiences are not paying to listen to their music. Also, the recorded music market in Spain declined by an estimated 22 percent in 2010, forcing record labels to cut back sharply on their investment in new artists. Investment in artists in Mexico has dropped by 69 percent since 2005 and domestic releases have declined by 45 percent. Harris Interactive reports that 76 percent of the music obtained online in the UK during 2010 was unlicensed. The IFPI report also cites a study by Adermon & Liang of Uppsala University in Sweden, which found that physical music sales would increase by 72 percent and digital music sales by 131 percent if piracy did not exist. The IFPI is campaigning for Internet service providers (ISPs) to agree to suspend voluntarily accounts used to publicly disseminate copyright infringing material and for government regulation to protect intellectual property rights. In 2010, the governments of France and South Korea implemented sanctions to engage ISPs in reducing peer-to-peer infringement on their networks. The European Union and the governments of the UK, New Zealand, and Malaysia are considering similar legislation. Another initiative strives to educate consumers about the need to pay for music in order to support artists.

Major record labels have been adapting to face these challenges by trying to increase revenue from other sources such as live performances, merchandise sales, and licensing. There is no guarantee this will compensate for the decline in revenue from record sales; according to Pollstar, during 2010, box office sales of the world's top 50 tours fell by 12 percent from 2009 sales to $2.9 billion. This could have been a temporary trend due to the worldwide economic recession or a permanent shift in the way audiences enjoy music. Some independent music visionaries believe that allowing free music on the Internet ultimately supports record sales by helping an artist become well known so that fans ultimately want to purchase studio-quality CDs and downloads. They foresee new business models in which fans willingly pay for personalized music experiences through subscription services, interactive devices, and sales of merchandise and event tickets. Others foresee free music services supported by advertising revenue. It is difficult to predict how audiences will be listening to their music in five years. One thing is certain: the record label that can adapt quickly, economize, capitalize on niche markets, and develop a widespread and flexible marketing network will have the most success.

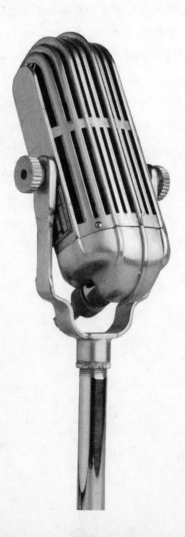

APPENDIX A

Further Reading

Industry Associations

American Association of Independent Musicians (A2im). **http://a2im.org**.

American Federation of musicians (AFM) **www.afm.org**.

The American Society of Composers, Authors And Publishers. **www.ascap.com**.

Association of Independent Music (AIM) (UK), **www.musicindie.com/home**.

Association of Independent Music Publishers (AIMP). **www.aimp.org**.

BMI (Broadcast Music, Inc.). **www.bmi.com**.

Digital Media Association (DiMA). **www.digmedia.org**.

Harry Fox Agency. **www.harryfox.com**.

IFPI (International Federation of the Phonographic Industry). **www.ifpi.org**.

National Music Publishers' Association (NMPA). **www.nmpa.org**.

Nashville Songwriters Association International (NSAI). **www.nashvillesongwriters.com**.

Songwriters Guild of America (SGA). **www.songwritersguild.com**.

SESAC. **www.sesac.com**.

Recording Industry Association of America (RIAA). **www.riaa.com**.

UK Music. **www.ukmusic.org**.

Business

Alternative Distribution Alliance. **www.ada-music.com**.

Business Licenses and Permits Search Tool. **www.sba.gov/content/search-business-licenses-and-permits** at the SBA.gov website.

Music Business Toolbox. **www.musicbusinesstoolbox.com**.

RecordLabelResouce.com. **www.recordlabelresource.com**.

U.S. Small Business Administration (SBA). **www.sba.gov**.

Legal

Donnelly, Bob. Lommen Abdo Cole King & Stageberg. *Why Artists Should "Do a 180" on "360 Deals."* **http://lefsetz.com/wordpress/index.php/archives/2010/04/19/360-deals-3**.

Lawyers by City — Directory of lawyers. **www.lawyers-by-city.com**.

Music Law Advice. **www.musiclawadvice.co.uk**.

NOLO. **www.nolo.com**.

The Arts Law Centre of Australia. **www.artslaw.com.au**.

U.S. Copyright Office. **www.loc.gov/copyright**.

U.S. Patent and Trademark Office. **www.uspto.gov**.

U.S. Senate Committee on the Judiciary Hearing on *"The Performance Rights Act and Parity among Music Delivery Platforms."* August 4, 2009, Testimony. **www.digmedia.org/resource-center**.

Wallace Collins Esq. Articles on legal topics. **http://wallacecollins.com**.

Contracts

101MusicBiz Contracts. **www.musiccontracts101.com**.

Law Depot. **www.lawdepot.com/contracts/music-recording-contract/?loc=US**.

Music Legal Contracts.com. **www.musiclegalcontracts.com**.

MusicLegalForms.com. **www.recordlabelstartup.com**.

Music Think Tank Downloadable 360 contracts. **www.musicthinktank. com/blog/download-music-business-legal-documents-for-creating-your-ow.html**.

Schornstein, Jay M. *Recording Contract Clauses.* Musicians Intellectual Law & Resources Links. 2006. **www.musiciansintellectuallaw.com/ rec_clauses.html**.

State of Texas Music Business Guide. **http://governor.state.tx.us/music/ guides/tmlp/tmlp_contractsextra**.

Books

BMI, *The Musician's Atlas Online.* **www.bmi.com**.

Cook, John, Laura Ballance and Mac McCaughan. 2009. *Our Noise: the Story of Merge Records.* Algonquin Paperbacks.

Escott, Colin, and Martin Hawkins. 1992. *Good Rockin Tonight: Sun Records and the Birth of Rock'n'Roll.* Virgin Bks.

Furht, Borko. *Encyclopedia of Multimedia.* Springer E-Books. Boston, MA: Springer Science+Business Media, Inc. 2006. **http://dx.doi. org/10.1007/0-387-30038-4**.

Gillett, Charlie. *Making Tracks: The Story of Atlantic Records.* 1974. Souvenir Press.

_____. *The Sound of the City.* 1970. Pantheon.

Halloran, Mark E. *The Musicians Business and Legal Guide, 4th Edition.* Beverly Hills Bar Association. Committee for the Arts. Prentice Hall.

Knab, Christopher, and Bartley F. Day. *Music is your business: the musician's FourFront strategy for success.* Seattle, Washington: FourFront Media & Music, 2007.

Krasilovsky, M. William, and Sidney Shemel. *This business of music.* New York: Billboard Books, 1995.

Passman, Donald S. *All you need to know about the music business.* New York: Free Press, 2006.

Wimble, David. *David Wimble's The indie bible: the all-in-one resource for recording artists.* New York: Schirmer Trade Books,

Agents

TAXI.com. **www.taxi.com/about.html**.

Name Search

U.S. Patent and Trademark Office. **www.uspto.gov/trademarks/index.jsp**.

Search Engines

A2G Music. **http://a2gmusic.com/content/record_label**.

All Record Labels.com. **http://allrecordlabels.com**.

Business.com. **www.business.com**.

DMOZ Open Directory Project. **http://search.dmoz.org**.

GoDaddy.com. **www.godaddy.com**.

Google. **www.google.com**.

InterNIC. **http://internic.net/whois.html**.

Microsoft's Bing. **www.bing.com**.

Network Solutions. **www.networksolutions.com**.

Wikipedia. **http://en.wikipedia.org/wiki/List_of_record_labels**.

WhoWhere.com. **www.whowhere.com**.

The Yellow Pages. **www.theyellowpages.com**.

Logo Design

Guru Corporation's Logosnap.com. **www.logosnap.com**.

HP's Logomaker. **www.logomaker.com**.

Licensing

ASCAP, BMI & SESAC (see Organizations above)

Sample Clearance Ltd. **www.sampleclearanceltd.com**.

The Music Bridge. **www.themusicbridge.com**.

Taxes

"Handy Reference Guide to the Fair Labor Act." **www.dol.gov**.

IRS Publication 541: Partnerships. **www.irs.gov/pub/irs-pdf/p541.pdf**.

Publication #15, circular "Employer's Tax Guide." **www.irs.gov/pub/irs-pdf/p15.pdf**.

Publication 334, "Tax Guide for Small Businesses." **www.irs.gov/pub/irs-pdf/p334.pdf**.

Self-Employed Individuals Tax Center. **www.irs.gov/businesses/small/article/0,,id=115045,00.html#obligations**.

State tax guide. **www.aicpa.org/members/div/tax/praguide.htm**.

Insurance

Allen Financial Insurance Group. **www.eqgroup.com/afrecpgm.htm**.

CSI Insurance Group. **http://csicoverage.com/recording-studio-insurance**.

Heath Lambert. **www.heathlambert.com**.

National Association of Insurance Commissioners (NAIC). **www.naic.org**.

Robertson Taylor. **www.robertson-taylor.us.com**.

Musicians Unions

AFTRA — American Federation of Television and Radio Artists. **www.aftra.org**.

American Federation of Musicians. **www.afm.org**.

Musicians Union: Local No. 6 (San Francisco, California). **www.afm6.org**.

Musicians' Union: Local 40-543 (Baltimore, Maryland). **www.musiciansunion.org.**.

Twin Cities Musicians Union (St. Paul, Minnesota). **www.musiciansunion.org**.

Songwriters and Music Publishers

Electronic Code of Federal Regulations, TITLE 37--Patents, Trademarks, and Copyrights. **http://ecfr.gpoaccess.gov/cgi/t/text/text-idx?c=ecfr&tpl=/ecfrbrowse/Title37/37cfr385_main_02.tpl**.

Guide to Record Label Companies. **www.record-labels-companies-guide.com/links-indie-record-cos.html**.

Hit Quarters. **www.hitquarters.com**.

Randall, David K. "The One Bright Spot In The Music Business." Forbes.com. January 9, 2009. **www.forbes.com/2009/01/09/music-publishing-itunes-biz-media_cz_dkr_0109music.html**.

Financing

3iC LLC. **www.help-finance.com/who1.htm**.

Fundingpost.com. **www.fundingpost.com**.

Cooperatives

Azalea City Recordings. **www.azaleacityrecordings.com**.

Sun Machine Cooperative. Minnesota, Iowa, Indiana and Illinois, **www.sunmachine.coop**.

Fund-raisers

Kickstarter. **www.kickstarter.com**.

PledgeMusic. **www.pledgemusic.com**.

Sellaband. **www.sellaband.com**.

Website Design

Buildfree.org. **www.buildfree.org**.

GoDaddy.com. **www.godaddy.com**.

Ten Top reviews: Shopping Cart Software. **http://shopping-cart-review.toptenreviews.com**.

Weebly.com. **www.weebly.com**.

Wix.com. **www.wix.com**.

Merchant Services

Durango Merchant Services. **http://durangomerchantservices.com**.

FastCharge. **www.fastcharge.com**.

Flagship Merchant Services. **www.cardservicesales.com**.

GoEmerchant. **www.goemerchant.com**.

Instamerchant. **www.instamerchant.com**.

Merchant Warehouse. **http://merchantwarehouse.com**.

Third Party Payment Systems

2Checkout. **www.2checkout.com**.

Adobe Web analytics powered by Omniture. **www.omniture.com/en/ products/online_analytics**.

Alexa. **www.alexa.com**.

ClickBank. **www.clickbank.com**.

Google Analytics. **http://www.google.com/support/analytics**.

Internet Corporation for Assigned Names and Numbers. **www.internic.net.**

Paypal. **www.paypal.com**.

Webtrends. **www.webtrends.com**.

Recording

Build a Recording Studio.com. **www.build-a-recording-studio.com**.

Studio Recording Engineer.com. **www.studiorecordingengineer.com**.

Manufacturing

Bison Disc. **www.bisondisc.com**.

CDBaby. **http://members.cdbaby.com**.

GS1 U.S. Bar Codes. **www.gs1us.org**.

IODA. **www.iodalliance.com**.

Isomedia Inc. **www.isomediainc.com**.

Nationwide Disc. **www.nationwidedisc.com/faq-s.html#general_q3**.

Rainbo Records. **www.rainborecords.com**.

Distribution

Beggars Group. **www.beggars.com**.

Caroline Distribution/EMI Label Services. **www.carolinedist.com**.

Hearn, Edward (Ned) R. "Digital Downloads and Streaming: Copyright and Distribution." **www.internetmedialaw.com/articles/ digital_downloads.pdf**.

One-stop. **www.sdcd.com**.

Record Store. **www.highwire.com**.

Select-O-Hits. **www.selectohits.com**.

Simply Gigantic. **http://simplygigantic.com**.

SmartCode. **www.technoriversoft.com/products.html** — generate bar codes.

Streaming Music Services

Amazon. **www.amazon.com**.

Amazon's Createspace. **www.createspace.com**.

betterPropaganada. **www.betterpropaganda.com**.

Epitonic. **www.epitonic.com**.

Facebook. **www.facebook.com**.

InGrooves. **www.ingrooves.com**.

iTunes. **www.itunes.com**.

Last.FM. **www.last.fm/music**.

MusicNet. **www.musicnet.com**.

MySpace. **www.myspace.com**.

Pandora. **www.pandora.com**.

RealNetworks' Rhapsody. **www.rhapsody.com**.

The Orchard. **www.theorchard.com**.

Tunecore. **www.tunecore.com**.

YouTube. **www.youtube.com**.

Music Websites for Social Networking Media

Amazon. **www.amazon.com**.

Bandcamp. **http://bandcamp.com**.

CDBaby. **www.cdbaby.com**.

Createspace. **www.createspace.com**.

EoneDistribution. **www.e1distribution.com**.

InGrooves. **www.ingrooves.com**.

Iodalliance. **www.iodalliance.com**.

Iris Distribution. **www.irisdistribution.com**.

Jango Music Network. **www.jango.com**.

Last Fm. **www.last.fm**.

MySpace Music. **www.myspace.com/music/artisthq**.

Pandora. **www.pandora.com**.

Pitchfork Media. **http://pitchfork.com**.

Playlist.com. **www.playlist.com**.

Red Eye. **www.redeyeusa.com**.

RootMusic. **www.rootmusic.com**.

SoundCloud. **www.soundcloud.com**.

Stereogum. **www.stereogum.com**.

The Orchard. **www.theorchard.com**.

Thesixtyone.com. **www.thesixtyone.com**.

Tunecore. **www.tunecore.com**.

Tunes Plus. **www.mytunesplus.com**.

Virtual Label. **www.virtuallabel.biz**.

Marketing

Bandcamp.com. **http://bandcamp.com**.

Elon University School of Communications. "The Evolution of IP Law and Copyright Protection." **www.elon.edu/e-web/predictions/ expertsurveys/2008survey/internet_and_IP_law_2020.xhtml**.

Pitchfork.com. **http://pitchfork.com**.

Roizen, Bambi Francisco. "Pandora banks on Advertising over Music." Vator TV. June 30, 2009. **http://vator.tv/news/2009-06-30-pandora- banks-on-advertising-over-music-sales**.

Stereogum. **http://stereogum.com**.

Demographics

Comscore. **www.comscore.com**.

Quantcast. **www.quantcast.com**.

Visible Measures. **http://corp.visiblemeasures.com//news-and-events/ blog**.

Future of Music

IFPI Digital Music Report 2011. IFPI. January 20, 2011. **www.ifpi.org/content/section_resources/dmr2011.html**.

Investing in Music: How Music Companies Discover, Develop & Promote Talent. International Federation of the Phonographic Industry. **www.ifpi.org/content/library/investing_in_music.pdf**.

Music Matters. **www.whymusicmatters.org**.

Pfanner, Eric. "Music Industry Counts the Cost of Piracy."

Pro-music. **www.pro-music.org**.

The New York Times. January 21, 2010. **www.nytimes.com/2010/01/22/business/global/22music.html**.

Young People, Music and the Internet. **www.childnet.com/downloading**.

Glossary

¾ rate — A discounted mechanical royalty rate equal to 75 percent of the statutory (technically legal) rate

360 deal — A contract in which a record label receives a share of earnings from all of an artist's activities in return for promoting the artist's career

á la carte music downloads — Downloads of individual songs chosen by the buyer.

A&R — Artists and Repertoire

Adobe Flash — A multimedia platform that allows streaming of audio and video on a website

aggregator — A middleman who compiles and formats digital music files and licenses them for retail sale

airplay — The playing of a song over the radio

alternative rock — A genre of rock that emerged from the independent music scene during the 1980s and encompasses a variety of sub-genres

ARG — Alternative reality game, a series of puzzles solved by collaboration of many individuals through Internet communities

assumed name — A business name that is different from the owner's personal name.

autotune — A feature that corrects irregularities in a sound recording

balance sheet — A financial document showing a company's assets, liabilities, and ownership equity at a given point in time

BHAG — Big Hairy Audacious Goal, a clear and compelling long-term goal that has the power to change your life as well as the way you do business

big-box store — A name for the large chain stores that sell multiple products under one roof, usually in a one-story warehouse-style building

bleed — The extension of color beyond the edges of a label to allow for cropping errors

bluegrass — An American genre developed in the Southeast from immigrant Scottish, Welsh, and Irish and African traditions, featuring stringed instruments such as guitar, violin, and banjo playing the melody in turn

blues — A music genre originating from African-American narrative ballads, spirituals, chants and works songs

brand — A name, symbol, sign, or slogan associated with a particular product or service

break-even analysis — A calculation of the amount of sales required to cover the costs or production and marketing

captive download — A music download restricted to a single listening device.

catalog — A portfolio of past recordings

chargeback insurance — Insurance that protects retailers from losses due to purchases made with stolen credit card numbers and customers who dispute credit card charges

clean — A CD intended for sale in a store, not given away as a promotional copy

click-through rate — The percentage of visitors who click a link on one page of a website to open and view another page

click track — A series of audio cues used to synchronize sound recordings

co-op ad — An advertisement that is shared by two or more related entities, such as a record label and a concert venue, that split the cost

college rock — Another name for alternative rock, which found its first audiences on college radio stations

container charge — A deduction from the price of a CD, DVD, or album to pay for the cost of packaging it

controlled composition clause — A clause in a recording contract granting the record label a lower mechanical royalty rate for songs written by the artist

copyright — Legal ownership of the rights to music

cover — A song performed by someone other than the songwriter

cross-collateralization — Using income from sources other than artist royalties, such as publishing rights or a second album, to pay for the recording costs of an album

delivery date — The date a master recording is completed and delivered to the record label

demo — Short for demonstration, a sample recording of an artist's work

DIY — Do-it-yourself

digital piracy — The illegal downloading of copyrighted material

digital warehouse — A collection of digital music by many artists, licensed to retail music sellers

digital rights management (DRM) — Access control technologies employed by hardware manufacturers, publishers, copyright holders, and individuals to inhibit the use of digital content

DI (direct input) line — A cable that carries sound from an electronic instrument directly into a recording device

door split deal — An agreement in which a venue pays the artist a percentage of the admission fees

EIN — Employer Identification Number, assigned by the IRS to partnerships, corporations and employers and used on all tax documents

EP — Extended play, a recording that includes more than a single song but is not long enough to be an album, often used to promote upcoming releases

e-zine — A magazine published on the Internet or through e-mail

emo — A style of rock music characterized by melodic expression and confessional or emotionally personal lyrics

fanzine — A small publication, blog, or website dedicated to a particular band or genre of music

fictitious name — A business name that is different from the owner's name

file sharing — Allowing others to use the Internet to access and download digital music files saved on a computer without paying

first contract period — The period that starts with the signing of an Artists Agreement and ends after the release of the artist's first album

folk music — Music from a particular region or culture, usually transmitted orally and performed to celebrate or entertain rather than for commercial purposes

graveyard block — Studio time during the night and early morning hours

hook — A musical passage or phrase that catches the listener's ear

imprint — A label that is a trademark or brand but not registered as a company

indie — A term meaning "independent" and referring to alternative music or an independent record label

initial period — Another legal term for period that starts with the signing of an Artists Agreement and ends after the release of the artist's first album

jazz — A style of music that originated in the U.S., characterized by solo and ensemble improvisations around flexible rhythms

lead time — The amount of time necessary to prepare for an event, activity, or publication

logo — A trademarked symbol that represents a company or an entity

long-playing record (LP) — A 33-$^1/_3$ rpm vinyl gramophone record (phonograph record), typically 10 or 12 inches in diameter and holding 45 to 60 minutes of recorded music

master — The completed, engineered, produced, final recording delivered to the record label for reproduction

mechanical royalties — Royalties collected on the use of an artist's original copyrighted songs on a record

metal — A genre of rock music characterized by loudness, heavy beats, extended guitar solos, and amplified distortion

multiple rights — Another name for a 360 deal

Nielsen SoundScan — The official method of tracking sales of music and music video products in the U.S. and Canada

nexus — A legal term referring to the physical presence of a business in a state for sales tax purposes

one-sheet — An advertising piece in which all the important information about a band or an album is concentrated on a single page

open-mic night — An event where amateurs are allowed to perform onstage for a few minutes each

option — The right of a record label, guaranteed in a contract, to extend the contract for an additional period

one-stop — A subdistributor that wholesales a large selection of CDs, movies, games and other entertainment media

pageview — A single visit to a Web page

payment gateway — A service that takes credit card information and validates it before transferring funds to your bank account

payola — The illegal practice of paying radio stations and disc jockeys to play a song

peer-to-peer network — A network of individuals who connect their computers through the Internet

persona — The on-stage personality created by a performer

playlist — A compilation on a listening device or music service of favorite songs or songs tied together by a particular theme or mood

phasing — Moving from one microphone to another

point-of-purchase (POP) — A term referring to items such one-sheets, cardboard stands, posters, and other items placed in retail stores where records are sold

Pressing and Distribution (P&D) — An arrangement in which a distributor pays the manufacturing costs for a record and subtracts them from the wholesale price

principal — An owner, partner, or executive who is responsible for business and policy decisions in a company

PRO — Performance rights organization, an agency that collects performance royalties on behalf of artists

pro forma — Done according to standard industry practice

promo — A promotional copy of a CD given away for free to DJs, music critics, media, and fans

pro-sumer — An adjective describing consumer products created for semiprofessionals or hobbyists

psychobilly — Popular music that is a loud, frantic blend of rock and bluegrass styles

punk rock — A genre developed between 1974 in 1976 with stripped-down rock instrumentation and political overtones, and a DIY ethic

R&B (rhythm and blues) — A genre of popular African-American music, with origins in blues and gospel, that contributed to the development of rock 'n' roll. The term is now used loosely to refer to several contemporary styles incorporating jazz and soul.

rack jobbers — Subdistributors that lease shelf space and sell records in retail outlets whose primary business is not selling music

recoupable expenses — Expenses that can be recovered by the record label from the artist's royalties

reggaeton — Latin urban music that incorporates many influences, including Spanish-language reggae, rap, hip-hop, electronica, and R&B

resellers permit — A certificate verifying that a merchant is buying goods for resale and does not have to pay sales tax

revenue — The total amount of money received by a company for its goods or services

rock — A diverse genre that emerged from rock 'n' roll during the 1960s, characterized by its use of amplified and electric instruments, a strong rhythm, and an appeal to young people

rock 'n' roll — A genre that originated in the 1950s from a blending of country and western with American rhythm and blues

rockabilly — An early from of rock 'n' roll blending blues, bluegrass, and country styles.

roots music — Traditional, or folk, music

royalty — The percentage paid to an artist from sales of his or her work

sample — A small digital clip taken from another artist's recording, digitally modified and used in a master recording

search engine optimization (SEO) — The process of optimizing a website so it appears near the top of search engines' result pages

self-employment tax (SE) — A Social Security and Medicare tax for individuals who work for themselves

shopping cart — Term for the area on a website that gathers and processes information for customers making purchases online

ska — A genre of Jamaican dance music developed from calypso with influences from American jazz and R&B and often featuring horns with percussion, guitar, and keyboard

soca — A modern form of calypso developed in Trinidad and Tobago and incorporating characteristics of hip-hop and reggae

soul — An American genre of music combining gospel styles with rhythm and blues

streaming — The playing of music or video on-demand or live directly from the Internet

street date — The date an album or CD is officially released

stakeholder — Someone who has a substantial interest in

your business, such as a partner, investor, or artist who signs with you

streaming — The active delivery of content to an electronic device through the Internet

string band — An ensemble composed entirely or almost entirely of string instruments such as guitar, banjo, and violin, typically playing country or jazz music

sublabel — A record label that is owned by a larger parent label

subscription service — A music download service that charges a monthly fee

sweet spot — The best location to capture the sound of an instrument.

term — The duration of a contract

tethered download — A music download restricted to a single listening device.

trim size — The dimensions of a CD label or record cover

trademark — A word or symbol the products or services of a particular company.

traditional music — A term used to refer to folk music

turn-around time — The time it takes to fill a sales order after it is received

user friendly — Easy to navigate or operate

vanity label — A label named for a particular artist but owned and controlled by a larger record label

widget — A small graphic symbol that launches an application or a link to a website

zine — A small publication produced unofficially by fans of a particular genre or cultural trend

zydeco — A genre that originated with fast-paced Louisiana Creole dance music and integrates many traditional and modern influences

BIBLIOGRAPHY

Arango, Tim. "Digital Sales Surpass CDs at Atlantic." *The New York Times.* November 25, 2008. **www.nytimes.com/2008/11/26/business/media/26music.html**.

Bertin, Michael. "Work for Hire: Mastering Intellectual Property Rights." *The Austin Chronicle.* August 25, 2000. **www.austinchronicle.com/music/2000-08-25/78379**.

Bloch, Michael. "Payment gateways, Internet merchant accounts and credit card processors — info and reviews." Taming the Beast.net. **www.tamingthebeast.net/articles2/back-end-ecommerce.htm**.

Britt, Shawnassey Howell. *The independent record label's plain and simple guide to contracting.* Lincoln, Nebraska: IUniverse, Inc., 2004.

"CAKE forms Upbeat Records and releases B-Sides and Rarities in October." RedEye.com. **www.redeyeusa.com/artist/166/news/4601**.

Christman, Ed, Ann Donahue, Gail Mitchell, Glenn Peoples and Ray Waddell. "How Michael Jackson Made $1 Billion Since His Death."

Billboard. June 21, 2010. **www.billboard.com/news/how-michael-jackson-made-1-billion-since-1004099450.story**.

Fitzgerald, Michael. "How Warner Music and Its Musicians Are Combating Declining Album Sales." Fast Company. July 1, 2010. **www.fastcompany.com/magazine/147/take-us-to-the-river.html**.

Frere-Jones, Sasha. "What Do Record Labels Do Now?" The Dotted Line. *The New York Times.* August 16, 2010. **www.newyorker.com/arts/critics/musical/2010/08/16/100816crmu_music_frerejone**.

Furht, Borko. Encyclopedia of Multimedia. Springer E-Books. Boston: Springer Science+Business Media, Inc., 2006. **http://dx.doi.org/10.1007/0-387-30038-4**.

"Hip Hop Legend and Twitter Star MC Hammer to Receive Gravity Summit 'Social Media Marketer of the Year' Award at UCLA Event on February 22, 2011." World Market Media. December 14, 2010. **www.worldmarketmedia.com/1876/section.aspx/3019009/hip-hop-legend-and-twitter-star-mc-hammer-to-receive-gravity-summit-social-media-marketer-of-the-year-award-at-ucla-event-on-february-22-2011**.

"History: The Soul You Know, The Music You Grew Up On." *Stax 50th Anniversary Blog.* **www.stax50.com/history/**.

"IFPI publishes Digital Music Report 2011." IFPI. January 20, 2011. **www.ifpi.org/content/section_resources/dmr2011.html**.

Jacobson, Jeffrey E. and Bruce E. Colfin. "Mechanical Royalties Today." TheFirm.com. **www.thefirm.com/articles/mechroyl.html**.

Knab, Christopher. "Inside Record Labels: Organizing Things." Music Biz Academy.com. April 2010. **www.musicbizacademy.com/ knab/articles/insidelabels.htm**.

Lublin, Nancy. "How to Write a Mission Statement That Isn't Dumb." Fast Company. November 1, 2009. **www.fastcompany.com/ magazine/140/do-something-wordplay.html**.

Moreno, Tonya, CPA. "The iTunes Tax: Several states tax digital downloads." About.com. February, 2011. **http://taxes.about.com/od/ statetaxes/a/sales-tax-for-digital-downloads.htm**.

Randall, David K. "The One Bright Spot In The Music Business." Forbes.com. January 9, 2009. **www.forbes.com/2009/01/09/music-publishing-itunes-biz-media_cz_dkr_0109music.html**.

Reeves, Martha. **http://mcapozzolijr.com/marthareeves.html**.

Review: "Here, My Dear." Marvin Gaye. **www.allmusic.com/album/ r8087**.

Rose, Frank. "Secret Websites, Coded Messages: The New World of Immersive Games." *Wired Magazine: Issue 16-01*. December 20, 2007. **www.wired.com/entertainment/music/magazine/16-01/ff_args**.

Rudsenske, J. Scott, and James P. Denk. *Start an independent record label.* New York: Schirmer Trade Books, 2005.

Schornstein, Jay M. *Recording Contract Clauses.* Musicians Intellectual Law & Resources Links. 2006. **www.musiciansintellectuallaw.com/ rec_clauses.html**.

Schwartz, Daylle Deanna. 2009. *Start & run your own record label: winning marketing strategies for today's music industry.* New York: Billboard Books.

Smith, Ethan. "Jackson Estate Steers to Next Challenge: Loan Refinancing." *The Wall Street Journal.* June 21, 2010. **http://online.wsj. com/article/SB10001424052748703438604575315364195884770. html**.

SPV Entering New Dimensions with a New Team. Blabbermouth.net. November 11, 2009. **www.roadrunnerrecords.com/blabbermouth.net/ news.aspx?mode=Article&newsitemID=123356**.

SPV Records Filing For Bankruptcy. Metal Underground.com. May 28, 2009. **www.metalunderground.com/news/details.cfm?newsid=44943**.

Steamhammer. The Corroseum. **www.thecorroseum.com/labels/ steamhammer.htmlp://www.spv.de/Company/Profile/Company_ Profile_US.php**.

Stross, Randall. "You Too Can Bankroll a Band." *The New York Times.* April 3, 2010. **www.nytimes.com/2010/04/04/business/04digi.html**.

AUTHOR BIOGRAPHY

After graduating from Northwestern University with a degree in history, Martha Maeda lived and worked in Africa, Latin America, Australia, and Japan. She currently lives in Orlando, Florida, and is the author of books on many topics, including *The Complete Guide to Spotting Accounting Fraud and Cover-ups; How to Solar Power Your Home; The Complete Guide to Green Building & Remodeling Your Home;* and *The Complete Guide to Currency Trading and Investing.*

INDEX

C

Capitol Records 26, 27, 50, 161
captive download 318
CBS Records 24, 25, 263, 280
chargeback insurance 203, 318
clean 50, 133, 227, 231, 319
click-through rate 211, 319
click track 230, 319
Columbia Records 17, 25, 254
container charge 156, 162, 319
controlled composition clause 167, 319
copublishing agreement 187
copyright registration 180, 192, 193
cover 165, 319
CRM software 247, 248
cross-collateralization 168, 319

D

Decca Records 22
delivery date 147, 319
demo 111, 209, 222, 319
developmental deal 39
DI (direct input) line 320
Digital
    Media Association (DiMA) 185, 305
    Phonorecord Deliveries 252
    rights management (DRM) 16, 159, 252, 254, 319
Dischord Records 30
door split deal 320
Dot Records 20, 23
D.S.P.s. (digital service platforms) 32

E

EMI Group 5, 17, 25, 26, 27
emo 13, 130, 320
employer identification number (EIN) 75

EP (extended play) 34, 320
Epic Records 24
Epitaph Records 30
Exclusive Songwriter Agreement 180, 188

F

force majeure clause 172
Form CO 195

G

Geffen Records 23
glass master 235
graveyard block 320
grunge 30, 35, 79

H

Harry Fox Agency 185, 305
heavy metal 16, 20, 23, 112, 120, 126
hip-hop 19, 49, 120, 133, 198, 199, 225, 272, 294, 323, 324, 328
hook 169

I

IFPI (International Federation of the Phonographic Industry) 22, 202, 306
indemnity clause 170
indie 13, 15, 18, 28, 31, 79, 197, 308, 310
initial public offering (IPO) 63
International Federation of the Phonographic Industry (IFPI) 301

L

leaving member option 173
license 25, 40, 42, 48, 52, 74, 76, 153, 166, 169, 173, 174, 180, 182, 186, 188, 189, 191, 254,